UNTAMED

UNTAMED

THE AUTOBIOGRAPHY OF

THE CIRCUS'S

GREATEST
ANIMAL TRAINER

GUNTHER
GEBEL-WILLIAMS, 1934 -

WITH

TONI REINHOLD

WILLIAM MORROW AND COMPANY, INC.
NEW YORK

Recognizing the importance of preserving what has been written, it is the policy of William Morrow and Company, Inc., and its imprints and affiliates to have the books it publishes printed on acid-free paper, and we exert our best efforts to that end.

Library of Congress Cataloging-in-Publication Data

Gebel-Williams, Gunther, 1934–
    Untamed : the autobiography of the circus's greatest animal
trainer / Gunther Gebel-Williams with Toni Reinhold.
        p.   cm.
    ISBN 0-688-08645-4
    1. Gebel-Williams, Gunther, 1934– 2. Animal trainers—United
States—Biography. I. Reinhold, Toni. II. Title.
    GV1811.G1811A3   1991
636.088′8—dc20
[B]   90-13539
                                                         CIP

Printed in the United States of America

First Edition

1 2 3 4 5 6 7 8 9 10

BOOK DESIGN BY CIRCA 86, INC.

To my wife,
SIGRID,
without whose devotion, patience, and determination
this book would not have been possible

PREFACE

By now, more than twenty years after his debut with Ringling Brothers and Barnum & Bailey Circus, all the world knows of Gunther Gebel-Williams's unparalleled greatness as a performer and animal trainer. There are, however, only a privileged few—and I count myself very lucky to be among them—who also know of Gunther's equal greatness as a man, his inestimable value as a colleague, and his unstinting generosity as a friend. His sense of humor and his ability to find the utmost enjoyment in even the simplest situation, added to his many talents, make him the most unique man I have ever known.

Gunther has a remarkable ability to walk into any performance space and, within moments, take in the new environment and understand what must be done to make it work. He sees instantly which sections of the audience will be the toughest to play to and can tell you, even before the show loads in, where certain props should be placed and if the customary rigging of guy lines will cause problems. He misses nothing.

He once honored me by naming his prized leopard

PREFACE

"Kenny." But the greatest and most enduring gift he has ever given me is his friendship. From the time he arrived in the United States I felt that my unqualified respect for Gunther was reciprocated, and it was not at all because I was the boss's son. A tremendous bond of friendship and affection grew from this mutual respect. Outside of my immediate family, I feel more comfortable and at ease with Gunther than anyone else I can think of, and knowing that he feels the same with me is certainly one of the most gratifying honors I will ever receive.

Gunther has given unselfishly of himself to over 150 million audience members in more than ten thousand performances in the United States. No one could be more deserving than he of all the acclaim he received on his recent farewell tour. Every standing ovation was just reward for the enormous amount of happiness he has brought to people of all ages in cities across America.

Because of the way he communicates with his animals, one would think that the phrase "kinder and gentler" originated with Gunther. His very special genius has changed the face of animal training throughout the world and will continue to influence circus artistry.

Although I'm certain that he had very mixed emotions about retiring from the ring, I feel nothing but excitement for the future. The important role that Gunther has assumed in the management of Ringling Brothers and Barnum & Bailey Circus means that we will be working together every day, scouting for acts and planning for the future. It's a new beginning for Gunther that is likely to bring our families even closer in the years to come.

—KENNETH FELD
President, Producer, and Owner
Ringling Brothers and Barnum &
Bailey Circus

ACKNOWLEDGMENTS

Special thanks to Kenneth Feld and Dr. Richard Houck for their contributions of time and words; to my children, Mark and Tina, for their encouragement and enthusiasm, and to Hans Holzer, our consulting editor.

FOREWORD

I met Gunther Gebel-Williams in late November 1984, on the day I was hired for the job as veterinarian for the Ringling Brothers and Barnum & Bailey Circus. The company was preparing a new production at its Venice, Florida, compound, and during my visit there with Kenneth Feld, the owner of the circus, I was charged with preparing the animals for the upcoming season. I asked what that entailed, and he said I should discuss it with the show manager. He, in turn, referred me to Gunther, whom I knew only by reputation.

I remember this meeting quite clearly because I did not know what to expect from the man who was, and still is, regarded as the foremost animal trainer in the world. As I walked from the darkened arena building into the intense sunlight, I was somewhat apprehensive. I spotted Gunther, shirtless and in a pair of faded jeans and cowboy boots. It took me several minutes to get his attention because he was barking orders and directing several activities at one time. He stopped long enough for me to introduce myself and ask what he wanted me to do for the animals. "Take care of the horses!" Gunther told me, then resumed his activities as if he had never been interrupted. Conversation with Gunther can be brief until one earns his respect, but our friendship, understanding, and mutual regard began that day.

The first several weeks of my circus job were hectic as I acquainted myself with the animals and people and tended to all the vaccinations, dentistry, and other procedures that were necessary for the animals prior to the circus train's departure from Venice. Then I was called on to treat the tiger, Prince, who rode with Gunther atop his elephant, Congo, in the show. He was so sick that I never left his side and, when I was unable to reverse his kidney failure, Prince died. Gunther had been terribly worried about him, and I was fearful that this incident, occurring so soon after my arrival at the circus, would affect the way he felt about me. The death of an animal is never easy for an owner or a veterinarian.

When I told Gunther that we had lost Prince, I could see from the look on his face that he ached inside, but otherwise he showed little emotion. He is not a man who freely displays his feelings, yet, as he has done consistently over the years, Gunther expressed genuine appreciation for my efforts on the animal's behalf. He slapped me on the shoulder and said, "Doc, thanks a lot for working so hard. You did a good job, even though he died. Get some rest." My fears of rejection vanished.

Many years have passed since this episode, and I have had the opportunity to discover firsthand some of what makes Gunther Gebel-Williams great. He is a trainer, performer, athlete, manager, father, and husband. He is an artistic and creative caretaker of animals, a friend, and organizer. He is a complex, high-energy person, and yet down-to-earth with an easy sense of humor and honest soul. Above all, he is a decent human being.

Most startling to me is his stamina. The circus puts on more than six hundred performances a year, and he never missed one in the more than twenty years he performed with Ringling. He has always been the first person to be up and ready for work and the last to leave at day's end. The effort he put into his work reflected how seriously he took his job, and that he recognized and accepted the scope of his responsibilities. He never shied away from any aspect of his work. Just as I had seen on the day I joined the circus, he was always out there working with his men. However, he not only directed their activities, but also looked after them, particularly those who were loyal to him. One of his favorite workers is an uneducated man in his late fifties who is rather irresponsible about money. Gunther was so concerned about his future that he banked part of the man's salary without telling him so that he would have a financial cushion for retirement. I was especially moved by this because it was a window into Gunther's nature. As busy as he was, he found time to care about people, and to put that concern into action.

Once we sat together on a bale of hay just talking about circus life. Gunther confided, "Doc, the easiest job I have on this circus is training the animals. The toughest job I have is tiptoeing through the minefields of circus politics." With that confession, I realized how well he has done this. There are many good animal trainers and performers, but few enjoy the kind of longevity Gunther has known, because they are unable to avoid personal conflicts and get along with others in the complex circus family. Gunther has done this with great aplomb.

He diligently looks after both his family and his workers, but he attends to his stewardship of the animals with even greater fervor. It is Gunther who has an ear for a high wind and runs to check the safety of a tent. It is he who gets up in the middle of a freezing night to check the heaters in the animals' quarters. He rarely delegated these tasks because he felt they were too important to trust to someone else.

My job was made easier by the special attention he gave to his animals. He tried to have a handle on each one's health so that he could stay ahead of illness and keep them well. I think his good judgment about their health was the result of knowing them so well, and possessing the ability to recognize subtle behavior changes. Because of this, he could identify problems that even my well-trained veterinarian's eye did not see. In the thirty-three years I have been working with owners, trainers, grooms, and even other veterinarians, I have never known anybody with his extraordinary ability to assess an animal's physical and mental state.

I believe the crux of Gunther's greatness is his power of observation. He sees things that other people do not see, and because they are so obvious to him, he probably wonders why we don't see them too. He can race through an area and spot an assortment of problems or potential problems without even slowing down. He snaps out orders—fix that, lock that, clean that—or stops and takes care of things himself the moment he becomes aware of them. He has the ability to see an entire picture at once and comprehend all that is in it, and that is what enabled him to have large numbers of dangerous animals under his control at any given time. He has this ability in all situations. He can walk through stables or tents and, with just a cursory glance at each animal, assess its condition. He can quickly scan an area and determine if one of his working men is absent. In the subdued light of the arena prior to the elephants' performance, he knew whether all the props were correctly positioned.

Gunther's ability to tune in to the behaviors of the different species enabled him to train many types of animals.

FOREWORD

This is extraordinary because most animal trainers must concentrate on only one species to become proficient. Coupled with this is his ability to concentrate on the moment. One second of lost concentration can bring disaster when handling exotic cats.

I have seen him perform in the center ring with twelve horses, notice his daughter, Tina, having a problem with her horse in another ring, jump over the ring curb, assist her, and then return, never losing control of his animals. I believe Gunther was able to have this kind of control because he trained and performed with his animals and did it with equal proficiency. I admire many aspects of his training methods, especially the way he studies a new animal. It is the policy of the circus to acquire only those born in captivity, not captured in the wild. When an animal joined Gunther, it was allowed to cavort in a corral. Gunther used this time to understand the animal's capabilities and what it could best do naturally, and he built on that during training.

Gunther has a special charisma and rapport with animals that is uncanny. There seems to be an energy flow that connects him with them. Once that connection is made, he controls them with his eyes, mannerisms, voice, and actions. I have marveled at the way he moves around an arena cage with so much grace and ease, and how he can move one step in an eighteen-foot ring to make a tiger that is eighteen feet away from him do something. His motives during training and performing were pure, for he wanted the animals to reach their highest potential, and not to merely bring attention to himself.

Over the years Gunther became the most famous circus performer and animal trainer in the world. He has received numerous awards from his native Germany for work he did on behalf of that country and circuses in Europe. From the time he came to America, he was the focal point of Ringling's Red Show. Over the years he was billed as a "superstar" and "a legendary circus performer" for doing what he enjoyed most in the world. The press dubbed him the "Lord of the Ring," and one newspaper said he had the "movements and flair of a danseur." I have come to understand that what people saw in his movements and style was the joy he felt inside.

Within five years of his arrival in the United States, Gunther received the 1973 American Guild of Variety Artists (AGVA) award as Outstanding Circus Performer of the Year. It was presented to him on national television by Ed Sullivan. He had already received the coveted Ernst Renz Plakette Award from Germany for all his contributions to the circus business, and three Circus World "Oscars" from Germany, Belgium, and France. His fame was rooted in Europe, and accolades were heaped upon him long before he came here. But he told me that he was proudest when he received the AGVA award because it came from America, and he loves this country so much. That award was preceded and followed by scores of presentations from organizations and local governments all over the United States. He has received at least forty keys to cities, and in 1989 and 1990, in almost every town where he performed, he received a plate or key, or a proclamation declaring a Gunther Gebel-Williams Day. Mayors and other officials showed up to thank him for all the work he has done as a performer and trainer. More than once he told me how grateful he is for these honors and that every item represents something wonderful to remember. I have been touched by his humility and the depth of his feelings for his fans.

This book was written during the final year of Gunther's performing career. I began by saying that I was not prepared to meet him, and I was even less prepared to face his retirement. I was stricken by the realization that he was taking this step when I watched him perform during the opening night of his farewell tour. The arena was filled with fans, and I stood in the back row so that I could take in the entire scene. Gunther made his entrance standing on his favorite elephant, Congo, who was draped in a splendid blanket on which "Gunther" was printed in large letters on both sides. As Congo circled the arena and the band played "Circus Man," I noticed that Gunther looked the same as he did the day I met him—tan, blond, and fit. He waved to his fans as he passed them, and people eagerly waved back. I knew he was seeing them for the last time and I was glad that I was standing behind everyone because I did not try to hold back my tears. I thought of the millions of people, the "children of all ages," who had seen him over the years and left the circus feeling better than when they arrived. I thought of the hundreds of animals who had been his friends and had lived under his compassionate care. I felt empty inside as I realized that after he retired, Gunther would not always be present when I cared for the animals!

Gunther Gebel-Williams has made an impact on my life. We have a great friendship, and I feel honored to have worked with him because he is such a special human being. This book will give you insight into the many facets that make up this complex man, who loves and trains animals and has so enjoyed his life as "Lord of the Ring."

—Richard I. Houck, DVM

CHAPTER 1

What made me go into a cage filled with tigers time and time again? This is the question I am most frequently asked by fans and friends alike. I could say that I was lured in by the danger and excitement of working with such wild and unpredictable animals. But that would not be true because I have never been stricken with the man-against-beast syndrome. I have never pitted myself against an animal in a test of endurance and will. Rather, I built a world around the animals with whom I worked, and in it I was their father and they were my children.

I went into the tigers' cage and worked with them for twenty-three years because of the sheer enjoyment they gave me. I never had second thoughts about going into a cage with any number of tigers or leopards. If I had ever feared them, even once, I would have stopped working with them, because one cannot be afraid and remain in control. As I tell the trainers and performers for whom I now act as a consultant and mentor, to work with animals that have rightly earned the moniker "man-eaters," one must always be in control. I have had some accidents—such as being thrown by an elephant and bitten by leopards—but the circumstances surrounding each one were different. The same thing did not happen to me over and over so that I became conditioned to fear a particular animal or situation. To be a successful tiger or leopard trainer, one must go into the cage and not take so much as a second to think about what may or may not happen or what happened last week or two weeks before.

I was always under pressure when I worked with the big cats, even though I had built a familial relationship with them, because everything had to be precise. There was no margin for error. Every movement I made had to be exact so that the acts went well and no one around me—animals or people—was hurt. Still, because the tigers and leopards and I worked so well together, I never emerged from the cage sweating or showing signs of nerves. I have actually been accused by the press of not having any nerves. Maybe I do not. But I believe the explanation lies in my approach to my work: I never went about it with the idea that something could or was going to happen to me.

Incidents, such as one that occurred in 1988, illustrate how unflappable I could be. After I discontinued the leopard act and my mascot, Kenny—whom I had trained to lie upon my shoulders—died, I gave a large panther named Zorro to a friend in Cleveland, who built a magnificent haven for him on his property. Zorro had been born in the circus and raised by me and my wife, but before we had an opportunity to work together, I stopped training leopards. I visited him a few years later and felt bad because he had nothing to do all day except lounge around. I asked my friend to give him back to me so that he could perform, and he did.

Zorro weighed 150 pounds compared with Kenny's 75. I weigh 140 pounds, so he looked even larger when I stood beside him. He was a beautiful animal, and I wanted to show

UNTAMED

him off, so I trained him to lie upon my shoulders. He was also an especially ornery leopard—he always had been—and he had not mellowed with age, but I never felt threatened by him, because I had known him since he was a cub. Then one day, during a rehearsal, I eased him onto my shoulders and brought him out of the cage and into the ring, as I planned to do during actual performances. Suddenly Zorro hissed and sank his teeth into the top of my head. The pain was excruciating, and I was bleeding profusely. I dropped Zorro and tried to get him into a nearby cage, but he refused to move. He was wearing a collar and leash, which was customary during training when a big cat was taken outside the arena cage, and I tugged on his leash, but Zorro stubbornly remained where he was. Don Grier, the general manager of the circus, wanted to rush me to a hospital, but I could not leave as long as a leopard was uncaged. It was difficult for me to see because blood was running over my face and into my eyes, but I wiped it with my hands and kept trying to cage the leopard. At one point Zorro almost slipped his head out of the collar while I was pulling on his leash. It was a very tense situation, but after several minutes he finally decided to return to his cage, and then I went to a hospital.

I have been hurt by animals so many times because of mistakes, always mistakes, but the mistakes of people, not animals. For example, whenever my workers got too close to the elephants, one of them was inevitably knocked down and I had to save him from being stepped on. I was injured several times under such circumstances.

I have a special kind of respect for my animals, and it is mutual. It is comparable to the kind of feeling parents and their children have for each other and is one of the two most important elements of training; the second is staying alert so that you can survive. I was always on my guard and did not do anything ridiculous to show off, such as putting my head into a tiger's or lion's mouth. I'm not stupid and never tried to be a hero. I understand the animals' capabilities.

Respect is the foundation of my training style. I worked with the tigers as a trainer, never as a tamer. I taught them to listen, but still be tigers. I never tried to break their spirits and so I did not use brutality. To train my animals, I used words, always words. I'd say, "Come here," to any one of the elephants, and it would walk right over to me. They knew that the command "Pick it up," spoken during an animal walk or exercise session, meant they had to quicken their pace. And they all understood the word "Good."

I spent many of my working hours talking to my animals, making certain that I spent some time every day with each of them. The voice means everything. Our relationships developed through talk, and not just on my part—some animals really do respond. Tigers and elephants make many sounds. Leopards never purr, lions do not answer, and giraffes are mute. But when I was training Dickie, the giraffe, for Ringling Brothers and Barnum & Bailey Circus, he communicated by giving me signals with his legs. For instance, when he kicked his front legs against the walls of his pen, it meant that he wanted a treat.

The tone of the voice is very important too. Whenever I use a harsh or firm tone, they know something is wrong. Actually animals know without being told when they have erred, but a harsh-sounding voice confirms it, especially with the elephants. I started working with elephants some forty years ago, and I believe they communicated with me more than any other animals. They absolutely know what I mean when I talk to them. I always refer to animals as if they are people because they have so many humanlike characteristics, and they have counted among my friends and family since I was a little boy.

UNTAMED

My lips and hands worked together when I performed, and everybody—all the animals—listened to me. That gave me an unbelievable sense of gratification and, I must confess, a feeling of power, too, because I was able to work that way with such strong animals.

Some people might believe that the tigers and other cats with whom I have worked did not have claws and teeth, or that they were given drugs to make them docile before they were brought out to perform. That is not so. Every one had claws and teeth, and none of my animals was ever drugged. If a tiger had jumped on me just once, I would have been a goner.

I not only protected my animals from the evils that can creep into training, I also worked hard throughout my life to protect them from each other. Animals can hurt each other very badly when they fight, and if given the opportunity, they will fight often. If a tiger was hurt by another tiger, the injured animal automatically blamed me because of my patriarchal role. They knew that I was in charge and expected me to make sure that nothing happened to them. I had to be ever-vigilant and keep everyone out of harm's way.

Having built a friendship with my animals, I was able to trust them, and they trusted me. It was not uncommon for me to work in a cage with eighteen or twenty tigers around me. Other trainers would not trust that many in a cage at one time, since they attack from the rear, and trainers want more manageable numbers. A tiger has to be really upset and hate you like hell, or somebody has to have hurt him from behind, for him to attack from the front. Otherwise he never does that. He is too smart; he stalks his prey and utilizes the element of surprise. But I knew I could turn my back on my tigers.

I carefully planned how my tigers would be positioned in an arena cage at any given time so that I could work freely and without worrying that something bad was going to happen to me or one of them. How could I work and do tricks with five tigers in front of me and five behind me if I was always fearfully looking over my shoulders?

Perhaps I was able to turn my back on them because I never gave them any reason to hate me. Still, I could have become a victim if a tiger had jumped on me simply for enjoyment and ended up shredding my arms, or face, or chest. Anything that involves grabbing on their part is dangerous because of their claws and teeth. And after they have reduced their trainer to a messy heap, they can't say they're sorry, that it was only done in fun.

People have marveled at the way I worked with my tigers, but most have not realized that it took years to build the kind of relationships we shared. I started when they were very young and small—between six months and one year old. I took them into my home and made them feel comfortable and safe; I let them play around me but not with me. Even when they were little, I never allowed them to jump on me or hug and wrestle with me, because I wanted them to respect me from the first day. I also did not want them to become accustomed to jumping on me and then try to do it when they weighed five hundred pounds.

People often take wild cubs into their homes, and when the cubs grow up, they cannot handle them. I have tried many times to help such people by taking the cats and trying to do something with them, but it never worked out, because there was no respect. The animals wanted to be in charge and to tell me what to do, because they had not been trained properly. Even when I had animals from the time they were young, there were no guarantees that every animal would work out, because wild is wild.

Another reason I worked so well with tigers is that I became one of them when I entered their cage. At that

UNTAMED

point I blocked out the rest of the world and all of its distracting influences, and saw only the tigers. I concentrated on their movements and responses to my presence and commands and paid close attention to how they reacted to each other, thereby enabling myself to think and act as they did. First, I was the father who was in charge, the dominant authority figure when the group was together, and then I was a brother, someone they could trust and with whom they could feel comfortable. It was difficult to fit tigers into this scheme, because they do not conform to family relationships, unlike lions, who are very family oriented. But the lion, who is more of a lover than other big cats, taking a female and building a family around her, tends to exhibit much more jealousy than a tiger, and that can lead to different problems for his trainer. Tigers do not experience as much jealousy, because they are real loners. After only two years they leave their mothers and must survive on their own. Their independence makes it tough for tigers to take orders and tough for trainers to bring them together in a cage and have them lie down next to each other and act friendly. They do not like being around each other, and this can lead to fights. That is why they must understand that someone is in charge and it is not one of them.

The tigers I worked with in the circus were not like animals we see in movies, who can be touched and petted for long periods of time. They would never allow a stranger to put a finger on them, though when I approached their cages and they heard my voice, many of them rubbed their heads and shoulders against the bars, purred loudly, and waited for me to scratch behind their ears. I always obliged them, but touches could not be prolonged. Long touches imply a kind of familiarity that leads to a breakdown of respect and could also lead to my being unintentionally hurt by a tiger who tries to return the affection.

Not every tiger likes to be touched. I had two very large Siberians who could not be touched at all. I could not even put a finger into their cages, because either one of them would have bitten it off. Still, they were beautiful tigers; they worked perfectly and never harassed me. I never tried to take their wildness away from them, not that I could do so anyway, for even in captivity, where they do not have to forage and kill for their food and they live in cages instead of in the bush, the wildness never really goes out of them.

Tigers are very proud, and they can be just as mean. There were times when I could not walk between their cages because they were so threatening. They would growl and roar and restlessly pace back and forth. And yet I had done nothing to aggravate them. The problem was that at certain times they felt more independent than others and they resented my being in charge, correcting them and telling them what to do. But when I went into the cage to work, they knew who was giving the orders and that we had to work together, and the relationship between us was renewed.

I believe my animals loved me very much and were as attached to me as I was to them—we were part of a big family. I gave them a great deal of time and love. Almost every waking hour of my life for forty-three years was spent working with them and for them, but they paid me back by being good workers and loyal friends. They did not call me in the morning with excuses about why they could not come to work or grab their stomachs in the middle of the day and say they were ill and had to go home. They did what they were supposed to do and learned what they were supposed to learn, and I think that is one of the reasons I respected them so much.

I do not know if they realized that they depended on me in particular, since they were more concerned with their care than their caregivers, but I personally attended to them every day anyway, so they never had to wait or want for anything. Animals, like people, respond to conditioning and external stimuli. When the tigers heard the sounds of the meat carts, they would jump to their feet because they knew it was dinnertime. But if they did not hear that noise, they just continued to laze around. They knew that a particular sound meant that food was on the way, so they became eager to get it. I tried to be the person who fed them all the time, because I hoped that in so doing, the animals would associate my arrival with their satisfaction, but I do not believe they really cared whether I fed them or someone else did, as long as they ate. Sometimes if I did not have the time to feed them, my assistant did it, and the reaction was always the same because they heard the wheels of the carts. For as long as I had tigers, I never believed that they felt they had to depend on me to survive.

I bought my first tiger, Bengal, for the equivalent of two hundred dollars in the summer of 1962. I was creating a new mixed act for Circus Williams in Cologne, Germany. Bengal came from India and was about six months old when he arrived in Germany. I had done very little work with big cats before then, but I built an unbelievable relationship with that animal. I spent time with him, lots of time. Countless hours are involved in building a relationship with an animal, then training and caring for it.

When you buy a wild animal, you must accept the enormous responsibility that goes with it. I did everything right for my animals. If my son was sick, I would ask my wife to take him to a doctor, but I would never ask anyone else to take care of a sick animal. They were my responsibility alone.

I was with my animals every day, whether we were on the road with the show or not. I could not get through a day if I did not know what was going on with them, even though I had people working for me who could see to their basic needs. The two men who assisted me with the tigers and horses had each worked with me for ten years, and my assistant for the elephants was with me for thirty years. But they did not have the same kind of relationships with the animals that I had, and many of the animals, especially the elephants, watched and waited for me all the time.

There are no books that can tell you how to build a loving and lasting relationship with wild animals. The key word is *wild*. Understanding how to work with them comes only from spending time with them and watching other good trainers at work. That is what I did from the time I was a young boy. I also believe that I was lucky to have performed with animals before I started training them, because it gave me the opportunity to understand their natures. After I became a trainer, I continued performing, which gave me an advantage over those who did not train their animals but only presented them. I spent so much time with mine that we knew each other exceptionally well, and that was illustrated by the smoothness of our work.

Every animal is different. They are like people—no two are the same. Some are smarter than others, some are nicer. Some are lazy, and some are not. Because of these differences I always had to find the right way to handle each one. Not every tiger, for instance, can be trained to jump through a ring of fire. When I incorporated that trick into the tiger act, I had to find several from among the twenty I was working with at the time who were not afraid of fire. That was no easy task, because most tigers will not go near flames.

I was usually able to move around the tiger and leopard cages with the ease of a dancer whose footwork was choreographed. I fortunately never found myself in the middle of an act thinking, "God, this is not going right. Get me out of here!" I have, however, been in a position where I thought, "Get the tigers out of here!"

This happened as recently as 1989, during a rehearsal. The cage we used was made of crisscrossed steel wires that looked like a hurricane fence wrapped around a circus ring. A tiger jumped onto a prop, the prop shifted, and the tiger started to lose his balance. He grabbed the cage with one paw to prevent himself from falling, and one of his claws got caught in the cage. Tigers' outer and inner claws are not retractable, so we were unable to free him right away, and he was just hanging there. I called to one of my watchers—people who stood around the outside of the cage to help me if I had a life-threatening problem—and asked him to pry the claw away. While we were trying to help, a very big tiger jumped down from his prop and tried to attack him. All they have to see is that one of the group is disabled, or sick and unable to defend itself, and right away they move in for a fight.

All the other tigers stayed on their props and watched the excitement from a safe distance, but we had to get the one who wanted to fight out of the cage right away so that we could help the other. I ordered my working men to open the side entrance/exit, and I moved the fighter out as quickly as I could. He growled and snarled and resisted all the way back to his own cage. We had to use wire cutters to free the other tiger, and when we got him loose, the whole cage almost collapsed under his weight. In more than twenty years of working with the tigers, that was the only time something like that happened to me, but I learned from the experience and kept a wire cutter on hand at all times.

I spent so many hours with the animals every day that I was present for virtually everything that happened in their lives. I learned a lot by spending so much time with them, including when I should make myself scarce. I used to make a point of being around whenever an animal had to be given an injection, whether it was a vaccination or medicine, until one day in the summer of 1968 when a tiger named Pasha became ill. I knew he was in some pain and I felt sorry for him, so while the veterinarian gave him a shot, I moved closer to him to be reassuring. When he felt the needle, Pasha became so upset that he lunged forward and practically jumped into my arms. By the time I brought him under control, my right arm had been badly bitten and clawed.

People expected me to be covered with blood after an incident like this, but whenever I was hit by claws or teeth, there was never a lot of blood. The blood vessels closed very quickly, but that did not protect my body from the poisons beneath a tiger's or leopard's claws. Infection began immediately, and I could feel it affecting me within moments. I sweated, and my throat and mouth became parched. My skin swelled and reddened, and I had to see a doctor right away to get injections to control the infection. Such wounds had to be watched carefully so that they would stay open to drain. These injuries always hurt like hell, and took a long time to heal, but I could never stay in bed until I was well. I had to practice, perform, and do all my other work, since there was no one who could present my acts for me.

What happened with Pasha was one of the worst accidents I ever had with the tigers, but it was my mistake. I was so emotionally involved with the situation that I dropped my guard and moved out of the safety range. And poor Pasha did not know what he was doing. Animals are like people. Some of them are scared to death of getting an injection. Some go crazy when they see a doctor. After that incident I decided that it was unwise for me to be around when the veterinarian was giving shots because I did not want the animals to get the idea that I was giving them the pain. I also did not want to end up in another Pasha-type situation. I learn from my mistakes.

I have always been lucky, even though I had some pretty bad accidents. I have never been in a position where I felt so bad that I had to be laid up and could not work. Most of my injuries have occurred when the tigers were fighting and I separated them. Either I did not duck my head down far enough, or I put my hands too close to them, and the normal reaction for a tiger is to slap.

When tigers fight, it is an unbelievable sight. There is nothing like it. They rip everything apart. They rip the flesh right up from the bone, leaving almost no skin behind, regardless of whether they are attacking a man or another animal. Imagine having to get between two of them to stop a fight. A tiger's claws are dangerous not only because of their slicing ability but also because bits of the meat they eat stay under their claws and become rancid. Plus, they do not have the kind of claws that go into flesh, then come right back out; theirs are like hooks and must be ripped out. Against their razor-edged claws human skin is like paper and just tears away.

In 1988, in Cleveland, while making a commercial for Ringling Brothers and Barnum & Bailey Circus, I got too close to one of the tigers, and he swiped at me and caught my hand. All the flesh on my hand was pushed back like an accordion, and the swelling was terrible. And God, any injury from a tiger is so painful! It took six weeks for my hand to heal.

People have often wondered whether I carried a weapon for protection. I never carried a gun or any other weapon into the ring to use when I practiced or performed, but we always had a gun backstage in case there was a disaster involving the audience and animals; thankfully we never had such a problem.

My son, Mark, and my other watchers always stood around the outside of the cage when I was working and provided my second, third, and fourth pairs of eyes. They watched for potential problems from the tigers and leopards and were ready to respond if I found myself in serious danger. They looked for any unrehearsed movements by the cats, especially those behind me—a tiger who starts to leave his prop, or signs of activity that might lead to a fight between two animals. Their job was to give immediate verbal commands to the troublesome animal to try to head off a problem and alert me.

I became extremely angry if someone yelled for no good reason, because I reacted instantly to the outcry by jumping around in the direction from which it came. A tiger or leopard can be shocked by such a rapid movement, and that could buy me enough time to bring an animal under control and get everybody back to where they belonged. I told my watchers over and over again that they were to yell only when it was absolutely necessary, because my first reaction could save my life. I wanted to move like that only in an emergency.

Being a watcher can be very boring, especially if you have seen an act a hundred times, and sometimes the watchers slack off. Once I chastised my own son for falling asleep while he was supposed to be watching for me outside the cage. I tried to impress upon all of them that they always had to stay alert, because their timely warning could prevent my untimely death. I understand that it is boring to sit around watching and waiting, especially when nothing happens. But their presence is crucial for that one time when something does happen. There were times when I was young and standing in as a watcher for a lion act when I dozed off, so I appreciate their position. It's a dirty job, but it is also an important one, and someone had to do it for me. I never

UNTAMED

asked anyone to do anything I would not do or had not done myself.

Since I spent almost my entire life in the circus business, there is little I have not done, or at least witnessed. I even understand performers who have problems with nerves, such as those who have to visit the rest room before every show, because when I was a youngster my nerves would go haywire every morning before practice, and I would have to run to the rest room like a nervous school kid. I would never tolerate that in myself today. If I had to run to the toilet before every show, I would have stopped performing many years ago.

Some people have said that I was tough to work with, and they were probably right. I believe I always worked more easily with animals than with people. I have a low tolerance for stupidity, especially in the care and treatment of animals, and people can sometimes act very stupidly. I was especially hard on people when they made deliberate mistakes. I forgave honest mistakes, but in our work a mistake caused by laziness or an attempt to cut corners could jeopardize an animal's well-being—something I have never tolerated. When a person assumes the responsibilities of an animal trainer, or accepts a job working around animals, he or she must have the attitude that the animals come first, because they rely on their trainers and keepers for survival. The people working with them must be responsible and caring enough to anticipate their basic needs.

Though I was always strict with my assistants, I never treated them badly. I treat people the way I want to be treated, and I taught my children to be the same way. I consider that rule especially important for my son, who is now an animal trainer himself and must deal with quite a few working men every day. I do not like it when somebody tries to push his or her weight around and acts like a big shot and tries to step on my toes, so why should I do that to other people?

I have a very strong work ethic, which I suppose comes from my European background. I always tried to treat people correctly, be well mannered, and keep things around me and my animals clean. One day someone is going to give me a golden broom in commemoration of all the times I've been behind one. It was not at all uncommon for me to sweep up behind the horses or elephants daily when we were on the road with them or even when we were in our winter quarters. One day when we were touring in Miami, some elderly men walked by the circus and noticed me sweeping. One of them mistook me for Siegfried, a member of the famous magic act, Siegfried and Roy, and said to me, "A couple of years ago I saw you in Vegas and now you have a broom in your hand." How could I explain? I simply smiled and said, "You have to take life as it comes."

My need for cleanliness extended beyond the animals' quarters. I even used to walk around checking the outside of employees' trailers to make sure that everything was neat. For years circuses in general had the reputation of employing slovenly people who stole everything in sight. That was not the case with our circus, and today outsiders steal from us.

I have been called a workaholic by people who confused commitment with overworking. I believed that where the animals were concerned, I was committed either to do the work myself or to be physically present to make sure it got done. There were times when I did not go home because I had a feeling that one of the animals was sick, so I stayed with him or her around the clock. If I had gone home, I would not have been able to sleep, and I would have gone back anyway to check on the animal in the middle of the night. Animals can be lost so easily, and it is very difficult to put so much time into raising them, become so attached to them, and then lose them. That is something many people do not understand.

Everything, from the quality of their food to Mother Nature, can affect wild animals. The weather was always a big concern for me, and I was constantly worried about extremes in temperature and whether or not the animals were too hot or too cold. I would have been very unhappy going home to a warm bed knowing the animals were cold. When the Ringling circus winters in Venice, Florida, some of the animals are kept at the fairgrounds in Tampa while others are brought to Venice. (Ringling has two separate shows, identified as the Red Show and the Blue Show. Productions are changed every two years, so when animals for one show are being trained at our winter quarters in Venice, those for the other show are housed in Tampa. I was with the Red Show.) There were times when I drove from my home in Venice 150 miles round-trip to Tampa when the weather changed to make sure the animals would not be cold. I would cover the tigers' cages, close the canvas doors on the hangars to shield the elephants and horses, set up special heaters, wait for additional deliveries of propane to keep the heaters running overnight, put blankets on the horses, and even blanket our little elephant, Prince. I was not able to rest unless I knew that I had done the most I could to make my animals comfortable.

I knew my animals. I knew how they ate, who stole whose food, what they liked and did not like, and I knew when they were sick. If an animal did not drink his or her water or eat normally, I knew right away that something was wrong. My greatest concern was when an animal did not eat. To be able to pick up on such things, I had to know each animal's individual habits. On more than one occasion my knowledge of their behavior proved vitally important.

All of our horses became sick in 1989, and it was caused

by something I had not encountered in my entire life. It all began with sawdust. In America we put sawdust under the horses so that the ground beneath their hooves feels softer and absorbs urine. Since I came here in 1968, we have used it without any problems, until we hit Chicago in 1989 during my farewell tour as a performer. We got into that city on a Monday, unloaded the animals, and used the sawdust we had left over from the previous town. In the meantime we received a new shipment of 450 bags from a factory in Chicago. The circus normally orders sawdust in each place it performs, instead of carting tons of it all over the country. On Tuesday night when I went to check on the horses, I noticed that one of them was sweating. I asked one of my workers about it and he pointed out that another horse had started acting strangely and still another had lain down and refused to move. I said, "Wait a minute. Something is wrong here. Bring me brooms. Get all the sawdust and hay out!" I thought the horses could have been sickened by something they ate. Then, two hours later, eight more horses were acting up, sweating and breathing hard, and I sought professional help.

The veterinarian first asked me if we had taken away their food, and I said we had. He then asked what kind of sawdust we were using. And that was the key. It turned out that the factory from which we received the sawdust had mistakenly included walnut shavings in it. The horses had been poisoned by the walnut and developed a sickness called laminitis, commonly known among horsemen as founder. I had never heard of this. They did not eat the sawdust, they only stood in it, but it was absorbed into their bloodstreams through their hooves. This particular illness is extremely serious because it affects the bone in the hoof, and it becomes so painful that horses are reluctant to walk. If the bone moves within the hoof, the animals rarely recover from the lameness. But the proper treatment administered quickly will alleviate the inflammation before the bone moves and reverse the other symptoms. We could have lost the entire herd.

As a result of this blight I gave away two twenty-thousand-dollar horses, one for five dollars and one for nothing, just so that they could live out their lives in comfort on farms. If, on that Tuesday night, I had gone straight home instead of going to the stable first, I would not have known about this problem until the morning, and I might have lost thirty horses.

I paid attention to tiny things that could make a big difference in the health of my animals, such as the temperature of their food. When I first came to this country, I ordered the men who work with the tigers to defrost their meat in the shade so that it would not spoil. They complied, but I noticed that as the day wore on and the sun shifted, they did not move the meat to keep it shaded, and it ended up standing in the sun. I moved the meat myself, and from that day on I ordered them to defrost the meat inside a tent, because I realized that I could not count on them to follow up on something so critical. Tigers should not eat rancid, sloppy meat that has stewed in the heat, nor can they eat meat that contains ice. I went so far as to jab my finger into their meat before they were fed to make sure it was thoroughly defrosted. I knew that if I did not do that, no one else would. To most grooms and handlers, working around the animals is just a job, but it was my whole life, and the animals were my special charges.

No one really knows how much work goes into caring for my animals. I had to be constantly alert, because none of them could say, "Hey, Gunther, my meat is not good! My hay is not good! I am standing in the wrong sawdust!" Every workday was twelve to thirteen hours long, and everybody wanted to go home when their jobs were done, but my day did not end with the show. Afterward I needed time with the animals. I had to make sure that everyone was fed, that all the cages were secure, and everything was in order before I could call it a day. I could not rush out and then worry all night if I had forgotten to do something back at the circus.

Chicago was the last town we toured in 1989. It was late in the year when we performed there and very cold, and Prince, our little elephant, became quite ill. I blamed myself for his illness and wondered if perhaps I had given him water that was too cold and it had upset him. The big elephants eat snow and ice and it does not have any ill effects, but it could disturb the little one. Then we learned that he did not have a simple upset stomach. Whatever ailed him had caused his white blood count to go sky high and then to drop dramatically low, which indicated that he had a massive infection, and he had to be treated with antibiotics. We almost lost him. I stayed with him the first couple of nights that he was sick, and then our veterinarian drove to the circus with me every day to give Prince an injection and check on his condition. As with the tigers I did not stay around when the elephants got their shots. They hate needles, too, and they yell and carry on whenever they get one. It took a lot of special care to bring Prince back to good health and get him to eat right again, but we did it.

I became physically distressed when I had sick animals. I stayed with them around the clock, even if the veterinarian was with them, because I had to know what was going on and be close by in case they needed me. And when we had bad weather—something that could lead to all sorts of problems—I did not go home, I just stayed with the animals. My wife and children understood how dependent they were and never objected to the attention I gave them. My family loved them, too, and was always concerned about their well-being.

In March 1990, Cincinnati was hit with four inches of snow while we were performing there. I stayed up throughout the night of the storm, spraying the elephants' tent with a gigantic fire hose to prevent snow from accumulating on the roof and collapsing the tent. By the time dawn came and the snow stopped falling, my arms and shoulders were so fatigued that I could barely lift them, and I felt a whopping head cold coming on, but at least I knew the elephants were safe. A few weeks later while we were in Lexington, Kentucky, the forecast called for severe thunderstorms, and I knew I would not be going home that night. Storms and animals do not mix.

Nobody taught me how to care for and train wild animals. Experience is an animal trainer's only teacher. I started learning when I was twelve years old, soon after my arrival at Circus Williams in Germany. Harry Williams, the owner, was a horse trainer, and he permitted me to spend time with the animals. Harry became like a father to me, and I learned a great deal from him. I began by working with a gentle little pony. From the first day I took care of him and was concerned about him and I built a special relationship with him. I brought him food, cleaned his stall, and kept him nicely groomed. He became my friend and often nuzzled up to me and put his face against mine when I visited him. That was the beginning of everything.

My life would have been much easier if I had been a horse trainer. The horses do not require the extreme attention that some other animals, like the elephants, need. They do not care one iota who brings them their water and food, as long as they get it. Although one can build a relationship with certain horses, after all the years I worked with them, just a couple of horses ever seemed happy to see me. Not the friendliest of creatures, they do not care about people one way or another, as long as they are not mistreated. But as fate would have it, and I am certain my life was molded by fate, I became more than a horse trainer. I seem to have chosen my work without any conscious effort, or perhaps I should say it chose me, and I have never wished that I had taken a different path. The more time I put into it, the more I wanted to do. Once a person starts in this business, and really loves it, he never comes out. I have never regretted my choices.

I absolutely like animals more than I like most people— I think I always have. Sure, a person needs friends. I have friends who would do anything for me as I would for them. But when compared to many people, animals win hands-down. They do not answer back; they are dependable and honest. If you do right by them and do not become careless and lax, they will do the right thing in return. One can never be 100 percent certain about people.

My family is different. I love them deeply and have always been very concerned about them. I have never worried about taking care of myself, but my first priority after I came to America was making certain that our house was paid for in case something happened to me. Today I am happy knowing that I have done everything right for my family, and they will never have to give up the things we earned together. For as long as we have been together, my wife, children, and I have worked hard. Not one of us is lazy. Everybody has a job to do, and we have done them well. That is why my greatest concern after all these years is to give something back to them.

My son began working with me when he was just a little tot, about two years old. His costumes were so tiny that my wife had to make them by hand. She painstakingly sewed piping and sequins on his colorful outfits so that he

would feel as much a part of the show as any other performer. As he grew older, we never pushed him into circus
work. He knew he could do whatever he wanted, whether
that meant joining the army or becoming a doctor, or whatever he dreamed of being. We did not want him to stay with
the circus against his will. But he chose to work with the
animals, and I am very proud of him, because once a person
makes that choice, it is usually his for life.

All the elephants with whom I worked have known Mark
for twenty years. He grew up with many of them and he
now works with them as a trainer and performer. Tina has
worked with the circus since she was thirteen, first as a
showgirl, then as an aerial dancer and presenter of horses,
and now she presents a beautiful dog act. And my wife,
Sigrid, not only performed with the horses for fifteen years
but also has had to be a homemaker, mother, and nurse-
maid to our children as well as to a long procession of little
animals who have passed through our home over the years.

Beyond one's family, one must be able to embrace other
people. I have understood this since I was a young boy and
have never been an outsider. I have always tried to be helpful and lend a hand to anybody who needed one. My wife
and I regularly bought knitted caps, scarfs, and gloves for
people who worked with us, so no one would have to suffer
from the cold. I paid close attention to the way my workers
dressed so that I could stay on top of their needs. If I saw
that someone needed shoes, I made sure he got them. And
nobody ever went hungry around me. Money was the last
thing I offered anyone, not because I am stingy, but because I believe it is something that can be earned through
hard work, just as I have earned it. Circus people become
an extension of one's own family, and that is why we help
one another, not to win a pat on the back.

I try to care equally for everyone, regardless of their

stature. Maybe that is appreciated by some and not by others, but at least I know I have tried to be the best possible person I can be. I do not believe I have any real enemies.

I like having friends around me. I never enjoyed being alone. Often when I was a child, and even as an adult, I turned to my animals for companionship, and they were always there for me. So were a handful of good human friends. I dread loneliness. I do not know if that is the result of my experiences during and immediately following the Second World War, but I always want to have people near me. That is one of the reasons why we regularly have dinner guests. Another is that I enjoy sharing the happiness we have. Almost every day of my life has truly been a happy day. We would all be tired by the time we finished our work, but we got up on time each morning and went to work because we enjoyed it. I am very grateful for everything I have, and I thank God for it.

I have never been a person who makes a point of going to church on Sunday. With few exceptions I worked every Sunday of my life for forty-three years, from early morning until late at night. I would say, "Lord, I did my job today, even if I did not go to church." I do believe in God. I believe that He has intervened in my life many times, such as when the weather was bad for days and cleared up only when we had to take the animals to the trains for a trip to the next town. I never forgot to say "thank you" for such favors.

I am also very thankful for all the people who have come to see us perform over the years, some of whom have become dear friends, but whether strangers or friends or both filled the stands, I have always given them my best. I tried to convey to the audience the great pleasure I got from working and performing with the animals. Some people, usually because they are poorly paid, don't give a damn about how they perform. But I so loved what I did that I

UNTAMED

wanted the audience to know it. My enthusiasm was evident to circusgoers, even when I first began training and performing. And the more I worked, the better I became.

A person becomes a much better animal trainer when he grows older. Maturity generally brings greater patience, and that is one of the keys to good training, especially when working with young animals. Creatures who are new and little need time to start understanding the world before they can even try to understand a trainer. A lack of patience may lead to brutality, and that is something one should never introduce into animal training. When a trainer does something wrong, an animal does not quickly forget.

I developed my own training style when I was very young, and it served me and my animals well for more than forty years. It is the style that enabled me to create acts that brought elephants and horses into direct contact with a fierce natural enemy, the tiger, and that led to my being able to drape a leopard over my shoulders without fear.

The leopard is the toughest animal I have ever trained, yet it was that animal, and not the tiger, that became my trademark. When people began associating me with leopards, it was like receiving a red badge of courage—they were that difficult to train and even harder to get to perform. But despite all the drawbacks of working with those sleek, beautiful creatures, they formed a unique act, and one of them became my best friend.

It is almost impossible to describe how dangerous a leopard really is. Tigers are dangerous, but leopards have a far worse reputation. They kill just for the pleasure of killing and fight for the pleasure of fighting. They fear absolutely nothing and are like living buzz saws when they get riled. They are more undependable than tigers or any of the other wild animals with which I have worked. They fight more than tigers, are more willful and have much stronger personalities than their striped cousins.

Once I started training leopards, I discovered that I felt much safer when I worked with the tigers, even though leopards are a fraction of their size. Average leopards weigh only 75 to 125 pounds. A man can feel like a giant when he stands among them. Tigers weigh between three hundred and six hundred pounds each. Yet I felt a greater sense of security when I walked between tigers than when I was surrounded by leopards.

I created many more acts with the tigers than I did with the leopards, but the imbalance was not because I was afraid of the leopards. If that had been the case, I would never have worked with them. I created fewer leopard acts because of the inordinate amount of time it took to train them.

A leopard's will stands in the way of his or her ability to learn quickly, so training and practice take longer. After one year of training the leopards, it was still like day one. I could train tigers in one third the amount of time. Plus, since leopards are so dangerous, I had to be extremely careful when working with them, and that consumed even more time. They were also very mean and spiteful, and always acting up. It is their nature to be this way. I regularly found myself having to take time away from practice to keep them apart and prevent them from fighting.

Once I introduced leopards to the Ringling community, I also had to take extra precautions to protect the audience and the men who worked with me. Unlike the cage in which the tigers perform, which has an open top, the leopard cage had to be completely enclosed to prevent them from jumping into the audience or attacking one of my workers or watchers. Leopards possess an incredible ability to leap great distances. Their long, thin tails act as stabilizers when they spring into action, and they seem to glide through the air. When a tiger suddenly finds itself uncaged, it becomes confused and hesitates. It does not immediately run. Not so with a leopard. The minute it is out of the cage, it takes a few bounding leaps and is gone.

UNTAMED

We had to be extra careful when passing between the leopard cages to feed and water them because, unlike the tigers, leopards will turn their paws sideways to slip them between the bars and swipe at people. They were always trying to get one of us. Everyone who worked with the leopards was always jittery, and I was extremely sensitive to their every move because they are so fast and so vicious.

I could never be satisfied duplicating the work of other animal trainers, so I did not rework old acts, or current ones. I always created something new and different that had never been seen in circuses before. The leopards presented a great challenge for me, and I determined to create one of the finest productions ever with those magnificent, deadly creatures. I used twenty-two cats—seventeen leopards, three black panthers, and two mountain lions. Not many people have trained leopards; not many people have wanted to. Certainly no one ever created an act with that many leopards, and I do not believe we will ever see it duplicated, because nobody wants to sacrifice the years it takes to train them, and few people have the requisite patience.

What made me different from other animal trainers is that I took the time to build a relationship with each leopard, regardless of how crazy they acted when I first got them and regardless of the fact that my days started at 7:30 A.M. and generally ended around midnight. Finding periods to work with the leopards meant adding extra hours to days already filled with training the horses, elephants, and tigers. It meant overseeing their transportation; loading and unloading them from the trains; taking them on walks; making sure that all their needs were attended to; and performing two, and often three, shows a day.

When I started working with the leopards, they were not even walking. I had to teach those guys to walk! They would come into the cage, lie down, and act as if they were dead. To get them moving, I would coax them to their feet by gently prodding them with my stick for a few feet. They would walk and lie down, then walk and lie down. They hated being made to move when all they wanted to do was lounge around as if they were in trees in the jungle, but when they snarled and resisted, I persisted. I sometimes had to laugh at their belligerence when I tried to get them to sit on props and they would freeze in defiance. They were so ornery that I could not please them even with a piece of meat. Their attitude was that they were so strong and self-reliant that they did not need to take meat or anything else from me.

Leopards can easily jump ten feet into the air, but the trick is to get them to do it on cue. As with training any other animals, success comes in finding the right one for the particular job. To get a leopard to jump when I wanted him to, I had to find a guy who liked to jump. This comes only through spending time in training, watching them carefully, and getting to know each animal individually.

A trainer must understand that his work does not take shape overnight. Sometimes I would come home after a practice session, frustrated and almost too tired to sleep, and I would tell my wife, "Damn it, Sigrid, I do not see anything. I see no progress." But I would be back at it the next day, and the day after, and all of a sudden it would come together.

In the beginning of my career it was tough to have the kind of patience needed to work with animals. But it came to me with time, and complemented my tenacity. I stuck with the leopards through two and a half grueling years of training until I got that act together. The first time I presented them was in Salt Lake City in 1979, and I had so many tricks in the act that it took a full twenty minutes. I had leopards standing on balls and walking on wires—feats that were highly unusual. I had set out to do something different with them, and I did. I was very proud of all I had accomplished with the leopards, but the act was much too long and took too long to practice. After a while I eliminated a lot of the tricks. I presented the act every day for five years, five of the toughest years of my career, because even after they were trained, the leopards remained difficult to handle.

Leopards are as beautiful as they are troublesome. Before I started working with them, I knew that I wanted people to marvel not only at what the leopards had learned to do but also at how magnificent-looking they are. When I began selecting animals for the act, I was lucky because most of the time I was able to acquire leopards in pairs, that is, two brothers or two sisters. This was something I wanted, because siblings have identical spots. When I designed the act, I put the black panthers on top, flanked them with mountain lions, then used two sister leopards with the same spots on either side of them, two identically spotted brothers on opposite sides of the girls, and so on. To achieve my original goal, it was important to have a nice-looking group of animals. As much as I looked after every one of them, I always felt sorry for the mountain lions, because the leopards were always trying to get them. Sometimes there would be three or four leopards chasing after one mountain lion. When one leopard started trouble, right away two or three others joined in. They would run around the cage sideways trying to catch the mountain lion, sometimes bounding from the sides of the cage to cut him off. I would have to jump between them and shout, "Hey! Stop!" and they would skid to a halt and skulk away angrily because I had spoiled their fun. Whenever I intervened on his behalf, the little lion would stop running, and I could almost see him catch his breath.

Sigrid raised the mountain lions in our house from the time they were cubs. They were her favorites, and I can understand why. They are such nice animals—the nicest animals I ever met. They never ripped anything apart like the leopards, who got crazy and tore up everything. Though a mountain lion's face looks mean when it becomes angry, they were timid around leopards and counted on me to protect them.

We did not raise any of the other animals that were part of this act. Most of them were between one and two years old when I acquired them. They were surplus animals from zoos, or they came from animal handlers, or as gifts and donations. (Many zoos do not like to give their animals to circuses for fear they will be maltreated, but they worked with me because of my reputation for kindness.)

When I first acquired the leopards, they did not want to know me. They hissed and swiped at me and rejected any efforts I made to break down the barriers between us. I looked for little windows—times when they dropped their guard, even if for only a split second—so that I could move in and give one of them a reward or a slight touch. They afforded me few opportunities to be affectionate and were so fierce that I became convinced that even if I got the act together, the leopards would never mellow.

I carried a small stick into their cage when we practiced so that I could give them directions or get them to move their butts without pushing them. I started my training by putting a few leopards in the cage at a time, then building up to where all twenty-two cats were together. If they were going to perform together, they had to practice that way. Being surrounded by tigers was dangerous enough, but having so many leopards around me was downright perilous.

I brought rewards—chunks of meat—into all our rehearsals, and eventually they started accepting them. But it was not meat that tempered the leopard's inbred hatred, it was my voice, and my refusal to let them beat me. I talked to them from the moment the first one stepped into the cage until the door closed behind the last leopard when practice was over. I never showed any signs of fear, and I met their defiance with equal boldness. After months of work they started respecting me, and more than a year later they started following orders without as much resistance. I was then able to teach them basic tricks, and we built the act from there. Gradually the individual personalities of each leopard emerged, and I was better able to work with them one on one. I took great personal satisfaction in this, because it meant that they were feeling comfortable enough around me to show themselves. I also discovered that I especially liked two of them—Kenny, who was spotted, and a panther named Blackie.

I found with Kenny and Blackie the kind of warm, close relationship that I tried to build with all my animals. They were different from their counterparts, and although they occasionally got into trouble, they listened better than the others and actually showed me signs of affection. They seemed to understand me, and in a curious way I felt they approved of me. They were my reward for sticking with the leopards.

I never identified what fueled the leopards' fiery tempers, so I could never get around it and coax them into being nice. Since I was not out to crush their spirits, I had to accept them for the mean little creatures that they were. Once I got them to move around and show some life, I wanted them to remain animated. With leopards that means staying nasty. Some of them were nicer than others, some more compliant than the rest, but I never trusted them the way I trusted the tigers. Although I assumed the position of authority inside the cage, I somehow always felt that it really was a draw.

Since leopards are so small, and I wanted the audience to get a good look at them, we had to have high-sitting props. Then, because the props were so high, we had to cover the top of the cage with a net so that they could not jump out. I used such props as bridges, and with them a mirrored ball, with everything set close together. No matter how familiar the cats were with the props, they would still fall off them when they started fighting. Working with the leopards was, at first, like being surrounded by a bunch of really bad school kids. They would fight, and fall down, and I would break up the fight, get them back up on the props, and then have a helluva time getting them down when practice was over.

Consequently I realized that they had to be well trained to respond to a voice command so that they would come down without prodding. Unlike the tigers, who can be physically pushed a bit to make them move, I could not safely push the leopards to get them down from their perches. But troublesome as it was, I never considered giving up. I would have felt thoroughly rotten if I had abandoned the act before it had been given a chance to fly. I would have had to get rid of everything—the animals, their cages, all the props, everything. That would have been tough to do. Knowing the kinds of personalities leopards have, I would have been very worried about where I placed them. I would not want the animals to be mistreated, nor would I want an inexperienced handler or trainer to fall victim to their nasty dispositions.

As difficult as the leopards were, Kenny became my best friend and one of my favorite animals, and it was he whom I trained to rest upon my shoulders. He even appeared with me in commercials I made for American Express. When he died many years later, I could not bear to bury or cremate his little body, so I had his skin tanned, and to this day he has a place of honor in the living room in our home.

I do not know if I would ever train leopards again. I am not saying that I would not—I simply cannot say that I would. Animal training is a highly individualized type of work. Some people would never consider working with tigers and would rather quit the business before working with leopards. Others stay away from elephants. I personally do not like to train bears. In all animal training, however, there seems to be a natural progression that almost always begins with horses or chimps, as I did watching seasoned European trainers with their own styles.

After I learned to train horses, I applied that knowledge to training other animals. It is extremely unusual for a trainer to work with as many different types of animals as I have. Trainers usually specialize in one area, and they do not digress from it. My progression from horses to elephants, to tigers and leopards, happened without deliberate planning on my part. I never sat down and said to myself, "It is now time for you to train elephants," or, "You have done enough with horses and zebras, go ahead and train a giraffe." I never planned and I never looked ahead when I was training horses and thought that tiger training was something I wanted to do in my life. It just happened.

Although I visited many circuses while working in Europe with Circus Williams, I never saw anyone work with leopards. I got the idea for the leopard act because I wanted to do something different, and I had been so successful with tigers that I thought I could surely handle other types of dangerous cats. Although I had several important mentors for horse and elephant training, there was no one I could watch to get pointers on working with leopards. To accomplish that, I drew on my years of experience training other kinds of animals, and then made adjustments as I learned about them firsthand.

Throughout my entire professional life I used my own style of training to teach all the animals with which I performed. I have been involved with llamas and camels, bison and zebras, giraffes and even yaks, and every animal is different. Every one of them provides a new experience, and because each type of animal is unique, and within groups each animal has its own personality, the way I train every animal is different. I could not use the same training style with the horses as I did with the elephants, or the same style with the tigers as I used with the leopards. A trainer must find the right way to handle each animal.

I trained a giraffe named Dickie, and he was able to work in many difficult situations. But working with a giraffe was unlike working with any other animal. I had to be careful about taking him on concrete floors, he always had to be on a rope, and he required special transportation. Before I began training Dickie, no one gave me instructions on how to work with a giraffe. I drew on my experience as a trainer and my own instincts to know the right things to do with him.

I do not know where my ability to work with the animals came from. I believe a good part of it stems from the fondness I have had for animals since I was a little boy. The rest comes from some place deep inside me—a place I cannot identify, but with which I have been in touch all my life.

Some of my grooms were with me for years and years. They watched me practice the horses, helped me bring them in and out of the ring, and of course cared for them throughout the day. But if I had said to one of them, "Let's go train a horse," they would not know where to begin. It might have been a little easier for me over the years if one or more of them had learned my style and had been able to work closely with me training the horses. They did not, so I did everything myself until my son became old enough to work with me. Because I did all my own training, I always looked for something different, such as an unusual act or new tricks for the animals, to challenge all of us and keep my interest high.

My first circus job as a performer was with the Circus Williams as a bareback rider. This kind of riding was called Cossack, the style used by Russians and cowboys. Once I became an accomplished Cossack rider, I started training my own horses—I was a teenager then. Later on I got five elephants to perform with my act and I slipped in horses that I had trained myself. I never looked to anyone to tell me how to do these things, because there was no place to learn. There are clown schools and acting schools and places to learn mime and juggling, but there are no schools for animal trainers. You must find your own way.

Once I became actively involved in training animals, it was my goal to do things differently from other trainers. I created my first really unusual act, a mixed performance with elephants and a tiger, long before I came to America. I used an Indian elephant, an African elephant (which is considered extremely difficult to train), and Bengal, my first tiger. Indian elephants and tigers are natural enemies, yet I was able to teach Bengal to jump onto the elephants' backs and stay there while they ran around the ring. Training these animals to work together was very difficult because I did not have the proper equipment at that time. We had no cages in which the tiger could live or work, and no special place to rehearse him safely. I had to start from scratch and buy the necessary equipment as I went along. Every time I did something new, I had to start from the ground up.

I have enjoyed training the animals to do different things. At one point I trained two horses to work with three tigers and an African elephant. Tigers and horses are natural ene-mies. This was something that had never been done before and took two years of practice before it could be incorpo-rated into the show.

Building new acts and making new additions are diffi-cult in the circus business because we do not have one site on which we can build. Because we are transient, we can-not plan on putting cages in one place, rings in another, and practice cages in another. We are always on the move, and everything we add must be portable. We have to have transportation space for extra cages, a place to put them when we reach each new destination, and be able to move everything from one town to the next. All this moving does not seem to bother the animals. I have never had to force any of them to get onto a train, and the elephants have always been especially compliant. As their names are called, they step up into the car without hesitation. One of my African elephants is always so anxious to ride the train that she tries to board before we are ready for her, and she has to be held back. I have found that after visiting the same towns for so many years, the lead elephants (those who are in the front of the line during animal walks) know the way from the trains to the buildings in which the circus per-forms, or the tents in which they are housed.

A passion for one's work plays an important role in successfully making additions to the circus because they in-volve tedious planning and those all-important attributes, patience and perseverance. If a person really wants some-thing and is willing to work hard at it, he will succeed. If he approaches this business with anything less, he will never make it. There might be many people who could do what I have done, but they are not willing to put in the tremendous amount of time it takes to learn, or to keep at it until they become really good. An animal trainer must do things cor-rectly—there can never be any compromises.

UNTAMED

The job also requires a great deal of self-discipline. I had to be alert every minute of every day. I could never let my guard down because I did not feel well or I was tired or out of sorts. And when I was performing, I always had to be in tip-top physical condition, regardless of how many shows I had done or how long I had been performing. Over the years I have also had to be patient with myself and be very flexible.

Whenever I started something new, I had no idea how it would turn out. New acts come together only through practice. If something looked good, I kept it. If not, I changed it. As I worked with the animals, the routines took on their own shape. Nothing was ever really planned ahead. Sometimes I started out with a basic idea, but then the act created itself.

I tried many things that never worked. For a time at Ringling Brothers I worked on an act in which six lions rode on the backs of six horses. (The horses, of course, wore protective coverings.) I gradually reduced the number of horses in the ring and had the six lions jump onto each horse's back several times. The lions were trained to enter the ring, jump onto a horse's back, ride a bit, then jump down, and leave the ring to make room for the next lion. The lions were not so bad, and one of the horses was excellent, but because the other horses did not work out, I had to buy four new horses to try to pull the act together. I never found the right horses, because most of them do not like to have lions on their backs. Eventually I had to stop rehearsing the act, and it was never presented in the circus. I did all that work for nothing.

I have never been upset when an act failed, because there is no limit to what one can do when training animals. If one thing is not successful, you move on to something else. There are a limited number of things a performer can do in a juggling act or a flying act, but there is no limit to the wonderful things that can be done by well-trained, healthy animals. The biggest stumbling block to training is that when one travels so much, there may only be two or three days a week in which to practice. This makes it very tough to create and refine new acts.

Rehearsal is a necessary part of all training. Without repetition nothing will go right, and everything will look like a mess. Just as human performers must do things over and over until they get them right, so must animal performers. The need for animals to practice must be respected by the trainer, and they must be given enough time to learn their jobs well.

I respected my animals and protected them as long as possible. All of my tigers lived an average of twenty to twenty-two years, which is a pretty long life span. That was the result of good care, and living and working with a purpose. It is true that circus animals live in confined spaces, but it would be dangerous for them and people if they roamed around at will. We cannot send the animals home at night and tell them to come back to work in the morning, so they must be kept in cages, stables, and pens. Tigers and leopards in zoos have bigger spaces than they have at the circus, but I do not believe that bigger spaces necessarily make for happier animals. I have seen tigers in zoos that seemed absolutely lifeless. They usually spend most of their time lying sleepily in their cages, alternately eating and dozing. Twenty-four hours is a long time for a creature with nothing to do.

My animals were active. Each of them had a job, and when they were not practicing or performing, they were being groomed, fed, exercised, and cleaned. We all worked equally hard, and I never had to push or prod any of my animals to get them to do their job. I believe this was because my training and treatment of them was right from the beginning, and they enjoyed what they were doing.

UNTAMED

They had no time to be bored. They had show time and time spent traveling back and forth to the trains, and the animal walks—there was always action. And the more action, the more the animals looked and acted alive. Tigers thrive on action. All animals do. When they are moving and doing things, some of the wildness comes out in them and people thrill to see that. When the little elephant, Prince, passes the crowds in the animal walks, everybody goes crazy. They love him. That is because he's not moping and dragging along. He is bouncy and animated.

Anyone who works around animals catches regular glimpses of their wildness, and that is thrilling as long as it does not involve fighting. The elephants and tigers were always kept relatively close to each other in the tents and arenas in which we performed. When the big elephants passed by the tigers' cages, nobody—not the tigers or elephants—became bothered or upset. But when little Prince went by, all the tigers went crazy. They knew he was a baby and virtually defenseless against them, and I knew that if the tigers got loose, every one of them would run for the little elephant.

I have never set a limit on the number of animals I would work with at any given time. I came to America with eight tigers and eight cages. Several years later I had forty cages filled with tigers and leopards. I trained and presented several mixed acts with horses, elephants, and tigers. I was the trainer and performer for three cage acts—a mixed act, the tigers, and the leopards—in each show, sometimes two and three shows a day. When I look back on those years, I really do not know how I did it all. Before me every animal trainer performed only one cage act, and that would leave them sweating and unnerved. I have been told that after he performed his lion act, nobody could talk to Clyde Beatty for an hour.

I never had time to sweat or go someplace for an hour

to unwind after doing one of the cage acts. In a typical show I would open with the tigers, present the leopards after intermission, and immediately go into the mixed act. Between those acts I would present the elephants and the horses. I was always running to change or bring in animals. There was never any time to be unsettled. I never really became unsettled while working with the leopards or tigers because I was never afraid of them. I would become mildly upset if something did not work out as planned, but I would tell myself not to worry because it could always be worse. I was glad that there was another show and another chance. If something goes wrong and you dwell on it, the entire act can go downhill right away. If you lose your concentration because one trick failed, the next will fall apart, and the next and the next. I seldom had problems during a show, but if I did, I just took things as they came and moved on.

Keeping so many acts going at one time took total concentration, especially for the mixed act. All the animals had to walk in perfectly every time. There was no margin for error. The horses had to be in certain positions, and on cue, the tigers had to move across the middle of the ring and jump onto the horses' backs. I had one situation where, during a performance, a tiger turned around when he was not supposed to and two tigers jumped on one horse. It was a touchy situation because neither tiger wanted to come down. My first concern was keeping the horse under control, so I held him until I got one of the tigers to jump down. The horse's eyes were not covered and he knew he had two tigers on his back. I kept him calm by talking to him and holding him. Fortunately he was wearing a leather blanket and a leather and metal neck cover so that the tigers could not hurt him. Because the horse did not become hysterical and the tigers finally did as they were told, I was able to hold the act together. We started once more from the beginning, and then it went as planned. Everything must be precise because in seconds the whole thing can fall apart. Once a horse is hurt, the act can come unglued. Nobody from the audience knew how much pressure was on me when I was performing such an act.

I spent so many months, and even years, putting these acts together that I tried to keep them alive as long as possible. In the past if one animal was lost, the entire act went with it. I trained many different animals to do the same tricks so that if something happened to one, the act could be kept intact. This was never done in America before I came here. I did something else that had never been done: I used the same animals in more than one act. For example, the tiger I used with the elephant was also used in the tiger act, or I would take a High School horse (an elegant form of riding, also known as Dressage, in which a rider moves a horse through complex maneuvers by using almost imperceptible hand, leg, and body-weight signals) and put him in the "Liberty" act, which involves a group of horses without riders moving in special formations. Each could do more than one thing.

I had to be careful about training the animals this way, because some of them interpreted my choices as favoritism. I could never let them feel that I liked one more than another. The elephants are especially jealous of each other and of people. From the first day an elephant named Tetchie met my wife and daughter, she never liked them. Tina rode her in the show many times, but it never worked well. Tetchie never bothered any of the other showgirls—only Sigrid and Tina. She is very jealous of them.

I also trained the animals for new acts every two years. This had never been done, even in Europe, until I started doing it at Circus Williams. When a circus performer had an act, he or she did not change it for at least twenty years and simply moved it from circus to circus and town to town. I have been in America for more than twenty years, and every two years I went to the same towns and did something different. I believe it gives people a reason to see a performer again and again and keeps their interest in the circus alive.

My audiences enjoyed everything they saw me do with the animals, including talking to them and giving verbal commands in my own strange "animal lingo," which is a combination of French, German, English, and Hindu, with a sprinkling of Spanish and Italian. It is difficult for a person to understand if they are not accustomed to hearing it. But my animals knew exactly what I was saying all the time, because they had been trained with this language of mine, and my workers used it too. After my son took over my elephants and horses when I stopped performing, he continued to use it.

The animals learn no matter what language is spoken to them, but once they become accustomed to a particular language and a certain set of commands, the same words must be used over and over again. Consistency is extremely important in animal training. Different trainers use different languages and commands, which is why it is difficult for one trainer to take over another's animals unless he or she knows the commands. There is no universal language in animal training. In Germany we spoke more English to the elephants than German, so most of my elephant commands are in English, with a little bit of Hindu thrown in. The main horse-training style is still French, and so are most of my commands for the horses. The animals knew when I directed words at them, and they used noises and body language to communicate with me. The way they looked at me or moved in my direction when I spoke to them showed me that they were listening and understood. I could tell

UNTAMED

from the way they cocked their heads and twitched their ears that they were listening for their names when I talked to them. Using their names is the most important thing of all when communicating with animals, whether casually or in training. When the tigers heard me speak their names, their ears went up, and the elephants flapped theirs.

Every animal was with me for months, and sometimes years, before we did an act together. Before I started training a tiger or leopard, we shared enjoyable moments in the cage, because a large part of that animal's life is spent in a cage and it should not be an unhappy place. I allowed them to play and run and jump in the cage and examine every inch of it at their leisure. Then I would introduce props in the cage and showed them how to sit on pedestals and stay there until I said they could come down. Some cats do not understand right away and think they can go up and down from a prop whenever they want. The most important element in training the cats is to teach them to sit and not come down. If they did not learn that, how could I make an act when everybody was walking around all the time? Once an animal learned to go up and down from the prop on command, I started teaching it other things, because by then we respected and understood each other.

I suppose I brought a lot more than my strange animal lingo to American audiences. People here were used to Clyde Beatty's famous style, the classic "man over beast" method, which employed a whip, gun, and chair. A friend of mine from Circus Williams, Charley Baumann, was the first person to bring a different style of training, which centered around hand signals and verbal commands, to the United States. Charley had a tiger act when he joined the Ringling Circus in 1964, long before I came to America. He gave people here a taste of something different by using a far less rough training style than they had seen in the past. But

I was the first person Americans actually recognized as having a distinct style, used with many different types of animals, that was a radical departure from what they were used to.

Until I came here, I did not know that Americans did not train as I did in Europe, mostly with voice commands. I had only seen Clyde Beatty in movies and had never met him or seen him perform in person, so I did not know that his style was really quite different from mine. It never occurred to me that if I came to America to work, I should bring along a chair and a pistol. I enjoyed my own way of training and did not change it in America. I discovered that audiences also liked it very much. In the latter part of the twentieth century, people would have stoned me if I went into a ring with a pistol, chair, and whip, and if Clyde Beatty were alive today, he would have to change his style of training to move ahead with the times.

I adapted my style of horse training to tiger training. I had trained the horses to do a lot of different tricks, such as waltzing and making unique formations, and I thought it would be wonderful and very different from what other trainers were doing if I could use the same type of training with the tigers. I performed with the horses using only two liberty whips—lightweight, long, thin whips with extended handles, one with a long leather lash, and the other with a short one. One whip is carried in each hand during a performance. The whips are used to signal the animals and help them with direction during an act, not to beat them. When I performed with the tigers, these were the only things I used. I also taught the tigers to do tricks that I had seen done by chimps. I mixed everything together and came up with an unusual tiger act. I put a teeterboard in the tiger cage, and the tigers jumped on the board, then went onto the high wire and walked the wire. I used tricks in that act that had never before been combined. That was the beginning of my doing everything differently with tigers—I didn't just train them to walk around the cage, sit up, and roll over, all of which were traditional tiger tricks.

One of the acts I created for Circus Williams was a mixed act with a tiger and an elephant, inspired by a nineteenth-century photograph I had seen that showed a lion on an elephant's back. Lion training dates back thousands of years to the Romans, but tiger training does not go back far at all, maybe a hundred years. Training tigers and elephants to work together was much more difficult and much more dangerous than working with lions and elephants. The temperaments of lions and tigers are very different.

I had seen acts with a tiger on a horse's back at Circus Belli and Circus Althoff in Europe and did not want to do the same thing, so I decided to put a tiger on an elephant's back. That would be different enough—but it also turned out to be difficult. The problem was that every time the tiger jumped on the elephant, it bit the elephant's blanket in an attempt to bite the elephant. One tiger attacked the blanket, breaking all his big teeth in the process. I had to find a solution and thought it would be in the training. I changed the training so that as soon as the tiger jumped onto the elephant, I fed him a piece of meat so that he would forget about biting the elephant. Bengal was the first tiger I trained for this act, and no matter what I did with him, he bit the elephant's blanket every time he jumped on its back. I never got him to break that habit. He would sit on the elephant's back without a problem, as long as he had bitten the blanket first.

I later expanded this act to include horses, but expansion took a lot of time, since the right animals had to be found. The first time I combined the horses, elephants, and a tiger in a single act in the United States, I had to find two horses who would not be afraid of the tiger. I drove all over Texas from one ranch to the next until I bought two geldings who worked out. The next time I needed horses for that act, I bought Belgians, and they did not work out. They were scared to death of the tiger. When a horse shows he is afraid, that is a signal to the tiger, who will waste no time going after him. But if the horses are calm, the tigers have no interest in harming them.

Because the animals were well trained, and I was tuned in to the way they interacted, I was able to keep them under control and get them settled down quickly when things went wrong. We had many problems with power failures caused by bad weather. During every show we kept Jeeps around the cage in which the tigers performed so that if the lights did go out, we could immediately shine the car lights into the cage and I could keep the animals in place. When it suddenly becomes dark, the cats jump down from their positions, run around the ring, and will not do anything they are told. The idea is to get light on them before they leave their props.

We were hit with a power failure in the Carolinas when I was the middle of my elephant act. All the elephants were standing in a pyramid, and the lights suddenly went out. That was the most frightening moment of my life, but we got lucky. An emergency generator went on right away, and the lights came back up in seconds. How long could the elephants have held their positions in the dark? Elephants, who have bad eyesight to begin with, are completely blind when they go from light to dark. They hear much better than they see. It might be dark for only seconds, but that causes great tension and problems for them.

I sometimes had to learn through trial and error the capabilities of various animals. I learned the hard way just how dangerous zebras can be. In 1956, in Sweden, I had an accident involving two zebras named Said and Sera, that left

UNTAMED

my arm in a cast for four months. I was holding the reins for both zebras in one hand leading them to a tent. A man held back the flap of the tent so that we could go through, and just as the zebras cleared it, he let the flap fall. Zebras react in a wild way to anything sudden. They kick and flail outward in all directions. As I held the animals, one zebra ran to the right and the other ran to the left, and they broke my arm like a piece of wood. I actually heard my bone crack. It was in a cast for two months before it was operated on, and two pins were put in to help it heal. Before that I went through the painful process of doctors trying to set and re-set my arm because it was not healing correctly. After the pins were put in, I wore a cast for another two months.

Every break and bite was very painful. I have been bitten where the teeth went through one side of my hand and came out the other. Often when one of my hands or arms would be injured and swollen, I would have to keep it elevated while working, which in itself is uncomfortable. But I would heal and then forget about it; after all, it was not as if someone came up behind me and tried to kill me. Whenever an animal hurt me, it was an accident.

I rarely scolded my animals. Since they were trained well and they performed well, mistakes seldom occurred. Some animals needed to be reminded about who was in charge, but I did that without brutalizing them. Most knew by the tone of my voice when they did something wrong. The horses were a little different. I trained the horses with whom my wife and daughter worked, but no matter how well one trains horses, after a while they think they can do what they want. They jump around and try to do their own thing. A touch of a whip in the right place at the right moment reminds a horse who is in charge. If a horse gave me problems, the next day I would train him a little longer, and the act was perfected again.

That kind of quick brushup cannot be done with elephants and tigers. They do not take quick correction. They must be trained to perfection from the beginning, because if they do something wrong once, then twice, the trick will never again work out the way you want. Elephants are very smart. They are so smart they would even take the hook right out of the trainer's hand and hit him or her on the head with it. They do not listen at all when they do not want to, which is one of the reasons a person must have their respect in order to work with them. To earn their respect, a person has to be around them with the shovel, pushing away the manure, giving them hay and water, and showing concern and fondness for them.

Bears are healthy, strong, dangerous animals, but they are too indifferent and distrusting for me. I prefer more open animals. A bear will never look a man in the eyes. They are not honest animals. I also do not think I could use my style of training on bears. Their trainers use a rough style, working not in cages but with the bears on leashes. That was not for me.

When I start training an act, I like to work gradually. I will put only one animal inside the cage or ring and practice with him. Then I introduce a second, and a third, and so on. When more than one animal is brought into a cage or ring too early in the training, they might jump around and want to play or fight with each other. They have to learn that the day has come for more serious business, and that only when we finished practicing would there be time to play. Animals need time to understand that, some more than others.

I treat them like children, respecting them but making sure they know they have to listen to me to get my respect. I was in charge. I was the parent. I brought the food, and, as I would say to a child, when you put your feet under my table, you have to do what I want and what I say. With-

UNTAMED

out such respect there is no chance of being a successful trainer. I rewarded the animals during practice and after shows just as children are rewarded when they successfully complete a job or do something good. My son rewards them the same way today: the horses and elephants get carrots and apples; the cats get meat during practice; and some animals who favor special things, such as bread, get rewarded with extra portions of such treats when they are very good. A tiger named Axel used to do special tricks for me, such as sitting on a mirrored ball, so he always got a special meat bonus after the last show.

I treated my animals like a part of my family. Maybe that was because I never really had a family of my own when I was a child. I was as protective of my animals as I am of my own children, and I tried to keep them around me, safe and contented, for as long as I could. When I was a little boy, I was always alone. My father was never home, first because of his work and then because of the war. My mother never had a good life, and after the war, when I was only eleven years old, I hardly ever saw her because she had to work so hard to keep food on the table. After the war everyone wanted to break out of the old ways and start new lives, and I had very little contact with my mother. Then, after my parents all but sold me to the circus, I had no one but the animals.

I never dreamed about things I wanted to become or do when I was growing up in the small town of Schweidnitz, Schlesien, in a part of Germany that was known as Silesia. I came into this world on September 12, 1934, when virtually every nation stood at the brink of war. From day one my life was filled with harsh realities, and there was no place in it for daydreams and childish fantasies.

The times in which we lived stole any hope for the future from me, and I suppose they did the same to my sister, Rita, and my parents. My father, Max Gebel, was a carpenter who built sets for our local theatre. He worked his way up to technical director before his career was interrupted by the war. When peace was finally restored, he worked at theaters in various towns around Germany. I remember seeing many performances at the theater in Schweidnitz where my father worked before he went into the army. I could have been easily influenced by his job, but I never talked of following in my father's footsteps. Instead I grew to hate the theater. I have only bad memories of show business from those days—the theater girls who were such a regular part of my father's life, the parties that kept him away from us, and how he would so often come home drunk and fight with my mother.

Theater people in those days were always poor, and they stuck together all the time, often to the detriment of their families. These are the things I remember most about my father's situation, and as far back as I can recall, I had the idea that I never wanted to be one of the show folk. But the way things turned out, it must have been in my blood.

Although my father was never physically abusive to me and my sister, his treatment of us was brutal in other ways. For some reason he never allowed us to drink anything with our meals. Sometimes my food would not go down properly, but still my father would not permit me to take even a sip of water. I would have to force the food down without any liquid, and it would come back up my throat and out my nose. When we were allowed to take a drink, we were never permitted to fill our glasses. That stayed with me throughout my life, and to this day I do not fill my glass.

The only good that came from this was that I learned how not to treat my own family. I am very protective of my children, and because of that there have been times when I did not give them enough freedom. I love them so much and am so happy to have a family of my own that I try to keep them close to me, and that is not always the best thing for them.

Before and during the war my father was a Socialist, and because of his party affiliation he had more than his share of problems with the Nazis. His political views led to his being jailed and beaten several times by the SS. Once, they beat him so severely that they damaged several of his ribs. My father always turned to the Church for help, but it never helped anyone. He became embittered by this and stopped going even for services. He felt that if he could not turn to the clergy for protection, and he had to be on his own anyway, then he did not need them for spiritual guidance. Because of my father's feelings, my sister and I were never baptized. My mother, Elfriede, had very little to say about this, but she still raised me as a Protestant in the privacy of our home.

As far back as I can remember, my parents never had a good relationship with each other. They may have loved each other once, but by the time I was old enough to understand what was going on around me, they were emotionally very far apart. By today's standards my father was an alcoholic. When he was drunk, my parents fought, and when they fought, he beat my mother. I was only a little boy of four or five, and I would be so frightened by the violence between them that I would hide under the table and watch him hit her. Sometimes I hid in a closet until the yelling and hitting stopped.

When I was very young, I rarely saw my father when he was not drunk. Consequently I spent little time with him, so he and I did not have a relationship, good or bad. I knew only that when I saw him walking home, I was scared because I knew he would be drunk. It was a terrible situation, and my mother took an awful lot of abuse from my father. When I was six, he was taken into the army and away from home, so I did not have an opportunity to be around him as I was growing up. I did not miss the fighting, but I did miss having a good, loving father.

Even though I saw these horrible things happening to my mother, I never developed a close relationship with her either. Children act strangely under such strained conditions, and although I do not know if I blamed her for the kind of home life we had, I do know that I never tried to protect her. My sister is six years older than I, and I do not think she was ever involved in our parents' fights. Rita, also, was not close to them. Some siblings turn to each other for love and companionship, but my sister and I did not try to comfort each other during these times. I was too young and she was too independent. We did not live as a family, but rather as a group of individuals playing out their own separate lives.

Even when I grew older, my sister and I were never drawn together by our home life. We only seemed to grow farther and farther apart as we sought ways to escape our collective nightmare. Even today we do not have the kind of close relationship that is shared by many brothers and sisters. I regret that. Rita still lives near Düsseldorf, Germany, in the town of Duisburg in which my mother lived for the last twenty years of her life. They lived only a couple of blocks from each other. Perhaps if Rita and I lived closer to each other, we would have time to talk, and I would get some answers about why our parents acted the way they did and why they were so indifferent toward their children. But we are worlds apart geographically, and in terms of our feelings.

My father completely disappeared from my life after he went into the army. I lost all contact with him. He was gone for five years, and in all that time he came home only two or three times for a couple of days. All the men in our community disappeared into the war. It was so strange to see a town without men. Germany had waged war against the whole world, and it needed all of its men in the fight. I was lucky, I was too young to be drafted, and years later when Germany formed an army again, I was too old.

I was eleven years old when Hitler was brought down in 1945, and I vividly remember what life was like during the war. Our tiny town was in the path the Russians were taking into Germany, so the fighting was all around us and grew more intense as the war dragged on. My mother tried hard to keep us together during that time, but my sister was seldom with us. Although she was not in the army, the military forced all the young girls and boys to go to the eastern front to build walls to hold back the Russian tanks. I had spent little time with my sister before the war, but after it started, I hardly ever saw her. When teenagers were not being used to build barriers, they were made to help in hospitals and elsewhere. All the children had to do it. They were not given a choice. We even saw youngsters carrying guns. I was spared that fate because I was too small and could not manage the weight of a gun.

My mother was a seamstress, and she kept us alive by taking in handiwork, for which she was paid not in money but in food. Unlike many of our neighbors, we always had something to eat. Today kids eat shrimp and steak as if they were commonplace foods. They go from a bicycle to a motorcycle to a car. They even have their own phones. When I was a child, our family never had a telephone. We never even had our own bathtub. We were able to take baths only on Saturdays, when a large steel tub would be hauled into the kitchen, and water, heated on the stove, would be poured inside for us to bathe in. We never had toilet paper during or after the war, only newspaper. It made me crazy when my children, as youngsters, wasted toilet paper. I can afford as much of it as I want, but that is not the point. The point is the waste and how vividly I recall those lean years.

Oddly enough I did not grow closer to my mother during the war years. And even after my disruptive father was gone, I really was not a good boy. I was a rebel. I refused to do anything to help my mother. When she wanted something, she always had to get somebody else to do it for her. She was pretty rough with me, which may account for why

I was not a little angel. My mother was quite physical when she became enraged. She used to hit me with heavy wooden clothes hangers and often broke them on my head. Once as a punishment, she forced me into a clothes closet and locked the door behind me. I was so upset with her that I ripped up all of her clothes hanging in that closet, which only led to more punishment.

I was a very angry person when I was young. Maybe that is what kept me alive. My difficult life made me tough and pushed me farther away from people and closer and closer to animals. Though some children in similar situations create imaginary playmates and friends, I never did. I was a very serious child. The seriousness of life never let go of me, and I had no time to escape harsh reality, not even in dreams. We struggled to have food and clean water every day. Nothing was pleasant or nice enough to foster a dream. I did not know that life could be different, so I did not dream about it being better.

I do not look back on those days and pine over things that I missed. You really cannot miss what you never had. But sometimes I am perturbed by the way children today, and even some adults, take things for granted. We had so little when I was a child, and appreciated what we did have so much.

I never finished grammar school, so there was no chance I could attend high school later on. The only formal education I had was during the war, when I attended the Pestalozzi School for four years. It was three miles from the suburb in which we lived, and naturally I walked there every day, which was extremely dangerous because the war was very close. It was so hard to learn anything with planes constantly flying overhead, bombs being dropped all around us, and the Russians coming closer and closer every day. Still, we had to go to school each morning. Hitler believed that school was the most important facet of a child's life because it could be used to indoctrinate young minds. In class we had to stand erect and "Heil Hitler" every day, whether we wanted to or not. I remember so many times when we had to stand for half an hour at a time with our arms in the air "Heiling Hitler." This was supposedly designed to toughen our young minds and bodies and give us endurance. I remember thinking how much I hated Hitler because I had to stand with my arm outstretched before me, not even able to hold it up with my other hand when it became tired.

There was also an emphasis on sports, because the Nazis believed that one had to be able to run and stay fit if one was to be a good soldier. We never did acrobatics or calisthenics, just running and related activities to build up the body. We were taught to march and sing, which was supposed to give us a sense of drive and nationalism.

I was not really afraid of the Gestapo, although their presence was constant. I knew, as did all other children, that if I did not go to school, they would be at my door looking for me, and I did not want that to happen. I still had memories of my father's bad experiences with the SS, and even though I did not live in fear of them, I did not want to incur their wrath. It became an accepted part of our lives to go to school, be there all day, and do what they wanted us to do, regardless of how painful or distasteful. Nobody was home to resist them. My father and most of the other men were gone, and a bunch of women and children could not have fought the Gestapo.

There were so many bad things around us, it was depressing for children. We did not know what to do with ourselves to have fun. I always felt so cold, and yet, for a diversion, my little friends and I would go swimming in the coldest weather in below-freezing water. My tolerance for the cold did not improve with age. Today I put on a coat if the temperature falls below 80 degrees.

In school everyone had to learn to play a musical instrument. My mother played the piano, my father played a zither, and I ended up with a violin. I had to walk four to five miles to get to the place where I took my music lessons. After the war I never wanted to play the violin again, even though I had taken lessons for a year. When I was very young, I would stand in front of the radio when it was playing and pretend that I was a conductor. I think that is why my mother decided to make the financial sacrifice and send me to violin lessons.

Our whole generation was brainwashed by the Nazis. Many parents listened to radio frequencies that were used by the Allies to broadcast news from the free world. We had only a little radio with maybe two channels, but when the Americans or the British talked, we listened. I knew of people who were turned in by their children for doing this. But I could never be that kind of person. I understood some of what was going on around me, and I hated it.

I was always afraid, always nervous. I was a physically small child, and I believe that I never grew to be very tall and broad because during the war, even though my mother exchanged work for food, I never had enough to eat nor enough sleep. I spent almost every night in the cellar because of the bombing. Each night we had to pile our shoes, socks, and clothes in the same spot near where we slept because we had to be able to find our things in the dark during an air raid. We were drilled and drilled—our entire life centered around drilling. Many, many nights we had to flee to the cellars because of the air raids by the Russians, and later the Americans.

The small airport near our home was always bombed, because it was used by the military. It was easy to spot the Russians because they used small planes with two men and flew low to the ground. One man would fly the plane and the other would drop a bomb by hand. But the Americans came with hundreds and hundreds of planes high in the sky. I used to look up and see those silver things glistening in the sunlight. They all flew over our little town because of the airport. Whenever the planes came, everyone had to run for cover, and that meant going to the cellar. To this day I still put my shoes and clothes in the same place at night.

Our region, Silesia, was positioned in such a way that it was surrounded by Russia, Poland, and the bulk of Germany. All the artillery, troop convoys, everything came through Silesia. Even when the Polish people were fleeing from the Russians, they passed through our area. Though I was not a soldier, I saw the war firsthand.

I was never able to have fun and play outside and do the things that other children do. During a war, children do what they must to survive. Adults and children were crying all the time, which was very upsetting. The worst time of the year for me was always Christmas, and to this day I do not like it. I remember all those Christmases during the war, hearing that the brother from one family was dead, and the father from another was not coming back, and some other neighbor had lost his legs, et cetera. Christmas is a very big family affair in Germany, but for us it was not a time for celebration. I only thought about who was dead and who was missing and how much pain it brought to the surviving family members, who could do nothing but cry.

I never wanted to be a German, and what happened during the war has bothered me all my life. I could not do anything to stop the atrocities, but my parents and other adults did nothing. I was in Litzmannstadt (Lódź), a big ghetto in Poland, and I saw what was happening to the people there, but I did not understand it. I thought they must be bad people. That is a child's logic. A child believes that if someone is locked up and punished, it is because they have been bad. Nobody told me the Jewish people were innocent victims. I saw them driven onto tramp trains along with their friends and families—children crying, women sobbing in the arms of their men—with nothing but the clothes on their backs. Today I ask myself how in the hell this went on without anybody in Germany rising up against it. Even if everyone rose up and ended up shot and bleeding, their attitude should have been, "Well, then let us die so that the next generation will live with pride."

This still weighs very heavily on me, and my feelings about Christmas disturb my family, but I am still dealing with these memories. My family often urges me to join in Christmas festivities, but it is very difficult for me to enjoy myself during that time of year. I am certain it was just as hard for my mother and sister to face Christmas during the war.

Contributing to my anxiety at Christmastime was that my mother never had time for us. A pair of handmade socks was the best she could do for us as Christmas presents. She was always too busy with the handiwork she did for others to do anything for us. Years later she never even made time for my children. She came to visit a couple of times in America when my son was small, but she never tried to build a relationship with him either.

Everything was scarce during the war, and I had few clothes. I always had to wear long, handmade socks with a rubber band around the top near the knee to prevent them from falling down around my ankles. I hated that. Every Sunday I would sit at the table and cry because I did not want to wear those same stockings on Sunday. I refused to go out, because I had to wear the same clothes I had worn all week. My mother worked constantly and was only slightly sympathetic about this, probably because she thought it was foolish in light of what was happening around us. Once, she bought fabric to make a shirt for me, and if she were alive today, the fabric would still be in her basket waiting to be cut. She took in a lot of work and promised each job by a certain day. Work came first. But we always had food, so I suppose that was the most important thing.

I was a bad eater as a child because I didn't like the food we had at home. We ate chicken on Sundays, and during the week our main course was soup. As an adult I ate five meals a day while performing. Sigrid would cook breakfast, lunch, and dinner, and I would eat snacks between shows and after the last show. But when I was a little boy, my mother would give us thin soup, a little bread, and some carrots, and if you did not eat, that was your problem. During the day all we had was some tea.

Even birthdays were nothing to look forward to when I was a child. I was born on the same day as my mother. My sister told me that my mother made the midwife hold back my birth so that I would be born on her birthday. As a child I was always upset that I did not have my own birthday and my own cake. All the fat ladies in town would come to the birthday party, but not for me, for my mother. I never had a party of my own.

All necessities, especially shoes, were very hard to come by. I had only a pair of sandals. Things like this change a person's life and the way one thinks. I believe this is one of the reasons I buy shoes for people in the circus who cannot afford them. It is another spillover from my childhood.

Lice was a big problem for soldiers and civilians during the war. It was brutal for soldiers in casts when lice got beneath the plaster. Everybody had head and body lice. This was especially disconcerting at bedtime because they were more irritating when a person was resting. The soldiers always tried to sleep in a horse blanket because, oddly enough, lice did not go inside those blankets. I never had a horse blanket, but when I got my hands on lice powder, I would sleep in drifts of it because I hated being bitten. Years later I found out that the DDT powder that was used during the war to control lice was very dangerous and caused many illnesses.

There were few diversions in those days, but one that brought me some peace from the fighting and hardships was skiing. We had small mountains about three miles from our town—practically in our backyard. I used to go skiing there with my friends. The first year I came to America, I took my family and a few circus friends to ski in the Sugar Mountains in North Carolina. Some of the people with us were high-wire performers, and I could not believe that anyone who worked the high wire would not be able to stand on two skis, but one of them could not. I thought I could stay on skis because I had done so as a child, but I was unable to keep my balance. I fell so many times that I had snow all over my clothes, even in my underwear. We laughed so much that we cried. It was a wonderful experience for me because I had not skied since I was a child, and it brought back some of the few happy memories I have from those years.

During the war, skiing offered only a brief escape. As the Russian front inched closer to our town, people began to leave. For months I watched as friends and neighbors collected their belongings and even their livestock—everything they could carry or cart—and left town. I would peer out our window in the direction of the airport, watch people passing as they left, and wonder what was to become of us. The Russian front was so close we could hear all the action every day. The constant bombing and fighting were becoming too much to bear, and finally one day we, too, had to leave. We packed whatever we could carry—for me that meant rolling a pair of socks into an extra pair of pants and packing it under my arm—and fled west to what was to become East Germany. Everything else was left in our apartment, unpacked, as if we were going on a short trip and intended to return. When we left, my father was a prisoner of war in Russia. Some of the prisoners came back before the war ended, but he was not one of them.

Rita, my mother, and I ended up in a town called Zwickau, which eventually the Russians invaded as well. I remember it as if it had happened yesterday, the night the Russian tanks came rolling in—hundreds and hundreds of tanks, and that terrible noise they made. We were stuck in East Germany under Russian control. My mother reckoned that if we were going to have to live under those conditions, we might as well try to make it home again. In 1945 mother, Rita, and I worked our way back to Schweidnitz through pockets of fighting and resistance. I was ten years old. I do not know how many miles we walked—it was very far—but we made it. When we got there, I was shocked to see that our entire apartment was as we had left it. It was not even slightly damaged, so we started over again. Our old friends were gone, and young people stayed away; mostly only the old people returned. But at least our surroundings were familiar. There was nothing for us in East Germany, and my mother had been unable to find work. At least when we went back to Silesia, she had a seamstress job.

We did not return with any special hopes—I do not think there was anything to hope for. Almost everything had been badly damaged by the bombing and had to be rebuilt. I was too young to be involved, and in retrospect it was for the best because a short time later I got hooked up with the circus.

One good thing about my mother was that she was always willing to work for a living. When we returned home, she worked for the Russians, making things for their women and mending and tailoring uniforms for the soldiers. We ended up living in a Russian community. That was very peculiar, since before the invasion, it had been a solidly German Protestant community. Kings, even Kaiser Wilhelm, had come from our area.

We lived in this town for one year. I learned to speak Russian fluently; we made good friends and always had food. I did not hate the Russian people. They were very poor but very nice, and they were devoted to their country. But they were also brainwashed for many years. It was the same thing that Hitler had done to us—they had no rights. Living among the Russians was a day-to-day existence, and we tolerated it, for that was all we could do. Then one day my mother became a casualty of war: she was raped in our home by several Russian soldiers. They did not know I was in the apartment, and five of them came in and attacked her. I was in another room when I heard her crying and yelling, and I was so frightened that I hid under the bed. When her screams became unbearable to hear, I ran to help her. One soldier was standing nearby while another was on top of her. A couple of them ran behind me, grabbed my arms, and held me. I felt as helpless as my poor mother. We knew that this had happened many times in our neighborhood, and now it was happening in our own home.

By this point in the occupation the Russians were a little more organized than they had been when they first took over. My mother reported the attack, and after that we never again saw the soldiers who were involved. My mother never talked to me about what had happened, even though she knew I had seen everything. I believe parents think ten-year-olds do not understand such things. But I did, and it was just another piece of what would be stored away in my young mind.

I did some bad things to the Russians during the early

part of their occupation because I was mischievous. The Russians kept two horses hooked up to a buggy and two military guards outside each occupied government building. Armed with my slingshot and a pocketful of stones, I would climb to the rooftops of nearby buildings and shoot the stones at the horses' backsides so that they would run away and the soldiers would have to chase them. Later on I organized four or five of my friends and we caught a Russian soldier whom we did not like and beat him up. When the Nazis were in power, we had to stay in line all the time. No allowances were made for mischief or childish pranks. When the Russians took over, I think we acted out of relief because we could do many things without the threat of punishment. But I really tested their tolerance with some of the things I did.

We acted out of stupidity, fun, and some hostility, but the Russians tried to overlook our pranks. They often invited us to eat with them, and they would sing and dance and try to be happy, even though times were hard. They chased after us when we pestered them too much, but we had dozens of great hiding places in old, empty houses and big barracks left behind from the old German army. We would scatter and hide, and the Russians never found us.

The Poles were more feared than the Russians because they hated the Germans even more than the Russians did. The Russians were forced into the war, but the Germans invaded Poland and did a lot of terrible things to those people. Polish animosity was so strong that we knew if we did something out of line, they would take our heads off, so as children we were very careful not to harass them.

Russian soldiers introduced me to several things, including vodka. To this day I do not drink it because of all the vodka I drank when I was ten years old. My friends and I were very impressionable, and since we always saw the

Poles and Russians drinking, we started drinking too. We began with a sip of this and a sip of that. After a while I was so heavily involved with drinking that I stole things from my mother, such as silverware, to have money for vodka. I threw the loot out the window of our apartment to a friend who would be waiting below, then we sold the stuff to the Polish people. My mother never knew what I was doing. She was always too busy to keep track of me or her belongings.

I drank so much vodka that I got falling-down drunk. I somehow managed to get home and slip into bed, but God help me if I tried to raise my head. The room would spin so crazily that I would be sick to my stomach.

I did not drink liquor long enough to become an alcoholic. After I finally stopped drinking, at the age of twelve, I did not drink so much as a glass of beer. Even today I drink very little.

As a child I also smoked, but I did not start out with regular cigarettes. The Russians smoked what they called *majorka,* which came not from the plush tobacco leaves but from their stems. They were chopped up, sometimes mixed with tea, and rolled into Russian newspaper. Anyone who wanted to smoke *majorka* had to roll it in Russian newspaper, since others did not burn as well. Later my friends and I graduated to Camel cigarettes, which we got from the Americans and the Russians.

Not long after we returned to our hometown in 1946, I started working for the Russians, tending their horses. I was the only child in town who worked for them. This was my first real job, though I received no pay. I had been hanging around the horses when one of the soldiers asked me if I wanted the job caring for two of them. I jumped at the chance, but I did not know where to find sufficient hay for them. There was no extra food in the area. But I remembered that before the war, everyone's backyards contained vegetable gardens and many people also kept rabbits. I looked in every rabbit house for hay to bring to the horses, and this was a source of tremendous enjoyment for me. I felt very responsible and important because I figured the horses were depending on me for food.

I then got a job on a farm controlled by the Russian military. I was a very slight boy, the work was very hard, and my mother let me travel thirty kilometers (about fifteen miles) away from home to live and work in that place. My first duty at the farm entailed working the soil with two horses on a plow. When the Russians realized that I was too small for that, they gave me two horses on a carriage, and I drove a Russian officer. The only reason I took the job was to be around the animals, and for that reason I worked there for several months. I worked very hard and did everything that was asked of me, regardless of how difficult it was.

I lived a day-to-day existence on the farm, without any schooling. I had my own room, but there were no other children for me to stay with, only old farmers. I was a very serious child and extremely diligent. I took care of the horses, watered and fed them. Most of the other work was very difficult for me, and I would cry when I could not do it.

Once a plow fell over while I was working, and I could not right it. It was so painful trying to pick it up. I did not have good horses who walked in straight lines, and so they would cause the plow to sway and move in different directions, making it difficult to keep it upright. My plow lines were always crooked because the horses would not walk straight. When it hit rocks, the plow jumped out of the ground, and I would become so frightened that I would let go of it and it would fall over.

Although I had food and shelter at the farm, it was a

very disheartening way of life. Everyone was filled with so much despair, so much anguish. Under the Russians and Polish people we Germans were like slaves, which perhaps was just. There seemed to be no future for anybody, so many people walked around like zombies, going through the motions to make a living, but few had the drive to leave and look for something better. When something went wrong in the fields, none of the workers cared.

Then I became very ill and had to be sent to a hospital. I developed eczema and a highly contagious fungus on my hands and fingers resulting in large blisters; my skin was raw. I think it was caused by the unsanitary conditions at the farm. I wanted to go back and work with the animals, but I could not because of my hands.

My mother seemed indifferent to my suffering. A Russian doctor sorely reprimanded her once because I had been very badly bitten in the leg by a German shepherd and my mother had waited several days before bringing me to a hospital. She finally had to push me there in an old baby carriage because I could not walk. The doctor was furious because the dog might have had rabies. It was not rabid after all, but a Russian soldier shot it anyway when it tried to bite him too.

My mother's indifference also extended to our daily activities. I do not believe she knew or cared where my sister and I were half the time. When we were forced to leave our home in Silesia a second time, Rita did not go with us, so after the war she never reunited with us as a family. It was many years later when she and our mother finally got together again.

I was eleven years old when we left our home for the second and last time. After the war ended, the Russians and Americans decided to turn Silesia over to Poland, and it became Świdnica. One day the Russians said, "We have to go home, and the Polish people are coming in to take over." The Polish people actually threw us out.

There was very little that my mother and I could take with us. I had a little toy horse with a buggy, which I had always handled very carefully because it was my only toy. We did not have room to take it when we left Silesia for good. I left my violin behind and stuffed the case with whatever clothes would fit. On our way out of town, we had to trek through very deep, spongy mud, and I was struggling so hard to move my legs that I wobbled, my violin case opened, and everything fell into the mud. What little I had was covered with dirt, and I had to put it back into the case in that condition. Then we trudged on to the stock cars.

Ironically we were herded into the same train cars the Jewish people had been forced into only a couple of months before. I remember sitting at a window, looking at the entire scene with detachment. The trains were now headed for East Germany, but they stopped along the way for us to be sprayed with DDT powder. We had to stand in a single line, and when it came our turn, each of us had to step under a loft. A cord was pulled, a hatch opened, and DDT powder fell onto us. We were snow white from the powder, and it got into our mouths and eyes. I often wondered later how many people died from being exposed to that stuff, but I suppose it was the only chemical available at the time to control the lice. We then got back into the stock cars to complete our trip. Many of the trains continued on to West Germany, but not ours. We ended up in the same damn spot in East Germany we had left only a year before.

We lived in the town of Zwickau, Sachsen, where everyone was dirt poor. As we expected, food was very scarce. I never ate so many potatoes in my life, and they were not even cooked. We would peel them, sprinkle them

with salt, and eat them raw. Whatever bread we could get
was always stale and filled with foreign matter, such as dirt
and rodent hair. My stomach used to turn when I put it into
my mouth. In East Germany everything was very bad. Forty
years later when the Berlin Wall was torn down, the people
were still poor.

My father came back to Germany within two years after
the war ended. At some point before his return, he and my
mother must have decided that they were not going to live
together again, because father did not join us in Zwickau.
My mother knew of his whereabouts and his plans through
correspondence from him. Although she never mentioned
getting a divorce, I am certain they did, because they both
remarried later on.

Life in Zwickau was miserable, so miserable that I decided I wanted to live with my father. Time had taken the
edge off my memory of him, and I believed that somehow
things would be different if I could only find him. I learned,
from a letter he had written to my mother, that he was
living in a place called Wanne-Eickel in West Germany. I
copied his street address from that letter and hid it away as
if it were some great treasure. I did not run away from
home; my mother knew where I was going when I set out
to look for my father, and she let me go. I left with only
the clothes I was wearing.

I had to take a train to the border that separated East
and West Germany. There I found a checkpoint that was
guarded by Russian soldiers. All the passengers from the
train were forced to stand in a single line and wait for the
Russians to check their papers and give them permission to
cross the border. I was only eleven years old and I was
terribly frightened as I waited there. Suddenly I saw three
young men break away from the line and run like mad across
the border. I did not know why they were running, but I

UNTAMED

bolted from the line and took off behind them. We were surrounded by farmland and open fields, which made it easy for the guards to see us as we ran. It was the early summer, and there had been much rain, so the ground was thick with more than a foot of mud. As we tried to run, the mud pulled at our feet, and I repeatedly fell until I was covered with mud from head to toe. The Russian guards began to chase us, all the while firing in our direction. I heard several bullets whiz over my head, but that did not stop me. I pushed on through the mud, so scared that I would not look back. After a while all I heard was the sound of my own heart beating.

I do not know what became of those other men, but I managed to keep going until I no longer heard the Russian soldiers. I cut across the wet fields to higher ground and walked the rest of the way. I was exhausted when I finally reached that little town, but my heart soared when I actually found my father's address and saw his name on the letter box. I did not know what to expect from him, whether he was living with someone or had remarried. All I knew for certain was that I had really found my father. It was one of the few times in my life that I allowed myself to become prematurely excited about anything.

I had dreamed of arriving at the door, ringing his bell, my father stepping out to see me, and his face breaking into a smile as I shouted, "Here I am!" But that did not happen. He was not home, and I was terribly disappointed. But I was making a new life for myself, and I was not about to go away. I sat at his front door for hours until I was so down and depressed that I did not expect anything anymore.

It was not very cold, but it was raining, and I was awfully uncomfortable after all I had been through to get there. My blond hair looked brown from the mud, and my clothes were caked with it. It was very demoralizing to have to wait on the street all day and into the night. When my father finally came home, it was after midnight. He was surprised to see me all right, but he did not take me in his arms and hug me and tell me how much he had missed me. He was not very happy at all. From the moment I explained my purpose, he made it quite clear that I could not live with him. He made excuses that there was no room for me and that he had to work every day and could not take care of me. He said I would have to go back to live with my mother because I would be a handicap for him.

I cannot recall how long I stayed in Wanne-Eickel with my father—it was not much more than a week or so—but I discovered some wonderful things while I was there. My father had a CARE package in his apartment, and in it I found my first bar of Hershey chocolate. He also had big, bright yellow bananas. I had never even seen bananas. And gum! He had gum, which he had gotten from the Americans, and I ate all of it. I later found out that you are supposed to throw the gum away when you are finished with it. I did not know that, so I swallowed it. I saw people standing in line for real bread. White bread. I ate white bread as if it were cake while I was with my father. I ate it as if I had never before seen bread.

It was a great experience for me to be able to discover all these new things. It was the only nice part of my stay in Wanne-Eickel. My father had only one bed, so I slept on the couch. He did not take me to work with him, so I never got to see the theatre where he spent most of his days and nights. We did not talk about the war or our experiences, or how we had lived before. He said nothing about why he did not come back to be with us when it was over, and I did not dare to question him about any of it. Young children were taught to accept things as they were. I never asked him why he wasn't happy to see me or if he even loved me.

UNTAMED

But it was a strange feeling to know that I was not wanted in his home and that I would have to leave soon.

We spent little time together, but one episode is memorable. We went into a shop, and I saw a hat that I wanted very badly, but I did not have enough money to buy it. My father watched me try it on, and it was clear that I wanted it. He finally said, "Well, if you do not have enough money to buy it now, buy it next time." I felt foolish and hurt.

Shortly afterward my mother came to West Germany on some business and took me back to live with her. I had no choice, because I was too young to live on my own. Soon my mother and I returned to West Germany for good and moved in with some friends. Our move to the West was the beginning of a new life for me, but as had been the case with our "new beginnings" in the past, this one started off on a bittersweet note.

Our situation hardly improved once we moved to West Germany. We were living with friends in cramped quarters in Cologne. Rita was on her own, having moved to the West before us, and my mother was without a job. She was not even taking in piecework as she had during the war. I never questioned my mother's actions, but I was not happy with our situation.

We had not been in Cologne long when my mother gave me the thrill of my life—she took me to see the circus for the first time! If she had known how drastically that outing was going to change our lives, she might have taken me there sooner, or perhaps never at all.

We saw an afternoon show of Circus Williams, and as we were leaving the grounds, I noticed a Help Wanted sign that stated the circus was looking for a dressmaker. I became excited and said, "Mom, there's a job for you! Let's go and find out about it." She was not very enthusiastic, but I insisted so strongly that she inquired about the position, and they offered it to her. For whatever reasons, my mother did not especially want the job, but I pleaded with her to take it. We needed the money desperately, and in those days in 1947, so soon after the war, jobs were not easy to find.

I was also thinking about myself, because I had been overwhelmed by the circus. I had never seen anything so wonderful! This was the first time that I was so completely taken in by anything. I was caught up in the excitement and color of it and consumed with the idea that it seemed like so much fun. I do not know what pushed me in that direction that day. Maybe the Lord was behind me.

Circus Williams actually hired both of us, and we lived and worked there. I was given a uniform the second day and put to work as an usher. They even included my picture in the program. I performed many different tasks right from the beginning. I was interested in learning, and I never complained about anything I was asked to do—I just did it. I was a hard worker for my years and anxious to please. I was also very respectful and well mannered, characteristics that were appreciated by the people who ran the circus.

I was with Circus Williams only a couple of days when I celebrated my thirteenth birthday. And I mean just that. I celebrated my birthday. There was no party for me, no hoopla, no cake, but this time it did not seem to matter. I was wildly happy that my mother and I were working for the circus. I had a job that I enjoyed, I was around animals every day, and there was enough food for us to eat.

My newfound happiness was short-lived, once again thanks to my parents. My mother and I had only been with the circus two or three weeks when she dropped a bombshell. She was quitting her job, but I was to stay on. She had already discussed this with the owners of the circus and asked them to draw up an employment contract for my services, which was like giving me away. She got in touch with my father, and they both signed the agreement. They could not have done a neater job if they had sold me outright and made a profit. When she told me, I felt as if I had fallen and it knocked all the wind out of my lungs. My eyes filled with hot tears, but she offered no explanation and showed no regrets. And because of my age I had nothing to say about it.

I could not understand why my mother was doing this to me. I tried and tried to figure out what I had done that was so bad to make her want to get rid of me. I was terribly distraught, but she did not change her mind. I do not remember if she kissed me when she left or even said goodbye. All I know is that one day she was gone. So I began life on my own.

A child caught up in such emotional turmoil cannot be expected to use reason to understand his plight. I have thought about this since I was thirteen, and now, as an adult, the only thing I can think of to justify my parents' actions is that after the war they wanted no part of the past. Everybody wanted to make a new life, and I did not fit into their plans.

Perhaps my mother had been through so much that she no longer wanted any responsibility. She was obviously looking for a new beginning, and nothing, not even her children, was going to hold her back.

It was terrible for me. I cried myself to sleep many nights, looking at her picture and feeling so alone. Despite everything we had been through, I still loved my mother and wanted to be with her. I was frightened to be away from her. She had not discussed her plans with me, and I had no idea where she was going. I did not feel particularly well or very strong at that time. Many evenings I sat by myself feeling despondent and helpless. I would go into the stables and sit near the horses and cry. I felt as if they understood what I was going through.

It was some time before I received a letter from my mother telling me where she was and what she was doing. But even in that letter she did not explain her actions or say she missed me and was sorry for leaving me behind. By the time she wrote to me, she had settled in Duisburg and was working in a dress shop, making alterations. The greatest irony is that years later, she ended up working for Circus Krone as the costume mistress. She stayed with that circus for a couple of years, then returned to Duisburg, where she remarried.

I did not understand the terms of my contract. I simply knew that I had to stay with the circus and accepted my fate. The circus provided me with food and lodging, and my contract called for me to be paid, not my parents. It stipulated that I was to do general work around the circus, including helping in the kitchen. From the day I started working for Circus Williams, I never cost my parents a single penny. I received my paycheck every week and never asked my family for anything, not even clothes, which the Williams family provided.

Although I did not know it at the time, I was very fortunate that my mother had chosen to abandon me at Circus Williams. Harry and Carola Williams liked me from the beginning and treated me as if I were a son. They had children of their own, however, and I never tried to put myself before them or take advantage of the way Harry and Carola felt about me. I developed a deep sense of loyalty to Mr. and Mrs. Williams. Many people move from circus to circus, taking different jobs, but I stayed with the Williams family and their circus until I came to America. I had many opportunities to do other things and could have come to America much sooner than I did, but Circus Williams was where I started, and I felt an allegiance to them. They became the family I never had.

UNTAMED

I made little money working for them, especially in the early years. I earned the equivalent of a quarter a day, then a dollar a day, and even after five years I hardly made much more than that. But in that family money was not necessary. Through their generosity I ate, had clothes, and a place to live. I did not need more than that, and so money became incidental to me. I did not carry money because I never had to buy anything, and I was actually able to save the little bit of money I earned. Even today I do not carry money in my pocket, and it does not even bother me to be without change because I am not the kind of person who stops during the day to buy a cup of coffee. Occasionally over the years I did not have enough money in my pocket to pay a highway toll. Now I carry money in my briefcase.

Quite a bit of time had passed before my mother came to see me at the circus. My father never came and never even wrote. It was as if he and I did not exist for each other. I desperately wanted him to be proud of even little things I did at that time, but he never saw any of it.

After they signed me over to the circus, I went to visit my father a few times. Children always hope that their parents are going to change and want them and like them. I kept hoping that would happen with my father, but it never did. As I grew older, I was less and less inclined to visit him, and after a while I no longer bothered.

My mother made an annual visit to Circus Williams, and whenever she showed up, it was an especially happy time for me. However, I eventually became accustomed to living without her. My days were so busy that after I got used to being alone, I no longer missed her. After a few years she stopped visiting me altogether and only showed up in the audience once after she remarried.

My mother seldom wrote to me, even though she was able to keep track of my whereabouts by following news of

Circus Williams. I tried to keep in touch through letters, but I did not always know where to write because she moved around so much. About seven years after she left me at the circus, I stopped writing to her. I hardly ever saw or heard from my sister.

Years later when my mother died, my sister found some of my letters among my mother's personal belongings. She had kept them in a neat little stack, tied together with a faded pale green ribbon. One was a Christmas greeting in a lovely card that I had sent her in 1948:

Dear Mother,

With all my heart I wish you well. Stay in good health. Don't be mad at me, a letter is following.

Your son, Gunther

There I was at Christmastime, deserted by my family, and I was concerned that she would be angry because I had only sent a card and not a letter. Below my signature I had covered the bottom of the card with symbols for hugs and kisses.

The circus did not make allowances for my age and permit me to work fewer hours than anyone else, and I would never have thought to ask for special treatment. I worked every day from early morning until late at night, and I hardly had time for anything else. I had so little free time that at one point, in early 1949, it took more than a week for me to complete a letter to my mother. I was in Cologne, where Circus Williams had its winter quarters. In my letter, dated February 27, I told her things I thought she would want to know about how I was living:

UNTAMED

Dear Mother,

Today, February 20, I had time to write you a few lines. Dear mother, I have had no news from you for a long time. Are things coming along in Hamburg? Is Rita planning to go to Hamburg? Here, where I am, nothing has changed, but there is much work because in a few days the season goes on. . . . In this season we will have short playing dates—only two or three days, sometimes five, in each place we visit—so we will have much to do. What is to become of me in respect to my apprenticeship I do not know yet. Today it is only a question of filling the pocket. . . .

A few days ago I took a trip to Castle Alberman, and these few days were some of the nicest I have known. . . . Dear mother, please excuse the bad writing, but it is almost midnight. You know, dear mother, how tired one gets. My eyes are almost falling shut. Dear mother, forgive me. Stay well . . . don't be mad at me that I have not written sooner. I will end this letter with my best regards. . . .

I closed my letters with many kisses across the page, and I would always tell her how much I missed her. I cried a lot when I was alone, knowing I really had nobody. When these letters were returned to me after my mother's death, I read them and thought, "How could a mother get something like this and not come and pick me up? How could she not want me to be with her?"

With my mother off and living on her own, work became my life. I immersed myself in it because it helped to keep my mind occupied. I did many things at Circus Williams in the beginning of my career, including cleaning up behind the animals. I never minded that job because it gave me an opportunity to be around them and to learn about taking care of them. I displayed a tremendous enthusiasm for them and jumped right into anything I was asked to do for them. Often, while I was caring for them or cleaning their stables, I would talk to them, and they got to know me quite well.

I wanted to be a part of everything, and some circus people started teaching me acrobatics when I was thirteen years old. They taught me to do handstands and somersaults, and although I had never participated in organized sports, I discovered that I was athletic. Many children at the circus in my age group were much more talented than I was, though. I was stiff as a board when I began this training, but everyone was nice to me and encouraged me to go on and try new things. They also laughed at me, sometimes out loud, sometimes behind my back. I did not like it when they laughed, but I stayed with it. After the handstands and somersaults, I graduated to more complicated work.

I also practiced with the trapeze act, but did not excel at it. But I tried everything, and I learned enough so that I was able to work my way into the acrobatic act. I was told that acrobatics was the best place to start learning to be a performer, and that was true. My early acrobatics training helped me throughout my career. I did not know exactly what I wanted to do. I just tried everything, discovering what I liked as I went along. I enjoyed every aspect of the work and never had to be forced to do anything—whether it was easy or not. And since I was most interested in animals, I spent as much time as possible working in and around their stalls, and watching them during practices.

No single person at the circus became my teacher. All the performers took me under their wing and taught me different things. After acrobatics I started learning to work with horses and ponies in short acts. In one of them four of us drove little ponies with sulkies behind them. We wore jockey costumes and had a lot of fun. I always got the last sulky, and in that position I was supposed to be a comedian and do slapstick things. I always did something to make the cart fall over, such as run behind it and jump for it, which made people laugh. I was also responsible for cleaning my own sulky and pony afterward.

Later on we had an act where we had to ride the ponies while wearing grand costumes with big hats. A girl was needed for this routine, and since we did not have one, the other boys made me dress in a girl's costume and wear a big wig. I hated that part. They always did everything to me because I was the youngest and they liked to tease me. I was not quite fourteen years old at that time. In another act they dressed me in a Hungarian national folk costume with a weird hat and had me present an act of six Austrian horses. I always had to carry that damned hat with the big feather sticking off the top of it. It looked so stupid, but no matter how much I complained, Carola said she wanted to see that hat because it belonged to the costume. However, I never put it on unless she was there.

After I had performed for about a year, I started learning bareback riding. An old man who was a retired bareback rider and trained the High School horses at the circus taught me from the beginning. Every morning I had to practice jumping onto a moving horse and staying on it. Harry Williams was a fine bareback rider and horse trainer, and he allowed me to be one of the helpers at his rehearsals. I began by bringing the horses back and forth to practice, cutting the carrots that would be used as rewards, and bringing Harry his whips. When Harry saw how much I loved working with the animals, he took over my bareback training and seemed to enjoy teaching me. This simple beginning with the horses proved to be rather important for me later on.

I was anxious about the things I was learning. I wanted to do well, but everything was so new to me. I used to become extremely nervous before my practices for bareback riding and acrobatics. I would get such pains in my stomach that I would have to go to the men's room. Some people never lose this nervousness. It wore off for me as I became more and more confident.

I liked working for Circus Williams. The days were exciting, and soon I started feeling grown up enough to handle my life. I was so busy with the animals and other circus duties that I never had to help in the kitchen, or polish boots, even though that was part of my contract. That pleased me greatly.

Although I took my meals with Harry and Carola, I never shared their family's living quarters. I lived in a circus wagon, which was tough. There were no showers. The only water connection was in the front wagon, and that is where we had to wash. It was not like today, when every trailer has its own shower and rest room. We washed in small buckets, and if we had to use the toilet in the middle of the night, we had to leave our wagon and go to what was the equivalent of an outhouse. Apart from that, I had everything I needed. The only thing that was missing was school. In those days circus children did not have special tutors. They either went away to school or did without it.

I got a different kind of education by working for the circus, and I learned every facet of the business. We did two shows every day. In addition to early-morning workouts with the horses and my other duties, I was an usher. There was no time to party or get into trouble, and when I got older, there was no time to go to dance halls or bars.

UNTAMED

The work pattern I developed during my early days with the circus is the one I followed all my life. At Circus Williams we began the day by rehearsing the horses at 8:00 A.M. and never went to sleep before 12:00 at night. The last show did not end until 10:30 P.M., and by the time we were finished at the stable and all the animals had been taken care of for the night, it was very late.

All the hard work paid off. I became such a good rider that Harry eventually allowed me to perform a bareback-riding act. My early training as a rider proved invaluable, and I went on to become a top High School (Dressage) rider. From the time I was thirteen until I was seventeen, I did not train the animals, because they had already been trained by Harry. I only cared for them and performed with them. It was a good experience to be able to handle animals that someone else trained. I had to pay close attention to the commands and signals used by Harry during practice so that I could duplicate them in the performance, and the closer I watched Harry, the more I learned about training in general.

The old style of training horses was to have riders on their backs repeating actions so many times that the horses got to know what to do. Eventually when I started training horses, I did everything with the longe, first with one horse, then two, then three, and so on. A longe is a long length of leather that is attached to a horse's bridle, then moved in different ways to give the horse direction. Sometimes I would have six longes in my hand at one time. I would train those six horses first, then another six, until all twelve could work together. In this, as in many other areas of training, necessity became the mother of invention. It had to done this way, because times had changed and we did not have twelve riders to train the horses for a couple of months until they knew what they were doing.

Harry did not give me special attention. It is not easy

to teach animals and the people who work around you at the same time. I learned by staying close to the animals and watching others work with them. I later spent one year with one of Carola's brothers, Franz Althoff, who was a famous animal trainer, and I learned even more by watching him. Over the years I learned a little from everybody and then created my own way of doing things. I spent so much time around the animals that I could not help but learn. Harry regularly performed the "Liberty" act. I had seen him practice and perform this act hundreds of times in the first year I was with Circus Williams, but I had never done it myself. One night at showtime Harry did not show up. Someone had to do the "Liberty" act, and at the age of fourteen it was I who went out with the horses that night. This was the first act I ever did alone, and I was ready to wet my pants from nerves, but I did a good job. Harry said he respected me because it took a lot of guts to do what I did.

I took to the circus animals in an uncanny way. They became friends whom I could always count on and trust. I liked feeding them and keeping their quarters clean. I knew where to find them at any hour of the day or night, and I could go there and be with them. They gave me a sense of security that I did not get from most people.

Harry never commented about my affinity for animals, but I am certain that he recognized it. I think he liked me so much because his background was so close to mine—not that he lost his father and mother in the same way I did, but he had come from poor beginnings and had to work his way up, build his own circus, and be there all the time to take care of it. Harry related to me, and I was always with him. I would even go with him in the car when he had to run errands and sit in it so that nobody would steal it. I was always up early and ready to work, and Harry knew he could count on me. This meant a lot to him, and we became very close. He was more like a father to me than Max Gebel had ever been, and I actually referred to Harry as my step-father.

Harry and other circus people taught me as much as they could about safety, a big part of which is common sense. I had little accidents, but nothing that I would consider serious. Once a horse fell on me, and my foot was badly hurt, but I always recovered quickly. I took things like that in stride. I never was hurt so badly that I wanted to leave. Once I started working for Circus Williams, I do not believe I ever wanted to do anything else. I worked day by day, and before I knew it a year had passed. My job took over my life so completely that I never had time to learn about other careers or even think about anything else. I loved what I was doing. If I did not love it, I could not do it every day, without weekends off and no summer vacations.

I had a lot of young friends at the circus, all of whom were much better performers than I. I was the newcomer; all the other children had been born and raised there, so they had a tremendous advantage over me. They were better riders and much more capable in other areas. The other kids were helpful and tried hard to teach me. Adi Enders was one of the greatest bareback riders in the business, and he and I and his brother Jacob built our own riding act. Adolf Althoff, another of Carola's brothers who was a fine horseman, trained us for years.

The Althoff family had been in the circus business for centuries. Franz, Adolf, and Carola had their own circuses before World War II, and Carola's became Circus Williams after she married Harry, since circuses were traditionally named for their owners. Circus Williams was the first to start up again after the war, and Harry put a lot of effort into making it a success. There was a great deal of competition inside the Althoff family. They all came together and talked and enjoyed each other's company, but there were times when they used each other's problems to their personal advantage in business.

Everybody was great to me, but I never took advantage of any of them. I was always exceedingly grateful for anything anyone did for me, and I think that has something to do with the way people treated me. I always tried to do the right thing and be polite, courteous, and cooperative. I was very popular, and later on I was able to travel to different places with my animals and spend time in cities around Europe because everybody liked me. In the wintertime I would spend months in Italy with Circus Togni, or I would go to Paris. Anyplace I went I was welcome.

Harry was very much like me. He always tried to be polite, but he was also trying to build the best circus of his time, so he had to be extremely demanding. Carola was demanding, commanding, and supertough. She was the eldest of eight children and grew up during the First World War. Harry was her second husband, and together they built one of the finest circuses in Germany. Even though she was such a tough lady, Carola and I developed a wonderful relationship, first as stepmother and stepson and later as my mother-in-law. I called her "mother" until her last day. She respected me tremendously, and she was confident that no matter what, I would always try to do the right thing.

I do not believe I could have had as much respect for my own mother and father, or ever felt such closeness, as I did for Harry and Carola. Carola and I had a lot of little arguments, but she always protected me. She often told me that she loved me, and I believed her.

Harry and Carola traveled with the circus. They had three children: Holdy Barlay, Carola's son from her previous marriage, who worked with Circus Williams, another son named Alphons, and a daughter, Jeanette. One of their

UNTAMED

children, Manuela, died when she was one and a half years old. Jeanette and Alphons were sent away to school and only joined us during the summertime. Many circus families want their children to learn an outside trade so that they do not feel their opportunities are limited. Jeanette and Alphons attended boarding schools, high school, and then went on for special training. Jeanette went to business school to learn secretarial duties, and Alphons studied the hotel business. They both joined the circus anyway, but Alphons was only with us about two years when he was killed in an auto accident. He was nineteen and a half years old. I had been rather fond of him, and I was shocked and saddened by his death.

Holdy worked with Circus Williams part-time. The rest of the time he worked as a single (a lone performer) and traveled around with his own act. I was on the road year-round, so I had the opportunity to spend much more time with Harry and Carola than their own children. And after Alphons's death, Carola became even closer to me. Harry and Carola never offered to send me to school, because they needed me at the circus.

The first couple of years after the war we might be in a town for months at a time because there was no other entertainment. When the country recovered and more and more entertainment became available, we found ourselves working that same town for two or three days. We were always coming and going, and this constant moving was backbreaking and tiring. Even though at that time we were only traveling around Germany, we never had time to do anything but work.

We had a seven-and-a-half-month season, then went to our winters quarters in Cologne. The first couple of seasons after the war were so good that we did not have to work in the wintertime, so I put those months to good use and learned other things. One winter I worked in the circus machine shop and learned to take auto engines apart, clean and repair them, and put them back together. The next season I learned carpentry. The only thing I passed up was welding, because I was not interested in it. I concentrated on things I liked and thought I would need later on.

At this time the Circus Williams only had horses. Harry and his people had created a number of fine horse acts, one of which involved a race between Roman chariots, each pulled by three horses. Harry worked in the chariot act with Charley Baumann, who was six years older than I. Harry had never taught me this act, but I used to watch them practice and perform it. One day Charley drove a truck somewhere on an errand, got tired, and pulled over to the side of the road to sleep. He slept so long that he never showed up for the show, and Harry needed someone to work with him in the chariot act. He looked at me, said, "Let's go," and I did it.

I was very short and had trouble staying on my feet inside the chariot. I would be hanging on to three horses, then I would fall and have to scramble to my feet, then I would fall again. The audience thought it was part of the show and enjoyed my antics so much that Harry said I should stay in the act. Charley later stopped working with horses and began training tigers.

We had a cowboy routine that involved riding and working with a lasso. Carola's son, Holdy, taught the act and worked in it. He became ill one night, so I had to stand in for him. I was able to do it only because I had watched Holdy for so many months. It was important to learn this way, because there was not enough time to teach and rehearse stand-ins. If a person was needed in a pinch, he or she had to be able to step right in.

I do not have many memories of Christmas with Harry

and Carola. Carola did as much as possible for everyone, but most of the time there was a show on Christmas, so we had only a short time to spend together afterward. I do not recall any big Christmas parties, but I do remember a party that meant more to me than any other: my first birthday party, organized by Harry.

Circus kids were always given birthday parties. In 1950, when I turned sixteen years old, I finally had mine, and that was very exciting for me. I was overjoyed by this display of affection. I had my own cake, and all the circus kids came to the celebration. Harry made it even more special by giving me the first birthday present I ever remember receiving—a brand-new red bicycle. When I was a little boy in Silesia after the war, I found a bicycle, but it had no tires on it. I rode it without tires and fell on my face every five minutes because the stones in the streets were so slippery beneath the bare metal. That was the only bicycle I had ever owned.

When Harry gave me the bike, he tried to make it sound as if he had given it to me to help me in my work, saying that I was to use it whenever he needed me so that I would not keep him waiting. But I knew that he had given it to me because he loved me. In those days bicycles were very expensive, so having one was really something special.

I hardly had a chance to enjoy this wonderful present when it was taken from me. There was no place at the circus to chain up anything or lock anything away, so I kept my bike in the stables with my faithful animals, and one night it was stolen. At first I thought it was a joke, that somebody had hidden it from me, but it had really been taken. I was horrified. I ran through the entire town desperately searching for my bike. I reported it to the police, and then for days I searched the streets because I believed it could have only been stolen by someone in the town. One day I saw a bike that looked exactly like mine, but I could not prove it. I never got my bike back, and I was terribly disappointed. It was the first really good thing anybody had ever given me.

It seemed as if I could not hold onto any of the material things that made me happy. This may account for why I developed such an attachment to the animals at Circus Williams and why I still have that kind of relationship with the animals at Ringling, some of whom have been with me since my Circus Williams days. The small material joys that came into my life were gone before I had a chance to savor them.

Disappointment was still dogging me, even in what little contact I had with my mother. On November 13, 1950, I wrote to her from Cologne after receiving two letters from her, one in which she scolded me for not writing often enough to let her know how I was. I replied:

> My dear mother,
>   . . . Your first letter did not make me happy
> . . . you can be quite satisfied and calm and sleep
> well and not worry about me. Your son is well. I
> am a good son. I was angry about your first letter,
> but your second letter is nicer. Dear mother, write
> again and send Rita's address. I would like to write
> to her again. . .

I closed my letter with a poem I had written for my mother:

> At the end of the day, think of me;
> When the morning comes, I am lonely for you.
> When you are far away, dear mother,
> I think of you in my dreams.
> I would love to be with you,

But fate wanted it otherwise.
May God arrange it as is best,
And may I see you again soon. . . .

I do not remember how my mother responded to such outpourings of my feelings; I certainly did not try to hide my loneliness or my desire to be with her. I only know that in many of my other letters to her I complained that I hardly ever heard from her.

A few years after the war, when Europe had finally settled down, Harry decided to take Circus Williams beyond the boundaries of Germany. Our first foreign tour was scheduled for the winter of 1950–51 in England. This was to be the first time Circus Williams had ever performed there, and the entire troupe was excited about the trip. I was all set to drive the chariot.

The chariot act was always dangerous. We could predict that the chariots would hit something—the stage, a ring, or each other—and tip and maybe even turn over. The intrinsic dangers of the act, however, did not stop Harry from keeping it in the show. When we got to London, he scheduled practices for morning and afternoon and insisted that we rehearse. I said that it was not necessary, since I had already worked in the act, but Harry was in charge. He wanted it to be perfect and felt that I needed the practice.

We were working in a spacious London arena called Harringay. Our crew had set up rings around stages, making sure that the outer ring was very large so that the horses would have enough room to run fast, as if they were at a racetrack. After all, the chariot act was a race. The horses managed to give the stage a wide enough berth so that they would not run into it or hit it, but on the turns the chariots swung out behind the horses and hit the stage. All of a sudden Harry's chariot clipped the stage and turned over.

Harry was thrown from the chariot, and the next one ran over him, hitting his shoulder and head.

I stopped as quickly as I could and ran over to where Harry was lying. My heart was beating so fast that I could scarcely swallow. I was immediately joined by other workers, who rushed from all over the arena to help. Harry was unconscious for a few moments, then he came to, stood up, and said he was all right. We had a lot of accidents, but nothing this serious had ever happened to Harry or anyone else.

Harry tried to carry on with the day's practice, but he could not. His injuries were much worse than he thought, and he was not able to shake them off as he had so many times in the past. He had to be taken to a hospital, and he ended up bedridden for a long time. For a while it looked as if he would recover, and we were very hopeful, even though he kept slipping in and out of a coma.

We worked our four-to-five-week engagement in London while waiting for Harry to recover. Carola came to England to be by his side and oversee the operation of the circus. Despite our prayers and fervent wishes, Harry never came back to us. After weeks of treatment he took a turn for the worse and died early in 1951.

I was devastated. After seeing so much death during the war I understood that dying is part of life, but to lose someone close to you is an awful thing. I felt as if I had lost the only father I ever knew. I had never known such deep sadness. I enjoyed being with Harry as a teenager, but I had often thought that he and I would have an even better relationship when I became a man—we would be able to do so much more together. The tragedy of losing Harry was compounded by the senseless nature of his death. It was not as if he had been sick for a long time and was expected to die. No one was prepared for Harry's death.

UNTAMED

Our tour of England, which was supposed to be for one or two seasons, had barely started when it was over. As soon as Harry died, Carola took Circus Williams back to Germany. She was so distraught when we got home that she could not attend her husband's funeral. Once we were back in Germany, we continued to work while Carola decided the fate of her circus.

We kept the chariot act in the show in spite of what had happened to Harry, and in the summer of 1951 I had a serious accident that was almost a repeat of the thing that brought Harry to his untimely end. The chariot I was driving turned over with me in it, and my head was badly injured. My whole body was convulsing as other workers tried to help me to my feet. Everyone at the circus, still unnerved over Harry's death, was greatly concerned for my life. I spent two days in a hospital suffering from amnesia and poor vision. I would have been hospitalized a lot longer than that, but I signed myself out because the circus was leaving that town and I was determined to leave with it. I ended up in bed for several weeks on the road.

We performed the chariot act until the end of that year, then sold everything from it and never did it again in Circus Williams. I would have kept the act in the show if it had not been for Carola. I think she feared I would end up like Harry. I told my mother about my accident in a letter I wrote to her from Braunschweig, Germany, that July:

My dear mother,

I have not had an answer from you yet, but I would like to write you again. I have had a fall again out of the Roman chariot, on my head and had a concussion. I had to be in bed for three weeks. But I am already better and handling the horses again. I have no headache anymore, so do not worry about it. Mrs. Williams says to say hello to you and that I am okay. Dear mother, where are you now? [She was traveling with Circus Krone.]

Mrs. Williams has sent me an angry letter because I flew from the chariot. She says if I fall off the chariot again, I will have to stop doing the act and they will give me a race car, so you do not have to worry about it. . . . I hope to hear from you soon. . . .

I had written to her from Hanover only a month before to tell her that a horse had kicked me with its front leg when I tried to get on its back and that I had broken a rib in another accident. The more active I became as a performer, the more I practiced, and the more likely it became for me to have accidents. But as I said, I took these episodes in stride and was grateful that I healed quickly.

Carola planned for the future of Circus Williams with Franz and Adolf Althoff. The circus was a family tradition, and her brothers knew that she loved it and was capable of running it without Harry. As long as Carola had some money and wanted to start again some time in the future, they wanted to give her the opportunity to keep her circus alive. Because of the cooperation she received from them, Carola decided that rather than fold the business, she would suspend Circus Williams for a year by sending all the animals to Franz at Circus Althoff so that they would stay alive and keep working. It was decided that I would go there too. We took the animals to Franz, and the rest of the circus stayed in Cologne at the winter quarters. Franz was in charge of everything I had to do, so I did not have to make any decisions immediately after Harry died. I did whatever Franz and Carola told me to do, and since I was still with a circus, my work basically remained unchanged.

Carola did not ask me to assume any new responsibilities after Harry died. She was always in charge, and I never questioned her authority. Carola had always handled the business end of the circus, while Harry took care of the technical part.

While Circus Williams was in suspension, Carola stayed home in Cologne. She visited us a few times at Circus Althoff, but basically she stayed by herself. She needed time to recover from Harry's death. She had taken it very hard. The most important thing for her, her children, and me was that our working relationship with Franz enabled us to make a living, and we did not have to sell our animals. We had a place for them and something for them to do. Circus Althoff was booked in Brussels late in 1951, and I had to get my father's consent to work in a foreign country. I wrote my mother to tell her of our plans:

> Dear Mother,
> The circus is going to Brussels and I am going along. I have just written to Papa for permission. I hope he will answer me soon. . . . Please do not be mad at me that I am not writing, but I always see you in front of me, and how you laugh, and then you cannot be mad at me. . . . Kisses,
> Your son.

I do not recall whether or not my father sent his permission to the circus, but when Franz Althoff went to Brussels, I was with him. I joined Franz late in 1951, when I was seventeen, and worked with him for one season—a full year. I had the opportunity to learn a great deal from him because he had many more animals than Circus Williams.

GUNTHER GEBEL-WILLIAMS

Franz was an elephant trainer of some renown, and while I was with his circus, I began what would become a lifelong love affair with pachyderms.

The learning situation with Franz was much the same as it had been with Harry: I had to stand by for hours and watch while Franz worked with the elephants. He did not give me any warnings or advice, but he knew how much I cared for animals, and he allowed me to be one of his helpers at practices. By being around the elephants I learned a lot about what to expect from them. I spent time in front of them for feedings and exercise, and behind them, sweeping up and keeping their area clean. I got to know all of his elephants by name and discovered firsthand how very smart they are.

The first time I saw two elephants fighting, I was amazed by their fury, strength, and endurance and how Franz and some of his helpers were able to separate them. There is no advice that can be given about something like that. They charge each other just as rams do and repeatedly bash their heads together with such force that their bodies shake. They push and try to knock each other to the ground, then step on each other. If the fighters are males, they use their tusks to draw blood. It is difficult to imagine what fighting elephants look like. To understand it, one must see it.

Franz had a great deal of patience with the elephants. He was not abusive or violent, and he worked quickly and effectively with them. From his method I came to understand that elephants would respond to something other than brute force. That was important for me later, when I introduced elephants to Circus Williams and trained them myself.

Every wound needs time to heal, and after a while Carola was ready to go back to work. When she revived Circus Williams, Carola relieved Franz of his responsibility for us, but she did not pass the reins to me. After the Williams horses and I had spent a season with Circus Althoff, Carola asked her other brother Adolf to close his circus temporarily and reopen hers. He agreed, and although he was running the show and was well known in the circus business, our name was out in front. I was eighteen years old when Adolf took Circus Williams back on the road. Because Carola had a good name, and the circus had been very popular and enjoyed a good reputation, she felt confident that we would be able to make a successful comeback.

For the previous year Franz had helped keep his sister going financially and emotionally. Once Circus Williams started up again, Carola went back on the road with us. She became closer to me than ever before, and I think in some ways she began to rely on me as much as she had relied on Harry. She counted on me to help whenever and wherever she needed me and to be a friend as well as a son.

GUNTHER GEBEL-WILLIAMS

I had lived with Franz for a year, and now it was time to live with Adolf. Both men took me into their families as if I were a blood relative. They displayed a kind of confidence in me that is generally reserved for family, and that made me feel warm inside. Being around Adolf and Franz was extremely helpful because I did not feel that I was all alone and on my own again after Harry's death. They became an extension of the love and closeness I had known with Harry and Carola, and this meant the world to me. When I was outside this circle, however, there were few people I felt I could depend on. I believe my childhood experiences and the things my parents did to me accounted for my general distrust of people.

We were a genuine family, and when Carola was traveling apart from the circus or staying in Cologne, I ate at Adolf's table. I was never treated like an outsider. Adolf's wife, Maria, cooked and did everything for us. If they had treated me differently, I would never have come so far. They made me feel that I was important and worthwhile to them.

I did not know what Carola had in store for me, and I hardly had time to discuss it with her since I went from the season with Franz right into the season with Adolf. There was much to be done to make Circus Williams successful again. I had learned a great deal from Franz and was looking forward to working with his brother because he, too, was a knowledgeable circus man and animal trainer.

My original employment contract with Circus Williams was for five years. When it expired, I did not sign a contract with Carola, nor was I asked to sign one with Franz. They would not have asked that of any member of their family, and they afforded me the same courtesy. (The next contract I signed was with Ringling Brothers when I came to America.) When Harry died, I was earning about ten marks

UNTAMED

a day and I felt like a millionaire. My raises continued to be small and far apart, but because the Althoffs were as good to me as Harry had been, I never felt a pressing need to earn more money. I was just glad to be working with the circus.

We traveled to Austria late in 1954, and while there I received a fabulous shirt that my mother had made for me by hand. With the shirt came news that my father had taken ill. I wrote with news of my trip and the unusual way I was living in Austria:

> Dear Mother,
>   . . . We have not had any rehearsals for two days because there is an exposition here and we must wait for it to be over. What are we going to do all day long? Mr. Althoff is here, so we really are not bored. I got up at 9:00 this morning and by 9:30 I was back in bed again with coffee. I just had lunch, and I suppose I will go back to bed. Every evening we go to the movies. What else can I do?
>   . . . The thing about Pa is very sad. I hope he will get well again. When Rita goes to him, let her give him my regards and that I said may he soon be well again.
>   . . . The shirt you made for me has pleased everyone here. It is very beautiful. I am well and thinking of you. The wind is very strong and it is not so nice here anymore. . . . I am sending you some money from the savings bank. Hopefully you can take 1,000 marks out of it for another shirt. . . .

I did not know that my father was so ill that his life was in danger, and I am not sure it would have mattered much to me if I had. One day he was dead. He had remarried, and his wife sent me a telegram telling me that he had died. My father was only forty-eight years old when he passed away on September 27, 1954. Carola offered to send me to his funeral, but I did not want to go. She said I had to go because he was my father, so I accepted the money to make the trip. I went through the motions of standing by his grave, but I did not feel any remorse or loss. I never even came close to shedding a tear. I would have felt like a jerk if I had done that. I stood there, and when it was over, it was over. I never returned to his grave, and I did not feel guilty about that. He was not a father. Harry had put him to shame as a father and as a human being.

As Europe regained stability, more and more markets opened up to our German circus, and we found ourselves booking engagements in many parts of the continent. We kept our winter quarters in Cologne, but traveled extensively outside of Germany. We had combined the animals from Circus Williams and Adolf's circus, so we were again working with horses and elephants, as we had at Franz's circus.

One year after Adolf and Carola resurrected Circus Williams, we headed back to England for bookings in London and Manchester. It was strange to return to London without Harry. Just being in that city revived all my memories of his accident. I missed him terribly.

I had learned so much since Harry died. I was handling elephants and horses now. I had become a much better performer, and I was becoming a trainer. I felt such ease around the animals. I still had the same kind of honest, even innocent relationship I had with the horses and ponies as a child, but I was developing a command of the skills necessary to teach the animals, and that was wondrous to me. I knew that Harry would have been so proud of me if he could

UNTAMED

watch me work now. I had come so far from the frail little boy who could hardly keep his footing in the chariot.

We went to England with five elephants and only the horses in the bareback-riding act. We did not take the Liberty horses. Although we were well received by audiences wherever we went, in some countries people in general were still bitter toward the Germans. I was always self-conscious because I was keenly aware of the atrocities my country had committed against humanity. I personally did not have any bad experiences during our travels, but the occasional hostility was not lost on me. Anytime I went to Holland, I felt bad because of the way the people there felt about us. Anti-German feelings did not run that high in France and Belgium, but the Dutch were very hostile. I believe the Dutch still hate the Germans, even today. We knew when we went to Holland that the authorities would do whatever they could to harass us. For instance, when we drove our cars with German license plates, we would be stopped. If one of us had committed even a minor infraction, we would certainly be penalized. Nothing was overlooked for us. I understood, because the Germans put those poor people through so much. The present generation may not remember what happened during the war, but in the early 1950s everyone remembered.

Going to England was not like traveling to one of the countries on the European mainland. We had to transport our animals, at least for part of the trip, by boat. We loaded the elephants and horses onto trains in Germany, which then traveled through Belgium and on to the port of Calais in France. There they were put onto a ship that took them to England. Fortunately there were only five elephants at that time and not many horses. It was quite a different crossing years later when I came to America with my own miniherd of elephants and other animals.

GUNTHER GEBEL-WILLIAMS

The animals arrived in Goole, England, and the elephants did not want to leave the boat. Out of everyone who was traveling with us, Adolf sent me to retrieve them. I was the smallest person in the troupe, I knew very little English, and I did not know my way around London. Although I was about nineteen years old, I was slight and looked much younger. There I was, scared to death to be among all those English people, and I had to travel by train to Goole. Although I was tired and would have relished the opportunity to sleep on the train, I was afraid to close my eyes for fear that I would miss the Goole station. I did not want to have to ask anyone for directions lest they discover from my speech that I was German. I forced myself to stay awake, eagerly watching every station as we pulled in and out. I will never forget being so frightened.

I took a taxi to the harbor, where I found the elephants, still in the boat. Before long I had our elephants on their way to the train that would take them to Manchester. Later on, when the animals and I were safe at the circus, I kept asking everyone how Adolf could have sent me off alone. I ranted that I was always the one who got the tough jobs, but I knew that was because Adolf trusted me to do things right; however, that did not eliminate the fear or frustration I felt that day.

England had changed since my first trip. The people seemed to be doing better. When I was there with Harry, the English people were still using food stamps for everything. I would stand on the shopping lines and people would give them to me to get food. People were so nice. There was enough food in England, but everything was still rationed. Not in Germany. The English people must have resented that we lost the war and they still had rationing. I always felt so strange being a German at that time.

While I was in England, I received a letter from my

mother in which she told me that she was contemplating suicide. She was unhappy with her life and feeling sorry for herself because she was alone and thought that she and Rita and I would never be together again. I answered her letter from Manchester early in January 1955:

> Dear Mother,
> . . . You should not have such silly ideas that we will not be together. It was always my desire to be with the circus and to get away from home. . . . It is not your fault. You have done every-thing you can for us, and I am grateful to you. You have your work. It may be difficult for you, of course, but you have your children, and you have to devote yourself to that, even if I am very far away. I love you just the same. I will again be in Cologne soon and we will see each other, even though we cannot do it for long. We will do what we can. . . .

I tried to console her. So many years had passed since she had signed me away to Circus Williams that it would have been senseless to chastise and blame her. I felt sorry for her. She knew what she had done and was feeling some remorse for it, even if she had a strange way of showing it. It was difficult not to worry about whether the next news I would have would be that my mother was dead. I could not run to be by her side. The best thing I could do was write and try to be reassuring. My mother did not kill herself.

Our foreign engagements were extremely successful, and over the three years that Adolf was with us, Circus Williams regained its place as one of the top circuses in Europe. Once we were on solid ground, Adolf told Carola that he wanted to leave us and revive his own circus. He assured Carola that I would be able to handle all the technical duties of running the circus as well as practicing and performing with the animals. Without any fanfare or grand announcements, I assumed much of what had been Harry's work. Carola and I ran the show, and by 1958 I had taken over the entire technical end of the circus and full responsibility for all of our animals.

Taking over the reins of Circus Williams felt like a natural progression for me. I had never seen Harry's death as a means of escaping the circus. I knew I would be needed more than ever by Carola personally and within the circus itself. Carola's giving me the responsibility of the daily operation of the circus reaffirmed that I was right where I belonged.

She continued to handle the business end of the circus and remained the sole owner. We discussed plans for Circus Williams in a general way, but basically she let me do whatever was necessary on the technical end and where the animals were concerned because she trusted my judgment. We had a great relationship, better, I think, than if I had been her biological child. There was a natural respect between us that is often lacking between many parents and their children. We were lucky to have the kind of relationship we shared, working together as closely as we did.

We had done so well in Europe that before Adolf left Circus Williams, we began an association with a Spanish circus called Feijoo-Castilla's. We tapped into the talent and resources of Circus Williams and Circus Feijoo-Castilla to create the Spanish National Circus. It worked in Germany for seven months out of the year for five years. We also worked with Circus Feijoo-Castilla and Circus Enis Togni to create the Circus Americano in Italy, which worked winters. By creating these circuses, we were able to cover

UNTAMED

greater areas than we could otherwise, and that meant more business. It also meant more responsibility for me when I took over Circus Williams.

We were busy twelve months a year. I met many people from other circuses over the years and worked with quite a few of them. Now I meet their children, who are also working in the business. I first met the owners of Circus Togni thirty years ago, and I used to eat at their house whenever I was in Italy. Now their children are performing, and when they are in America, they come to our house. It is very important to me to maintain these relationships and keep our business a family affair.

I had never been so busy. I did everything, from taking care of the animals to overseeing the movement of the circus from town to town and country to country. My job stayed that way until the day I left for America. I had my own ideas about how I wanted to do things and was perfectly willing to carry the load as long as nobody gave me orders. From the beginning I recognized that I needed advice, but I did not need somebody to tell me what to do. I had been able to make decisions since I was young, even if I then changed my mind many times. I still do that constantly, and this drives people who work with me crazy. One of my helpers, Piccolo, a three-foot-tall dwarf, always complained about how often I reversed myself. I did not do it because I lacked confidence in my decisions, but because I was always looking for better, safer ways of doing things. I was only changeable when it came to the animals, not in my private life, where, if I say something, I do it.

I did not hesitate to seek advice from Carola, but most of the time I got answers by watching people work inside and outside the circus, by using common sense, and by always searching for solutions and thinking things out. I never waited for anyone to tell me what to do. If something had to be done, I found a way to do it. If there was a problem, I found a way to correct it.

By its very nature the circus is in a constant state of change. In Europe, first we regularly traveled in circus wagons and by train, then overland through the streets when new tracks were being laid, and later we went back to trains. Circus life itself never really changes, but the way we do things changes. You make a bigger tent, you create a different kind of show, but the basics remain the same. Before too long the basics for me included all the jobs contingent with moving the circus around, handling the staff, hiring, firing, raises, and all the technical work, plus training, creating new acts, and practicing as much as possible.

Circus life is stressful for the person running the operation. You go from one town to the next and do the same things over and over again and hope that business is good. You even have to be involved in the publicity. In Germany, before we had television, the circus had to publicize itself. We made posters and put them up everywhere we could to spread the news of our arrival.

When I first took over, I was too busy with everyday responsibilities to make any major changes in the animal acts. I did only what was necessary to keep the animals healthy and working. I had so much to do that it was a great chore just to hold regular practices. We had the horses and an elephant act. Later I bought and trained new horses, and when I really wanted to do something different, I started working with a tiger.

In 1956 we opened our season in Berlin at the Deutschlandhalle, a popular arena that had been destroyed during the war and rebuilt. This engagement was announced in all the newspapers, and we had a lot of advance publicity. Just before we opened there, Carola came to me privately and asked if I wanted to take the name Williams.

She said she knew I would be proud of it and that she believed it was something Harry would have wanted if he had lived. She said, "I want you to carry this name always. You have been a part of the family, people know you are a part of the family, and I want you to have the family name." Everybody believed Carola was my real mother and always referred to her as my mother. Thus I proudly took the name, out of respect for Harry and so that his name would stay alive. I thanked Carola and have kept his name to this day. I think her daughter, Jeanette, is proud that I carried on the Williams name, and I always did right by Carola. I was honored to be associated with her family.

Circus Williams did much more traveling after I took over. Before, we had to be based in Germany because it was difficult to move around Europe. But by the late 1950s it became easier to travel with the circus, and often I would have to go ahead to the next town to make sure everything was all right so that we could bring in the animals.

Carola was very good to me. She stood by me in every situation, even if I did something wrong or said something out of place to someone. She never corrected me or complained about me to others. If she had something to say to me, she said it when no one else was around. We discussed many things in private, and that gave Carola an opportunity to air any grievances she had.

One of her big complaints was that I seldom honored clauses in our contracts that demanded we keep off the grass. When a circus is built, it is very big, and almost every contract called for us to not put certain things on the grass. Sometimes I would have to disregard those stipulations and do it anyway. Carola was always upset when I did that. She would tell me, "You say to yourself, 'Let the old lady talk, I'm going to do it anyway.' " I would defend myself by saying, "Carola, that is not true. Why do you talk like that? I

never think like that. I have to do it my way so it works."
We had a lot of arguments in private, but we never reached
the point where I said, "I'm getting out of here," or Carola
said, "Get out."

Carola and I argued about business matters, not personal things, and we never took our business disagree-
ments personally. When an argument is over, it is over; I
do not carry a grudge. Carola was that way too. After an
argument between me and my children, we hug each other.
That is very important. Like a real mother, Carola taught
me more than just the ins and outs of the business.

We had about one hundred working men and fifty performers associated with Circus Williams. We had two shows
every day, fourteen shows a week, and two days off per
year. In America we have one day off each week, and that
is usually spent traveling between engagements—four
hundred, five hundred, even one thousand miles, because it
is such a large country. In Germany we never had to travel
more than twenty miles to the next town, so it was not
necessary to have a day off. We dismantled the circus at
10:30 P.M., after the 8:00 show, and finished by 1:00 or
2:00 A.M. I would go to the train to make sure that everything was loaded and then drive ahead to the next town.
When we reached our next destination, we would have to
set up two tents for the horses, one for the elephants, and
one big top with a fence around it, and seating areas.
Everything would have to be perfect in every town, because it would be inspected by the local safety authorities.

Every day was a challenge, and in many ways every
day was different. For instance, on some days there was
sunshine and on others rain (and in Germany there was more
rain than sunshine). Weather changes presented a whole
new set of problems, and the thicker the mud, the greater
these obstacles were. We also had a lot of fun and many

UNTAMED

laughs watching each other maneuver on foot or in vehicles through mud. I always drove a big tractor, which we used to get things out of the mud and keep everyone moving. I was also always on hand to raise the tents and to put everything into place. When we finished, we went to the train and unloaded the animals. We do the same thing today—we set up, then go for the animals. By doing that we have a safe place to put them when they reach the circus grounds. I always loaded and unloaded the animals myself; that way I could be sure there were no problems.

I did not know what to expect from the other employees of Circus Williams when I stepped to the helm, so I just assumed command and never acted in a hesitant way. There were many people who had been with the circus and in the business much longer than I—people who were there when it was Circus Althoff, long before Harry and Carola married. The old electrician and the man who was in charge of all the Jeeps had been there thirty and forty years, respectively. Sometimes I was surprised that people like them took orders from me, but it worked, and I was surprised that it worked so well. I think it was because I had earned their respect. Many of them had known me since I was twelve years old, when I first joined the circus with my mother. They knew how hard I had worked all those years, and they had seen me work with the animals and knew that I could handle them.

In Germany we were lucky because the trains were never far away from where we set up the circus, and it was always a short walk for the animals. But after a while Circus Williams had so many animals that we had to make two or three trips to the train to collect all of them.

By the end of the 1950s we had at least fifty horses and had started a children's menagerie with everything from buffaloes and zebras to camels, ponies, giraffes, and llamas.

After the animals were loaded and unloaded, we had to make sure they had food and water. It takes more than one person to do that, but I always checked on everything myself to make sure it was done right. I never felt I could depend on anyone 100 percent.

Once, we had an accident in which a wagon filled with horses flipped over. We were traveling overland from town to town, and workers always fell asleep while they were driving. There were some fifteen horses in that wagon, and two of them were injured and had to be replaced, which meant that I somehow had to find the time to train two new horses. We were always lucky that nothing happened with the elephants, because they are so big that the consequences could have been far more serious, but we had many accidents with the horses.

Bad weather was a problem no matter where we were because it made it especially tough to travel with animals. My stomach always turned when the weather was inclement. I had to worry about the big top and the elephant tents when the wind was bad. Some elephants do not care if the wind is strong and the tent they are in moves, while other elephants become nervous wrecks. I always had to protect the nervous ones, because they can become so upset that they get crazy and lose control.

With all of these things to worry about, I always knew that I could turn in many directions for help. In every circus, big or small, everybody always told me that if I needed something, I should call on them, so I never felt alone.

When I was nineteen, problems with bad weather were even more serious than they are today, because back then we were not as well equipped. Today circuses have efficient portable heaters to use inside the animals' tents when it is cold. At Circus Williams we heated tents by lighting coal inside barrels in which we had made many holes. If someone accidentally knocked a barrel over, the whole tent could go up in flames. Circus Williams never had a fire, but there was a serious one in Munich at Circus Krone in their elephant tent, and they lost eight elephants from smoke inhalation and the burning tent falling on top of them. It was one of the most terrible things I ever heard of in my life. Circus Williams was performing in a nearby town, and the day after the fire Carl Sembach, who owned Circus Krone, picked me up and drove me to Munich to see the tragic results.

Critical things can happen at any time. In Europe we were always confronted with the threat of snow. Circus Williams was traveling in Austria one season and had snow in the middle of the summer. We were also always faced with problems caused by high winds. Often we got up in the middle of the night to circle the wagons around the animal tents so that they would not blow over. Once, in Rome, Italy, we were in the middle of a show with a full audience when one of my workers rushed into the big top to tell me there was a fire. The whole generator was in flames and it was dangerously close to a tent. I had to get a Jeep, hook it to the burning generator, and haul it away from the tents. I was driving like a madman with this burning thing behind me and a tank filled with gasoline. Afterward my colleagues respected me for taking such a risk, but I only did what seemed necessary to me at the time.

Things that might never bother us affect animals. Elephants, for instance, are afraid of going through a tunnel or overpass where traffic or trains are passing overhead. They react terribly to sounds and movements from things they cannot see. Horses get spooked by this too. Once, in Cologne, when we had only five elephants, we were on an elephant walk from the trains to our headquarters and all five of them became alarmed in a tunnel and quickly turned around at the same time (they always move in groups). A man riding past on a bicycle was knocked down when the elephants did their about-face. The shocked cyclist had barely managed to scramble to safety when the elephants trampled his bike. Elephants do not turn around and say, "Stand aside, I am coming," and run single-file. They like to run together.

Although we had our share of upsets in Germany, it was much easier to travel with the animals, and the circus as a whole, in those early years. Today, in the United States, we are allowed to travel with only two trailers behind a tractor. In Germany we could haul as many as ten behind one tractor. We did not have to worry about police at every turn, as we do today.

We almost always traveled by train in Europe and we had sixty cars to load, but they were small flat cars, and every flat car held two circus wagons. Circus people did not live in train cars at that time but in trailers or circus wagons, and we had to travel without light until we set up the circus and got the generator going again. We could not work that way today. People would complain and not show up for work. Maybe they were not the good old days after all; maybe today is much better.

I had a lot of accidents while driving different vehicles. In Austria, while hauling two heavy circus vehicles down a hill by truck, I tried to brake, but nothing happened. I told my passenger to jump out and then I aimed the truck for a big tree and crashed it. I walked away basically unharmed, but the equipment I had been hauling was not in such good shape.

Driving for the circus was taxing even without accidents. Moving from town to town overnight in Europe kept me on the road for many nights without any sleep at all, or at the most one or two hours. I could not always go to bed, so I slept briefly on a rolled-up canvas, then got up, and we started all over again. We had this schedule in Germany, as well as Italy and Spain.

Regardless of these dangers and inconveniences, I think

the riskiest thing I did in those days was eating the available food on the road. Once, right after the war, I unknowingly ate a dog. It was during the time when the Russians were in our town, and I was surprised to see that our neighbor had meat on the table. All the while I was eating, I was trying to figure out where it came from because it was virtually impossible to get. After dinner I realized that the woman's dog was missing and that he had been the main course. I survived, but I never ate there again.

Circus food was another story. I was lucky enough to eat most meals with the family, first with Mr. and Mrs. Williams and later with the Althoffs. We always had a kitchen where food was prepared only for us, which I greatly appreciated, since I never had time to cook for myself and there were no fast-food places where I could eat. Our main meals consisted of soup, salad, an entrée, dessert, and a platter of cheese and fruit. The rest of the employees ate in their own kitchen, equipped to feed one hundred people or more, but I was always lucky enough never to eat there. The meals were often hastily prepared in large batches, they tasted bland or reheated, and they looked unappetizing. Everyone lined up army-style and the food was dropped onto individual trays. When we were on the road, we had a food wagon for the working men, and when I was not able to be with the family, I ate there. It was often difficult for me to find something to eat in the food wagon or even a restaurant after the war because I will not eat what I do not like or cannot identify.

As if eating on the road was not risky enough, I started creating dangerous situations for myself when I began riding bucking broncos, camels, and buffaloes in our circus acts. Some animals do not like to have anyone on their backs, and they buck like hell, but I and several other performers rode them anyway. Although this was dangerous, it was the most fun we had when we were young. Adi, Jacob, and I would ride the animals to train them, and were thrown from their backs so often that we appeared to be sitting on springs. We all ended up having black-and-blue rumps, but we laughed like mad. The more somebody was thrown, the more fun we had. Sometimes we rode these animals just because we knew they were going to buck and throw us. That was our only risky recreation since we did not have time to leave the circus and do outside things, such as participating in organized sports and we did not drink and carouse.

Adi and his brother, Jacob, were two of my best friends. They were good-humored and easygoing with gentle natures, and they often treated me like a brother. They taught me circus etiquette, which is based on sharing and caring for each other as if we were all members of the same family, and how to approach the trainers and people who were in charge of us so that we could get what we wanted, which usually was a better act or more performance time. Adi and Jacob knew when to be serious about work and when it was okay to play, and when I first joined the circus, I took many of my cues from them. After I became a bareback rider, I worked with them in many of Circus Williams's riding acts.

Circus kids—later teenagers and young men—pulled innocent pranks and antics to have fun, but we always stayed around the circus. When I became a man, I did not have any outside interests, so I had no hobbies or sports to pursue. I never went fishing, and I was never really interested in soccer. That is rare for a German, because most Germans are crazy about soccer. I am more interested in American football. I was never involved in anything that was a pastime. My attention and free time had to be directed somewhere, so it went to the animals.

When I got older, whenever I wanted a diversion or something that would give me genuine pleasure, I turned to my animals, and we spent some wonderful times together.

This photograph was taken shortly after Circus Williams hired my mother as a seamstress. I was twelve years old. Within months after this deceiving photograph was taken, my mother all but sold me to the circus.

My father, Max Gebel, c. 1940

I began my circus career as a thirteen-year-old usher for Circus Williams. I never planned on becoming an animal trainer—it just happened.

Harry Williams, owner of Circus Williams, enjoyed a Chinese dinner in celebration of his birthday in Heidelberg on October 26, 1945. Pictured, *left to right,* are Karl Kossmayer, Harry Williams, and Max Radutzsky.

Carola Williams

My chariot was led into the ring in 1949 by a circus helper. Carola Williams hated this act because it was so dangerous, and finally banned it from Circus Williams.

During one of our few reunions, my sister, Rita (*left*), and my mother, Elfriede, visited me at the Circus Williams winter quarters in Cologne in 1950. Rita and I were separated by the war, and never reunited as brothers and sisters do.

I started training this pony after I had been performing with him for about a year. By 1951 the two of us were good friends.

Courtesy Horst G. Lehmann/Lomont/APB

Tini Berman was my first big love. She presented a lion act for Circus Williams for many years.

In 1960 with Alfons Williams (*left*), and his sister, Jeanette. Alfons died in an auto accident and later I married Jeanette.

Courtesy Hermann Sagemüller

In 1962 I opened the western riding act in Circus Williams by carrying an American flag in my hand. From the time I was a young boy, I had a secret desire to be an American, a dream that was realized in 1976.

Courtesy Lutz R. Schoellkopf

Getting ready to land on an elephant's back after being sent into the air on the teeterboard.

Courtesy Julius Römer

Bengal was my first tiger, and one of my favorite animals. He and I shared a special friendship and love.

Courtesy E. G. Schweizer Bottrop

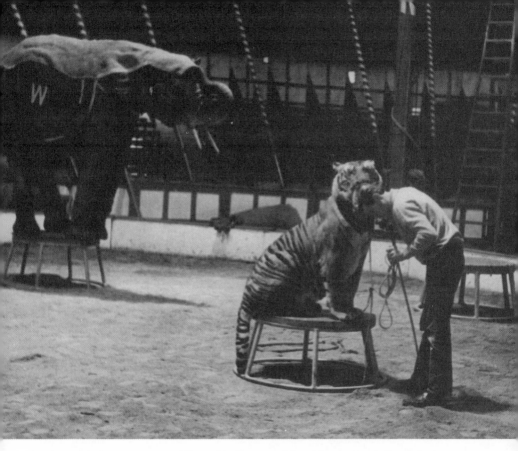

A private talk between me and Bengal before practicing the mixed act. Congo waits patiently in the background.

Courtesy Wilhelm Pabst

I expanded the mixed act to include two elephants—Congo and Thaila—and Bengal.

During the mixed act in 1964 I joined Bengal on Congo's back and ended the act by kissing the tiger's face. Something upset Bengal one day and he lurched and one of his teeth caught me in the face very close to my eye. That was the last time I kissed him during the act.

Here I am with Sigrid and Mark.
Courtesy Sam Siegel/
Metropolitan Photo Service, Inc.

Once I was secure in my ability to handle the technical end of Circus Williams and still train and perform with the animals, I created routines that would ultimately become my standards. In a bold move to put Circus Williams on top, I made a big break with European circus tradition. Instead of keeping the same acts season after season, which had been the accepted way of presenting a circus, I added new elements each season. I introduced different styles of training, created imaginative tricks for the elephants, and gave them a well-rounded program of exercise and special care, created the mixed act with an elephant and a tiger, and initiated many other features that were challenging for me and attractive to audiences. News of my innovations spread quickly, and people were interested in coming to see what Circus Williams was doing. It was a way of keeping business strong and gave me the opportunity to work closely with many types of animals.

I also changed the appearance of the circus. I updated equipment, and when we needed something new, we bought it. And to suit my new animal acts, we got different cages for performing inside the tents. When we needed new tents, we sold the old ones to another circus and replaced ours. Piece by piece, we made Circus Williams bigger and better, with new layers and dimensions each season, and audiences always had a reason to come again.

My popularity and reputation grew, and I became quite successful as a performer and trainer in Germany and elsewhere in Europe as we worked with our Spanish and Italian arms in Spain, Italy, and Portugal. We spent one winter in the Iberian countries and five winters, for five months at a time, in Italy. Circus Togni had its winter quarters in Verona, but each winter we would start our tour in Milan and crisscross the country. We worked out of arenas and tents in all of the major Italian cities.

Despite the good fortune I found at home, I had one burning desire that had been in my heart since I was a young boy. I wanted to be an American. I loved American cars and clothes, and I even found my heroes among American movie stars. Whenever I was not working, and for certain of our presentations such as our cowboys-and-Indians bareback-riding act, I wore cowboy boots, a cowboy hat, and a Western-style jacket or coat, especially in Italy, where American clothes were popular.

I admired many Americans and longed for the day when I, too, could be one. I learned as much English as I could, which at that time in Europe was not very much. I even took to telling tall tales about my origins, never realizing that my accent was a dead giveaway. One day in Italy, when I was about twenty years old, a stranger asked me whether I was an American, and I said I was. He then asked where I came from, and I proudly answered, "Sarasota." I knew that many American circus performers lived there, because at the time it was the winter quarters for Ringling Brothers and Barnum & Bailey Circus. The man with whom I was speaking was delighted when he heard that I was from Sarasota. He said, "No kidding! I worked there once." I left so abruptly I practically fled. The last thing I could do was have a conversation about a place I had not even seen.

Perhaps I projected my secret passion into my own future, or maybe I was just destined to live in America. My mother once told me that a Gypsy woman read her palm and said that her son would travel all over the world. Although I was doing a great deal of traveling each year, it was confined to Europe, and I am not sure if America was even a possibility in those days. All my efforts were concentrated on Circus Williams, but I still indulged in my dream every time I donned my boots and hat.

By the late 1950s and early 1960s it was easy to buy American-made goods in Luxembourg, and when I had saved enough money, I bought a spanking-new Chevrolet. I was very proud of my car and kept it looking as if it had just rolled off an assembly line. Not long after I bought the Chevy, when I was working in Sweden, I saw a beautiful gold-colored Cadillac convertible with big bumpers. It belonged to Kate Bronett, the owner of the Swedish Circus Scott. What a beautiful car! I told Mrs. Bronett that if she ever wanted to sell, I would buy it. A few months later I bought it and sold my Chevy to another performer.

Mrs. Bronett had bought the Caddy in New Jersey, which at that time issued license plates that did not bear any dates. I kept the Jersey plates on the car, and one night the police stopped me and asked why I was driving an American car with American plates when it was not allowed in Germany. I quickly bluffed: "Wait a minute. I worked in America and I can buy whatever I want in different countries." I guess I surprised the officer by answering so quickly, because he apologized and let me go. I figured I had better get rid of the plates soon, but I could not bring myself to part with them.

Not long after this I had to drive overnight from one

German town to another with three other men, two in the back and one in the front. I filled up the gas tank before setting out on the trip because I was very tired and did not want to stop on the road for fuel. A short distance into the drive I fell asleep, hit a lamppost, and knocked it over. The light pole crashed across the car, stretching electrical wires over the metal surface. When the wires began sparking, I told everyone to jump out because I was afraid the sparks would ignite the gasoline. I was the only one who got hurt. When I struck the pole, my face hit the steering wheel, and my mouth and gums were bleeding. My Cadillac was so badly damaged that I ended up losing the car. After that I decided that the loss was too painful, and I did not buy any more American cars. But I still drove with my American license plates, regardless of the law against doing so.

I never was in any really serious trouble with the law, though I came close a few times for driving too fast or getting into fights at the circus. When I fought, it was with circus working men who disobeyed instructions or deliberately neglected a task and then became defiant when questioned about their actions. We would fight on the spot, and then my opponent either apologized and did his work correctly or was fired. The boss not only has to have a big mouth, he has to be as tough as he talks.

I was involved in a few other brawls that led to brushes with the law. Once, in Naples, I got into a fistfight with a German man, and he went to the police, who arrested me and brought me into a station house for questioning. While they were taking their report, I was so dumb that I talked to the man with whom I had fought in German, warning him that when I got out, if I saw him again, I would kill him. One of the police officers understood German and wanted to put me in jail for threatening the man. I somehow managed to talk my way out of that one.

UNTAMED

The German police and I were not good friends at all. I hated their domineering, arrogant attitude. Many people in uniform have a bad attitude. They hide behind a uniform and a badge and forget that they are in power to protect people's rights, not take them away. Police should command a certain amount of respect, but many of the German police acted like bullies, snapping at people and making judgments before they gave anyone a chance to explain. I also think that I balk at this kind of authority as a reaction to the Nazis during the Second World War, when people were deathly afraid of even voicing their opinions.

The police were not my only nemeses. The German border guards and I did not get along either. Every time I drove from West to East Germany, I had trouble. The guards always made me pull over to the side of the road and remove my sunglasses; then they would search me and my car, sometimes even taking my car apart—anything to harass me. My name also bothered them. I would say Gebel, and they reacted as if I had said Goebels. Nobody else from our company was ever pulled over by them, only me. I may have displayed a bad attitude, too, because I did not like this checkpoint business. Maybe I was a little too smart-alecky, a little too commanding toward them.

Also, I often drove on the left side of the road, even though we were only allowed to drive on the right, because the road leading from East to West Germany was so bad, especially on the right. Whenever a guard questioned me— and one of them always did—about why I drove on the wrong side of the road, I explained, then he would say, "We do not have bad streets in the German Democratic Republic." They certainly did, but I knew that if I did not keep my mouth shut at such times, I would land in jail and nobody would be able to help me. Often, after soft-talking my way out of trouble, I would drive away seething because I despised those people. I hate any kind of extreme authority without reason.

The most serious border incident in which I was involved almost led to my being jailed. It happened in Berlin. Circus Williams had a small-bird act with pigeons and parrots that we leased to other circuses. At this particular time it was with the Circus Barlay in East Germany. It was my responsibility to collect the payment from them. One week, instead of having me bring the devalued East German marks to the West, Carola asked me to buy china in East Germany. (Even though East German money was worth less than West German marks, we leased acts to circuses in the East because work was work and we still made some profits.) In those days we could buy expensive china in the East for relatively little money. We were working in West Berlin and I had to pass several checkpoints to get into the eastern part of the city. I drove across the border in my Mercedes without incident and picked up the money at Circus Barlay. When I got to the store, I discovered that as cheap as the dishes were, I did not have enough money, so I headed back to West Berlin for more cash.

Before crossing the border, I stopped at a circus to see an old friend named Werner, a jovial, quick-witted man who had worked with me and Charley Baumann training animals at Circus Williams. He was wearing large boots because he had been working with polar bears that day and he said he did not have time to talk. I would not take no for an answer and finally convinced him to ride with me to West Berlin and then back to the East so that we could talk for a while.

Werner and I crossed into the western part of the city without any problems, picked up more money from Carola, converted it to East German marks, then returned to the border. I do not know if I aroused the border guards' suspicions by going back and forth so many times in one day, or if somebody had blown the whistle on me because I was taking so much money into East Germany. At the time we were only allowed to bring a certain amount of cash into East Germany, and I had a lot more than what was allowed. Whatever the reason, as soon as we got to the East German border, an officer with a machine pistol immediately stopped my car. He opened the back door, got inside, and said, "Let's go, down there." He pointed to a guardhouse on the side of the road. I had not done anything overtly wrong, but if the officer intended to search me, he would have discovered the money.

As I drove to the guardhouse, I used a secret lingo to communicate with Werner. In Germany we have a special circus language that is sort of like pig Latin. In this jargon *lobi* means "money." I asked Werner, "What should I do with my lobi?" In the same lingo he told me to give it to him and he would put it in his boots. I carefully slipped the roll of bills out of my pocket and into Werner's hand. He slid it into one of his rubber boots just as the officer ordered us to stop talking.

When we got to the guardhouse, both my car and I were completely stripped and searched. They did nothing to Werner because he was East German. The guards found nothing illegal, so they put my car back together again—seat, bumpers, hubcaps—and let us go.

This was the closest call I had at the border. I was very concerned while I was detained because I knew that there was no embassy to turn to for help. A person could be held for months, even years, and nobody but their family and friends would care. I knew that if they grabbed me, nobody would start a war to get me out of prison. I was especially angry about this incident because it never would have happened if I had not had to buy that damned china for Carola.

My aversion to following orders accounted for some of

the problems I had with police and border guards. I even hate to receive orders on paper. Anyone can talk to me and ask me to do something reasonable, and I will do it. But if somebody orders me to do something, I immediately become difficult. Orders upset me. I was pushed around all of my young life, and once I was considered an adult, I refused to let anyone order me around. Harry Williams used a different approach with me and did not order me to do things. Besides, he was not domineering, which made it easier to comply with Harry's wishes. He was a big person, and I was a little guy, but I admired, rather than feared, him.

I also admired Carola's father, Dominick Althoff, himself an old circus man who commanded a lot of respect and got people around him to do the things he wanted without making them feel as if they were in a work camp. I happily called Dominick "Grandpa," and since he approved of the relationship I had with his daughter, he did not seem to mind. Grandpa was a burly, rugged-looking man, who stood erect and kept his lips set tightly while working. He was precise, demanding, and strict with his workers, but under his stern appearance there beat a good heart. He was affectionate toward me, and I had a lot of fun with him.

I did not know my mother's parents, and I only knew my father's mother. I loved my grandmother. She was the only person I remember being close to when I was a child. We lived in the same town, but at least ten miles apart. I would spend nights with her during my vacation from school, and they were really the only happy times I knew in those days. She made the best apple strudel in all of Germany, and she enjoyed watching me eat it, because I loved it so much. Grandma was not a tall woman, and she always kept her soft, wavy, ash-brown hair, which was flecked with blond, pushed back from her face. She was pretty, but I thought that, second to my mother, she was the most beautiful woman I had ever seen. My grandmother's true beauty came from within. I can still recall the touch of her hand against my forehead as she pushed my hair from my face, and feel her lips against my cheek.

I do not believe my mother told her what our lives where like at the hands of her son. She might have been able to do something about his treatment of us if she had known. Instead she and I just went along as grandson and grandmother, and she was one of my favorite people. When the war broke out, she went to live in a tiny mountain town called Hirschberg with one of her brothers. We had already left Silesia the first time when my mother and I were summoned to my grandmother's side because she became ill. I felt so helpless and confused as I sat in her hospital room, hoping she would be all right. She looked very weak and was too ill to speak, but I whispered her name so she would know I was near. My throat tightened as I fought back tears—I did not want my grandmother to see me cry because then she would know how frightened I was by the thought of losing her. I remember hearing a big clock toll the hour and thinking that I had better get closer to my grandmother because she was going to die. I inched my way to her bedside and gently caressed her hand, then I backed away and resumed my watch from a chair. She left me soon after. This is still vivid in my memory—the sound of the clock and then losing her. I felt very bad when she died.

Grandpa Althoff came to Circus Williams the year Harry died. He was retired from his own circus and needed something to do. He was a good horse trainer, so he took over the training and practicing sessions with our horses. I had a relationship with Grandpa long before he started working at our circus. He often came to visit Carola and was well aware of my situation. Grandpa treated me nicely; he was kind to me and liked the way I worked with the animals. Because we were not strangers when he came to our circus, we had a good working relationship, much the same as I had with Harry.

I never laughed as often as when Grandpa was working with the horses. When he was around, it was easy to laugh over little things, and I had such a nice time with him. He used the old style of training, which was to bring the horses out of the stable, then to return them when practice or the performance was over. (Today we set up a ring close to where the horses are housed and practice there.) Frequently we sent the horses back after practice, and Grandpa would say, "One more time." We would then have to get the horses back into the ring for another rehearsal. This drove all of the grooms mad. Sometimes when Grandpa ordered the horses back for a second time, we would tell him that the groom refused to bring the horses back and forth any more. Grandpa would march right over to the groom and hit him on the head. It was a mean trick, but it made us laugh so hard we cried.

Of all the young men who worked with him, I was Grandpa's favorite, which made me feel very special and good about myself. He showed his favoritism in different ways. At practices, for example, when Adi Enders, his brother Jacob, and another rider named Mark did something wrong, Grandpa would charge up behind them with the whip and let them have it. He did not hit to hurt, but to show them that they had made a mistake. Once he asked me, "Do you think that I am afraid to hit you too? I am not!" But he never hit me.

Carola and Franz gave Grandpa money every week, in exchange for which he became one of our horse trainers. Grandpa also trained our pony act, which was called "The *Kinderstuben*," or "The Children's Nursery." In that part of the show each pony was required to do something different. One pony would lie down, another would sit on a chair, another pony would pull a cab, and another would pretend to sleep as a clown came along ringing a bell and pretended to wake the pony. It was a pleasant, endearing act.

We had a lot of fun when Grandpa led the ponies' rehearsals. All of them were black and greatly resembled each other, and that made it easy to confuse Grandpa. The only difference was their heights. We often fooled Grandpa by deliberately giving him the wrong ponies. Grandpa would become confused because the ponies would not follow his commands. When we finally told him that they were the wrong ponies, he would be furious, but not for long.

I think he liked being the object of our attention and affection. We pulled one trick on him regularly, and he fell for it every time. He wanted to be home by a certain hour each day, and every once in a while we would rush him out early, telling him that it was late and if he did not leave right away, he would miss the train. Grandpa would rush to collect himself and then hurry to the train station. The next day he would come back furious, calling us swine because he had gotten to the station an hour early and had had nothing to do until the train arrived.

Grandpa was an effective trainer and did not abuse the horses, but he stuck to the old methods, which were completely different from today's. The old style ruined the horses and ran them to death. Adolf would watch his father work with them and say, "Let me take a picture of this before the horses die, so I have something to remember them by."

I knew that if I were training the horses, I would not do it that way. Still, I learned the basics by watching, how to make a horse sit and lie down and how to make them do the kinds of things that were included in "The Children's Nursery." These are things one would never see in America, because in a big arena they would be considered boring. They have to be done in a one-ring circus, which is smaller and more intimate, and audiences expect to see very personal, involved acts. Still, it was a good time, and there was always something to make me laugh.

I made some friendships back in those days that have lasted all these years. Adi Enders is now with Circus Williams-Althoff in Germany, which is owned by Franz Althoff, Jr., an elephant and horse trainer. Adi's brother Rudi also became a horse and elephant trainer, and their brother Jacob is a circus clown. Two other old friends, Willie Mark and Klaus Liereck, are in circus management. Holdy Barlay, Carola's son, and I were like brothers. Holdy had his own rodeo riding act and worked in Italy for a long time. He is still working in Europe.

Romance, like friendships, almost always had to be found among the girls who worked for the circus, or whose families were associated with it, because of our transient lives. It was difficult to maintain an outside relationship. Usually if one of us met a girl in a town where we were performing, we would be able to keep company only for the length of our visit, which generally was for anywhere from a few days to a few weeks. Then we would move on to our next venue, and that would be the end of that.

We always had nice-looking girls at the circus, but their mothers and fathers were protective of them and warned them about us young bucks. Their parents wanted them to have secure futures, and they knew that the circus business was anything but. Occasionally a friendship with a girl did turn into something special, but usually her family would have to leave to go somewhere else, since most performers were contract players. When their contracts expired, it was time for them to move on, so the relationship would have to end anyway.

UNTAMED

A man would have to be lucky to meet a girl who was with the circus long enough for the two of them to stay together for years. I never had a relationship in my youth that lasted any great length of time. My love interests would always come and go, and I could not keep in touch or go to visit a girl because I worked seven days a week.

On occasion I had brief yet intimate relationships with women I met inside or outside the circus. Once, in Brussels, we had incorporated a fashion show into the circus for publicity. I met one of the models and she became my girlfriend. She worked for Bon Marché, a large department store in the city. After one of the shows she and I went back to her place and spent the night, and she did not go to work the next morning. This was unusual, and someone from Bon Marché showed up at her door to find out why she had not reported for work. I was naked when the knock came on the door. Instead of running for a closet, I grabbed all my clothes and ran into the backyard, because I was scared to death that I would get into trouble for having stayed there. Fortunately, because of what I had been taught as a child, my clothes and shoes were in one neat pile and I was able to snatch them up in one swift motion. I dressed quietly in the backyard and from there exited unnoticed.

When I was nineteen years old, a lovely girl came into my life, and she and I quickly became a couple. Tini Berman, a blond beauty from the Netherlands, who used Yvonne as her stage name, was one year older than I when she arrived at Circus Williams. She brought along a lion act, which we had agreed to lease from the Swiss Circus Knie. Tini and I hit it off right away and developed an intimate, but comfortable relationship. My position as animal trainer with Circus Williams enabled me to spend considerable time with her because I watched her performance to make sure it was well rehearsed. I also hung around the cage during practices so that if something happened, I could protect her.

I became one of her watchers after a while, and whenever she worked, I was always at the back door of the cage ready to help her. A few times when the lions started acting up, I stepped into the cage, even though I had never worked with big cats. I paid close attention and learned the commands Tini used so that I could control the lions if the need arose. It was she who inadvertently provided me with my first opportunity to perform with big cats when she became ill one night and I replaced her.

I am certain that I was not afraid of the lions, otherwise I would not have gone into a cage with them. They had been trained well, but not by Tini; she only performed with them. She had been hurt just once doing this act, when a lion bit her hand, and she had to go to the hospital for treatment. Otherwise she had had no major problems. There were four male and four female lions, and it was a good act. However, I did not leave the cage saying, "That is definitely something I want to do." Even though I was not crazy about them, my experiences with the lions did not end when Tini returned the next day.

She had come to Circus Williams with a trainer. When he left to go back to Czechoslovakia, she was alone. I helped with the lions because I had a personal interest in her—we were living together in the same trailer. When one of her lions died, I trained its replacement. I decided to do this because all our animal trainers were such prima donnas. They would refuse to work at the drop of a hat and even quit without giving notice. I was so irritated that I decided to train the cats myself.

I worked with the new lion by using the same commands that had been used to train the others. Since I had never seen anyone train a big cat, it never occurred to me to go into the cage armed with all sorts of nightmarish instruments. I decided to use verbal commands in the same calm, commanding approach I used with the elephants and horses. I was patient. He was a good animal, and after a while we were able to integrate him into the act.

I had the idea that the cats were there to perform, and I thought the way to accomplish that was by taking a commonsense approach. Although I was successful in training that new lion, I did not work with cats again for at least four years, when I decided to create an act with a tiger.

When Tini and I first met, she was married. We became so close that she got a divorce and stayed with Circus Williams for seven years. She wanted to marry me, but I was not ready for that kind of permanent commitment. I thought things between us were great the way they were, but Tini had other ideas. We began having frequent arguments, mostly about other women, and every time we fought, Tini threw me out of her trailer. I used to say, "Tini, you've thrown me out so many times that one day I'm never going to come back." We got into a big argument one night, and I said I was not going to marry her. She threw me out, and I refused to go back. She tried to patch up our relationship, but I had had enough. Tini worked with Circus Williams until her contract expired, then moved on to Circus Krone. We saw each other twice after that, and we kept in touch for a while, but the spark was gone. She visited me once in America years later; eventually she stopped performing and married someone outside the circus business.

Our parting was painful. We were good friends, better lovers, and, as an added bonus, we worked very well together. I cared a great deal about her, but I was still young and had a tremendous responsibility with the circus. I was not ready to take on the additional responsibility of a wife, which to me was more than just living together. I felt empty and alone when Tini left, having grown accustomed to having someone I could depend on for love and affection. But, as always, there was little time to be sad about something so personal. There was too much work to be done.

Carola knew I was having an affair with Tini, but she did not question me about it or show any signs of disapproval. As long as Tini and I did our jobs efficiently, Carola did not care if we played a little on our own time. She knew I was distraught when Tini went away, but Carola had few words of comfort. I would get over it, she promised.

Carola's daughter, Jeanette, had spent very little time at the circus while she was growing up. We basically only saw her once a year, during summer recess when she came home from school. After graduating high school, she went to a business college, and then took a job in an office in Cologne.

Jeanette found office work boring, so when she was eighteen, she decided to join our circus just as her brother Alphons had done. I was surprised to see what a worldly young woman came home to Circus Williams. She certainly had grown up. Jeanette was slender and dainty, with fragile features, milky skin, and honey-colored hair—looks that belied her strong personality and somewhat spoiled nature. I had seen her in various stages of maturity, but in my mind she was still a little girl. Suddenly here was this beautiful young woman, and, what was more exciting, she was going to be working with us.

We had spent so much time apart when we were youngsters that I never really thought of Jeanette as my stepsister, but since I considered Harry and Carola to be my stepparents, Jeanette had a rightful place in the family order. I could have been old-world about it and steered clear of Jeanette whenever my thoughts of her were more than brotherly; however, because we had grown up in relatively different worlds, we did not have the kind of relationship that brothers and sisters share. Actually we were not much more than acquaintances, and in my mind that made her fair game.

I did not have to go out of my way to court Jeanette. When she joined Circus Williams, it was decided that I would teach her to work with the High School horses—which is considered the ultimate form of riding and requires the wearing of formal black riding attire—and to present the "Liberty" act. It seemed a natural slot for her since she was Harry's daughter. Our relationship developed quickly, and it was pretty clear to everyone at the circus, including Carola, that Jeanette and I were sweet on each other.

Carola did nothing to interfere with our budding romance. She did not even discuss it with me. Carola was a sly old fox, and in many ways I think she was quite pleased to see that I took to Jeanette in a romantic way. Any close relationship between me and her daughter would be good for the business: A marriage would really cement my long-term association with Circus Williams, and it would discourage other suitors and potential interlopers, who might be able to lay claim to the circus if they married Carola's daughter. The thought of an outsider taking over made Carola extremely uneasy.

I was twenty-six years old then, and I no longer lamented losing Tini after Jeanette came on the scene. Nothing stood in the way of our relationship, and after a while she and I started talking about marriage. Carola was partially responsible for the idea of a union between me and Jeanette, which she encouraged by talking about how natural and logical it would be if Jeanette and I married. As for my own reasons, I saw a nice-looking young girl who would not have to leave the circus when her contract was up, and Jeanette chose me because I was so attentive to her. We also believed that we were in love. I practiced the horses for her, worked on her act every day, and catered to her. What young girl would not like such attention? Finally it was decided that Jeanette and I would definitely marry. I did not make a sweeping proposal; it sort of evolved into the thing we should do.

One important factor stood in the way of our union: Jeanette was a Catholic and I had never been baptized in any faith. I would have been happy with a civil ceremony, but not Carola. She wanted me to become a Catholic because she wanted us to be married by a priest. To accomplish that, I had to embrace the faith. I did not find the idea of being baptized a Catholic unpleasant or objectionable, I simply did not feel it was as important as Carola said, and I certainly did not have time to study or prepare in any special way for baptism. I believed in God, and I did not think it was necessary to be sprinkled with water to prove it.

I discussed this with Carola before arrangements were made for me to see a priest. I told her that I did not feel I had to commit myself to an organized religion in order to believe in God. I wanted to believe in Somebody all the time, not just when I felt terrible, or was in a bad situation, or because Carola wanted me and Jeanette to be married in a church. I always had the feeling that I was protected by a higher power. I consistently tried to do the right thing, and I believed I was rewarded for that.

Despite my protests, Carola was set on a big, fancy church wedding (and I think Jeanette was too), and that meant baptism for me. I wanted to make Carola happy, so I did it for her. Shortly before my marriage, I was baptized privately in the presence of Carola and Jeanette at our winter quarters in Cologne. The priest was the same one who said mass on Sundays for our circus employees. He knew how I felt about it and why I was allowing myself to be baptized, but he was unperturbed.

Carola had been born in Cologne and she was considered a celebrity there. She was part of the cream of society, a prominent businesswoman who knew everyone who was anyone. She was proud that I was marrying her daughter, and I had little to say about any of it. I decided to let her do whatever made her happy. The wedding was planned for the late fall when the circus would be at its winter quarters. Carola planned and paid for the entire wedding. She had to. I was too poor to buy Jeanette an engagement ring.

This was an exciting time in my life. I was rapidly becoming a famous circus star, and now I was anticipating my wedding day. The wedding was a bit overdone for my taste, but Carola wanted it, and that was the way it was. It would have been much smaller and intimate if I had had something to say about it. I was a bit excited by all the hoopla, but also self-conscious because I was embarrassed by the opulence.

On November 12, 1960, Jeanette became my wife in the society wedding of the year in Germany. The church was aglow with candles, and huge baskets of flowers were everywhere. The men wore tuxedos and the ladies fine gowns. I wore tails, and Jeanette was resplendent in a fabulous wedding gown that had been designed especially for her. I had no thoughts about the propriety or impropriety of my actions as I looked up at the towers of the church before going inside. I was glad to be taking a bride and was looking forward to our life together. I was jittery before the ceremony, but my uneasiness was caused more by the extravagance than the marriage. Much of my apprehension disappeared when I saw Jeanette walk down the aisle. She looked beautiful, and I was very much in love with her.

From the look on Carola's face, this was one of the happiest and proudest days of her life. She must have invited half of Cologne to the ceremony, because the crowd was damn near overwhelming. She sent out only an exclusive 150 invitations, however, to our reception, which was held at a country club. My mother and sister and some of my circus friends were there, but Carola primarily invited her family and friends. She invited my mother and Rita because she said it was the correct thing to do. I felt saddened by their presence because they were so indifferent toward me, but my mother told me that she was happy for us and wished me luck. I do not remember seeing her smile at me while we were in church, and she seemed to barely enjoy herself at the reception. Her attitude made me unhappy, but I honestly did not expect more from her. She was civil toward Jeanette, and that is what mattered most to me. I was certain that if Harry had been alive, he would have approved of my marriage to his daughter. He had been proud of me and would have known that Jeanette was in good hands. I regretted that Harry and his son, Alphons, could not share our joy, but Holdy was present and wished us much happiness. He and I enjoyed a warm and friendly relationship and he did not object to my marrying his stepsister. Of course Franz and Adolf Althoff were present, and I was glad they could be a part of such an important day.

My responsibilities at the circus stood in the way of a honeymoon, so we spent our wedding night at a local hotel in a grand suite. Jeanette was happy that we were not in a circus trailer, but it did not matter to me where we were so long as we were husband and wife. When we got back the next day, our own trailer was waiting for us, and we lived and worked together. We simply picked up where we had left off the day before our wedding. Carola lived by herself next door to us, but we were so busy all day that we only got together at lunch and dinner time. She never questioned me about anything, even when our marriage went on the skids and Jeanette was accusing me of all sorts of things, including infidelity. Carola was too smart to interfere in my personal business. She told me, "As long as my business works out and you do not do anything wrong with the circus, I do not care what else you do." She stood behind me, but of course she also stood behind her daughter. Carola knew how to walk that fine line without falling off in either direction.

I never saw my marriage to Jeanette as a way to own Circus Williams, and even after we were married, I did not function any differently in my work than I had in the past. I always worked as if the circus were my own and I took care of the animals as if I had bought them with my own money. I did not hope to garner Carola's favors by working that way—I simply did not know any other way to work. In the last couple of years I worked there, my pay increased, but the circus always belonged to Carola after Harry died, and Carola knew that I was not a threat to her ownership.

Jeanette and I continued to work professionally as we had before we were married, but neither of us really worked at our marriage. After three years we began quarreling, which turned into screaming matches and long periods of silence and anger. We often argued about my long working hours; I spent more time with the animals than I did with her. Our marriage crumbled because I was too busy and she was too young. She was also better educated than I and perhaps expected more of me. I think she missed something in our relationship from the beginning. She wanted to live her life as other young women did, going out to dinner and dancing and reaching beyond the borders of the circus, where my life ended.

Soon after our wedding we tried to have children, but Jeanette never conceived a child while we were married.

We went to doctors and specialists because we thought something was wrong with one of us. We were told that we should have been able to have children, but for some unknown reason we could not. Perhaps fate had intervened. We might have stayed together if we had had a child. As it happened, after six years our marriage fell apart. We just could not stand to live at odds any longer. We separated for a while, then divorced in the spring of 1968.

Carola knew better than to try to keep us together when our marriage was not working. She said, "You have to make your own decisions." Jeanette moved out of our trailer, and we went right back to working as we had before, she with the horses and me with everything else. All we did was destroy our marriage papers and stop sleeping together. All else, including the rehearsals and performing we did together, remained the same, if somewhat strained. When Jeanette and I separated, some of our fellow performers gossiped and speculated about the reasons for our break up, but that did not bother me. They had gossiped every time we had an argument, so I was used to the raised eyebrows and occasional snickers. In such a small community it is almost impossible to have much privacy, and colleagues had known for a long time that things were not quite right between me and Jeanette.

My relationship with Carola did not end, but it was a bit tense after Jeanette left me. Carola tried not to be judgmental, but she was obviously unhappy with me. I was not, however, concerned about the chill between us because we still loved and respected each other, and I knew that in time she would accept Jeanette's and my decision to lead separate lives. I was confident about my position with the circus. Carola never imagined I would leave Circus Williams if my marriage to her daughter did not last.

Although we have taken separate paths, Jeanette and I

are doing better today than ever before—we can talk without screaming at each other, and I have helped her whenever she needed me. Ironically our relationship now is more like brother and sister than it was thirty years ago.

In the early months after our divorce it was not easy to continue working with Jeanette; it was difficult to be emotionally detached. As in the past I immersed myself in my work, and that helped me to get through yet another difficult time. I had become widely known all over Europe, and I concentrated on creating spectacular animal acts for Circus Williams.

I started training the elephants with voice commands in Germany late in 1957. The idea arose out of necessity, but it quickly became the basis for all my training. If a trainer is going to use a hook and physical forms of command, such as hand signals, the elephants must be close enough to see him and to be touched by him. That limits what a trainer can teach, and I did not want to be limited by anything. I wanted total freedom to create different kinds of acts, things that had never been seen before. To accomplish this, I had to be able to move elephants around without having to be a foot away from them, and without having to run back and forth as if I were mad. If elephants were to be successfully spread out in elaborate formations and even put into more than one ring, they had to be taught to respond to something other than touch or hand signals. Voice was the reasonable alternative because of the way it carries. I had always spent a lot of time talking to my animals, especially the elephants, and I knew that they responded to my voice because they became animated whenever they heard me. They looked directly at me and seemed to be paying close attention when I spoke to them. I knew from my daily talks with them that I would have to use the same intonations in my voice that I would with children—I would have to be firm with some commands and soft with others, and use a scolding tone when necessary.

Franz Althoff was the first animal trainer to spread out the elephants to create bigger acts, but he never worked with more than twelve at a time and he still used hand signals and touch. Franz was one of the greatest elephant trainers who ever lived, and I learned from him.

I started out with five elephants, then gradually increased the number to twelve, and then twenty. I introduced them to voice training slowly and in small, close groups. I would bring two or three elephants into a ring and have them stand several feet apart. Then, instead of using hand signals, I would give them verbal commands, and touch them to get them to lift a leg or turn in a particular direction, so that they would associate each command with a different action. Repetition was the key. I used very little touch so that they would become accustomed to listening and responding instead of waiting to be pushed or given a hand signal. By my talking to them constantly they grew to recognize the sound and intonation of my voice, and by my frequently addressing them by their names they learned to respond without any other cues. Although they fancied the attention, they were slow to react to this new form of training. They are smart but also extremely stubborn, and my method was completely foreign to them.

Gradually I spread them out, positioning them farther and farther apart, so that each had to listen more carefully. It was much easier when they were close together and I could give them signs, but I was not looking for an easy way to train them, I was looking for a different way. I wanted the audience to see the elephants using their minds. I was looking for something that would make them exceptionally responsive, good performers, and I found it. This proved to be useful when I came to America with twenty elephants and had to spread them out over three rings because it was impossible to fit them into one or two. This was a real challenge. The closer the animals are to a trainer, the easier it is to get them to perform. The farther away they are, the more detached and independent they feel. By working almost exclusively with voice commands, I could keep the animals aware of my presence even when I was not near them. The first time I presented an elephant act using voice commands only, the audience was astounded. People audibly gasped when I shouted at an elephant forty yards away and he immediately responded by standing on his hind legs. They marveled at the intelligence that was displayed by my elephants.

I also started creating more acts that revolved around individuals. Elephants are extremely group oriented, and because of that it was difficult to get an individual elephant to follow commands and listen. I worked on this because it was something unusual, and I trained several elephants to be the stars of their own acts.

When I was learning to train elephants at Circus Althoff, I discovered that African elephants cannot be trained in the same fashion as Indian elephants. They require much more patience and are far less dependable. There was no way to train African elephants to do whatever I wanted because they are so strong-willed. I had two African elephants. I taught them as best I could and hoped they would do the right thing. Most of the time they did.

As I said before, there was no standard language for training elephants, so I created my own elephant talk by combining words and languages. I do not think it made a difference what I said to them as long as I was consistent. Consistency in the sounds of the commands and the intonation of the voice are very important. When I called an elephant by name and said, in a voice so fast that the words almost ran together, "Pick it up, pick it up, schnell, schnell,"

UNTAMED

that elephant knew that he or she was lagging behind and had to quicken his or her step. If I shouted to an elephant by name and said, in a voice that went from a low to a high pitch, "Up!" that elephant knew it had to stand on its hind legs.

After a while I worked primarily with voice commands, but I still carried an elephant hook as a prop because I would have felt lost without it. The hook will not get them to move faster when they do not want to move, and it will not get them to perform if they are feeling lazy and stubborn. The hook does come in handy, though, when used to protect workers and the audience from the elephants, and to protect the elephants from each other. When trouble erupted between elephants, I needed the hook when I moved in to separate them.

Our performance showed the audience that the animals and I were used to working together and were having a lot of fun. Some of the elephants and I, such as Suzie, Congo, Tetchie, and Nellie, developed close relationships and we were openly affectionate toward one another, which also thrilled circusgoers. What the audience did not realize was that without the slightest provocation one of those elephants, no matter how well trained, could have turned in a minute from a gentle giant to a wild and dangerous creature. There was always an element of danger involved.

Once I had trained the elephants to respond to voice commands, I decided to create a mixed act with a tiger and an elephant. I wanted the animals and I to work together. I did not want simply to put a tiger on an elephant's back, parade him around the ring, and then stick him back in a cage. I wanted the tiger to do such things as jump down from the elephant, jump through a fire hoop from one elephant to another, and really give a performance. This had never been done before.

In 1962 I bought Bengal, my first tiger, for one thousand German marks, from an animal dealer in Belgium who had sold me some of our elephants. I told him I wanted a little tiger with a nice disposition so that I could get close to him, and he introduced me to six-month-old Bengal, who was like an outsized, frisky kitten. Although the temptation to play with Bengal and be a pal was great, I knew that I had to build a certain amount of respect between us if I was going to be able to get into a cage with him when he was big enough to rip my head off.

Every time I saw him, I talked to Bengal. I sat in a cage with him for hours at a time and even slept there some nights so that he would get used to me being around and feel safe. There were no reference books that I could turn to for advice on training a tiger. I had to use common sense and the know-how I had acquired by working with other animals. I did not want to break his spirit, but I did not want him to become unapproachable.

I wanted him to know that he was a tiger and to act like one, but I could not say, "You are a tiger. You must be a tiger. This is what you are supposed to do." I knew I had to give him a certain amount of freedom to discover what he was, and to do that, our relationship had to be rooted in trust. He had to know that I was not going to threaten or hurt him, and I showed him that by sitting and sleeping with him.

Bengal also had to know that I was in charge, so he was not allowed to play all day. By not playing with him every time he romped over and jumped at my legs, I taught him that there was a time for play and a time for work, and he could not treat me like another baby tiger. He had to treat me as he would treat a father tiger. I introduced discipline into his life gradually by making him sit until he was told to move and by having him do simple tasks, such as moving from one pedestal to another on command. As with the elephants, I used primarily voice commands with Bengal, sprinkled with some hand signals and the occasional shove on the rump.

So many times I sat with him, staring into his face and wondering what he was thinking, what he was going to do next. I sometimes tried to second-guess him just to test myself to see how well I was getting to know him. I would move toward him and imagine how he was going to react if I touched his side or put food near him. Bengal and I got to know each other very well. I tried to think as he did so that I would understand how to approach him with commands and so that I would recognize when he was getting tired, when he was not feeling well, when something was too difficult for him, or when he was just acting like a silly kid.

There were fleeting moments when I got so close to Bengal mentally that all distinctions fell aside and we were on the same wavelength. One night while I was sitting in his cage, I started to doze off. Each time my eye lids closed, I quickly opened them and picked up my head so that I could see Bengal. He watched me for a long time, never taking his wide eyes off me; then I noticed that, from watching me, he was growing weary and having a devil of a time keeping his eyes open. We both relaxed our guards and fell asleep together. At those times I do not know if he became a man or I became a tiger. I nurtured him and watched him grow as a father watches his child. I became just as protective of him, too.

Training for the mixed act had to take into account that elephants and tigers are natural enemies. To avoid any serious problems, I started creating the act by putting a dog on the elephant's back to get it used to having another animal on board. I chose my best African elephant, Congo, for this job, and let my own dog, a large, black standard poodle named Mohrchen, do the riding. After a few practices like this, I switched between the dog and Bengal. I would let the dog ride on Congo's back first, then quickly put Bengal up there, then take him down and put the poodle up again. This was designed to give the elephant confidence that nothing was going to happen to him. Congo and Bengal actually grew up together, but they did not start working together until they were four years old.

After performing this act for a period of time, I was ready to try something different again, so I added an Indian elephant named Thaila. Bengal would jump from one elephant to the other and do tricks, such as jumping through a fire hoop while moving between elephants. All three of them were very smart and well trained with voice commands. Congo never made a big deal about working with the tiger, but Thaila always acted worried and was much more skittish whenever she heard noises from the tiger. I believe they react this way because there are no tigers to fear in Africa, but in India, elephants and tigers share the same habitat, so fear of the tiger is in the Indian elephants' genes. Still, the act was extremely successful, and all three of them managed to get along.

I trained the mixed act for about a year before presenting it. The first year they performed together, I always made sure that I had someone in the ring with me to help separate the elephants if they got into a scrape. Thereafter I performed with them alone. Elephants are difficult to separate, but easier to command and get to stop than horses.

The tiger was new to the circus; none had ever been trained to perform, whereas lions were being trained a thousand years ago. I worried every time I practiced with Bengal because we had not yet purchased the proper cages to work in, and I had to rig a cage and keep him on a leash at all times. It was dangerous to have so strong and fierce an animal on a leash, and I was lucky that there were no mishaps. He did not react badly to being on a leash because, I believe, he knew that he was powerful enough to easily break away.

I was very proud of all my mixed acts and I presented them wherever we toured. Audiences were thrilled; but once, I was given a strange introduction while appearing at the Cirque d'Hiver, one of the most famous circuses in Paris. The director, Ringmaster Bouglione, who hired our trained acts for his winter season, came out into the ring and spoke through a megaphone. He introduced me, then told the audience that it was too bad I was only German and not Russian. Apparently during the Cold War people were fascinated by the Russians, and I would have therefore been even more sensational than I was.

I changed the mixed act several times. My training of Bengal had been so successful that I bought two more tigers. I did not have to spend as much time training them as I had Bengal because I had learned by working with him. I knew how to approach tigers now and discovered more and more about them, but I still invested a great deal of time in training and practicing with them. When I next did something different with the mixed act, I combined three tigers with horses and Congo.

I had to be careful about putting horses into a ring with tigers because they are more afraid of the big cats than Indian elephants are. The easiest thing would have been to keep the horses stationary as much as possible. Generally a horse is kept from moving by being put on a pedestal. My emphasis was always on doing things differently, so instead of putting a horse on a pedestal, I had a horse standing on the ground and the tiger sitting on its back. If the horse made the slightest move, the tiger would fall off, and there would be hell to pay in the form of a ferocious fight if they confronted each other. This presentation had to be perfect for everyone's safety.

In the 1950s I had seen an excellent horse-and-tiger

act presented by a trainer named Harry Belli. The animals were very precise and worked beautifully together. Later Adolf Althoff created a horse-and-tiger act, which was performed at Circus Althoff and then brought to America and presented by Adolf, Franz, and Evy Althoff in one of Ringling Brothers' shows. That act was still appearing when I came to America. I did not want to duplicate these feats, I wanted to do more, so I put two horses, three tigers, and one elephant together. I trained them to enter the ring at different times, move in various formations, and the tigers jumped from the elephant's back onto the backs of running horses with great precision. The mixed acts contributed to the notoriety that was being enjoyed by Circus Williams, and I discovered that I was becoming known throughout Europe.

Unlike other circuses, which saw some fairly hard times, we were always working. We never stayed in our winter quarters. When our season was over, we performed in other countries during the winter months. On the rare occasions we were home, I worked on changing the acts to keep them fresh. That became my trademark, and I was never angry when people tried to copy my work. I was proud.

I do not know exactly when I became famous. I started collecting newspaper articles about myself in Germany because it was fun. Then it mushroomed into the kind of fame that movie stars have. Suddenly it was upon me. People stopped me in the streets or waited backstage for an autograph. Newspapers requested interviews with me, and foreign news agencies contacted Circus Williams for information about me. Cameramen came to rehearsals and shows to photograph me and my animals. The important thing was not to let it go to my head. I shied away from the publicity, but Carola loved it because, she said, it was good for business. Although I appeared on posters and television shows and received keys to cities, I still went to the animals in the morning and cleaned up their stalls. It was also sobering for me to know that if I died, the circus would live on.

By the time we started traveling with Circus Williams to Spain and Italy, audiences recognized me, but it did not change my life-style, except that I bought better cars. My home was a circus trailer, I dressed in Western-style clothes, ate simple foods, and spent most of my waking hours working. I seldom had a lot of money. Carola hardly ever gave me raises. I guess I was a bad businessman in that respect, but I honestly did not strive to make a fortune. When Jeanette and I were married, the circus belonged to our family, and everything I did was for us, so I did not look for more money in those years. When the marriage was over, I still considered that I was working for the three of us—Carola, Jeanette, and myself—so I never asked for any large sums of money as recompense.

Later, when I joined Ringling and went to America, I had ten thousand marks in my pocket, equal to about four thousand dollars, which was a small amount of money to have saved after working for twenty-two years, night and day. I was underpaid until the last two years I was in Germany, when I made some very good money, and that is what I put into savings. One reason I never griped about my salary was that Carola bought anything I needed for the animals, regardless of the price. This made me happy, so I did not ask for more money for myself. Carola was so much like a mother to me, I would have felt peculiar asking her for more money.

In retrospect Carola could have done better by me. When we formed a partnership with Circus Scott in Sweden to work winters, Carola got 50 percent of everything. From our partnerships with Circus Togni and Circus Feijoo-Castilla for the Spanish, Portuguese, and Italian work, she got

25 percent. When the Spanish National Circus worked in Germany, she got 50 percent. We had twenty elephants and two flying acts in that circus, and it was a really big show. I was in the forefront of all of those deals, and I was the one doing all the extra work with the animals. But I never got anything extra, even though I was a major attraction in all three of those circuses and worked as if they were my own.

A few years before we came to America, Carola gave me a choice between a substantial raise or a piece of Circus Williams. Carola's friends advised me not to take it because she would still retain control over the money and could invest it any way she saw fit. They said I would never see an extra penny and that I would always have to worry about taxes and other obligations. They also pointed out that ultimately the circus would be divided between Jeanette, Holdy, and me. They advised me to take a pay raise, which I did.

Later, when I came to the United States with my wife, Sigrid, and daughter, Tina, I was concerned about how much money I was going to make because I wanted to be certain that if anything happened to me, my family would be provided for. I tried to be tough when I was negotiating my contract with Ringling. I said I could do everything they wanted me to do, as long as I was paid for it. So what happened? I went and did the extra work anyway and was not compensated for it. I was not very highly paid for the first ten years I was in America. During that time I created many new acts that went beyond what my contract required me to do and never received additional compensation for any of them. I could have honored my contract by creating a camel act, but I did what I thought was best by creating acts that involved leopards, lions, tigers, and even a giraffe. After ten years I negotiated another contract, and it was a different story.

UNTAMED

I never made demands of Circus Williams or Ringling Brothers, and I believe that was the right way to go, because I have had much luck. I may not have been overpaid when I started working for Ringling, but the owners provided superior accommodations for me and my family on the circus train and in trailers—things they did not have to do—and later on I was made part of the company.

Other circuses, including Circus Scott in Sweden, tried to steal me away from Circus Williams once I became well known. Kate Bronett, who owned Circus Scott, asked if I wanted to go to America, because she could have leased my act to Ringling Brothers. At that time the Ringling circus was still owned by the Ringling family, and they were always looking for new, up-and-coming performers and animal trainers. I turned down many offers because I felt a responsibility toward Circus Williams, and throughout my career I have only been with two circuses, Williams and Ringling.

I did help to train other circuses' animals whenever they asked me and I was available. I did it for Circus Togni in Italy and for Bouglione in France, and they paid me directly for this work. They were interested in my methods, and by working with their animals I was teaching their trainers my style, which soon spread all over Europe. I did not encounter jealousy or resentment because I was doing things differently. People saw how far I could go (I once presented a pyramid with twelve elephants in a small ring—a most difficult, unprecedented act for elephants), and they appreciated it.

CHAPTER

8

I have always had an eye for beautiful women. I spied them easily in a crowd and was not shy about approaching them— that is, unless they were with children. I saw other women after I broke up with Jeanette, some casually, some more seriously. I did not really have marriage on my mind when I met Sigrid, who became my second wife, devoted partner, and the mother of my son and stepdaughter.

The Circus Williams was working in Berlin one cold April day in 1966 when I spotted a svelte, beautiful blonde in the audience, accompanied by an adorable little girl, who was about four or five years old. Her hair was the color of pale yellow corn, and she had finely chiseled Germanic features, high cheekbones, and alert, smiling eyes. I was smitten with this woman the minute I saw her, and every free minute I had during that show I spent watching her and the child, who looked like a porcelain doll with light brown hair, large eyes, fair skin, and rosy cheeks. The girl delighted in walking up and down the aisle, and the woman seemed to spend more time looking after her than at the show. She was very stylish and well turned out, from her hair and makeup to her shoes. I was always attracted to women who cared about how they looked. Women who looked plain or average and wore no makeup did not get a second glance from me since I was surrounded by beautiful showgirls and performers all day, and I never felt that I had to settle for anything less in my private life.

When I saw an opportunity to get a little closer to this intriguing woman, I took it. I went to the top of the bleachers, closed the canvas door to block the chilling winds, then sat down a few rows behind them. I noticed that when she finally got the child to sit down, she wrapped her arms around her as if trying to warm the girl. I would have happily warmed the two of them.

I wanted to know if she was married before approaching her, so I sent a performer friend of mine on a fact-finding mission. He sat beside the woman and made small talk that was peppered with questions about her and the child. I continued to look on as he engaged her in conversation, and was very anxious to know what was being said. She turned only once to see where the little girl was, and we made eye contact, but our glances were not lingering.

When he had enough information, my friend and I met outside and he told me that this woman, Sigrid Fuls (her maiden name was Neubauer), was a widow, and the child was her four-year-old daughter, Tina. That was all I needed to know. I could approach her with a clear conscience.

This was one of the few times in my life when I was distracted from what was going on with the circus. I presented my acts, then positioned myself in various strategic places around the arena so that I could watch Sigrid. I wanted to be sure I did not miss her when the show was over, because I wanted to introduce myself and see if I could spark a relationship. I watched until Sigrid and her child left the arena, shortly before the end of the show, then followed her out to the parking lot, where I tried to talk to her. Sigrid was aloof as she got into her car, but I ignored her cold shoulder and asked if she would like to come back the following day to see the children's menagerie. She said she had other plans, so I asked about the next day, and she declined. I pressed on and asked if she would come back on Saturday. I was elated when she said she would. We agreed to meet at a certain time, but when I left her that day, I was not sure I would ever see Sigrid again.

I was wrong. True to her word, Sigrid returned on Saturday with her daughter, but they strode through the menagerie without me. Animals in cages and stables were out in the open in the menagerie, which was located in a small tent outside the big top, so people could see them before and after the show. This especially appealed to children, who were able to get close views of camels, giraffes, llamas, and even buffaloes. I had been detained on business outside the circus and was frantic when I rushed into the tent because I thought I had missed them. Fortunately I arrived just as they were leaving, and I apologized for being so late.

Sigrid and I spent some time talking, and we got along well. She was polite, courteous, and well spoken, and that counted for a lot with me since I always tried to be very correct and well-mannered. I was certain that I wanted to see more of this woman, so I invited her to visit me at my trailer the next day. I had to have at least one break during the day, and I thought I would use that time to get to know Sigrid better.

Sigrid was very prompt and arrived on schedule, but she was extremely upset after having seen a promotional picture of me and Jeanette in a local newspaper. "You are married, and I don't like this," she told me, then headed for the door of the trailer. I sprang to my feet with all the speed and agility of one of my big cats. With great dramatic flare, I opened all the closets and drawers to show her that there were no women's clothes anywhere in my trailer, because Jeanette had moved out. My quick thinking convinced her to stay awhile longer, and that gave me the opportunity to explain that I was separated. I asked Sigrid to come back the following day, and she said she would.

Sigrid never struck me as being anything less than a smart, quick-witted woman, and she proved it when next we met. She kept our appointment but did not come to visit me by herself. She invited her mother-in-law to come along. Sigrid was close to her in-law from her first marriage, and she wanted her to check me out. I guess I got a seal of approval because after that Sigrid and I tried to see each other on a daily basis. The Circus Williams was booked in Berlin for only four weeks—not a very long time to cement any relationship, but I gave it my best effort.

I was initially attracted to Sigrid by her beauty and pleasant nature. I was not surprised to learn that she was a fashion model. As we got to know each other better, I discovered that her worth extended far below her surface. She had been warm from the beginning of our relationship, helpful, and kind. She was patient, understanding, and always willing to listen. She did not find my work dirty or unpleasant, and that was of critical importance to me in any long-term relationship; from the outset this felt as if it should and could be long-term.

Sigrid made no demands on me, and that was something I needed. I was working so many hours a day that I did not have time to meet or worry about her every need. She understood that. In the little time we were able to spend together in Berlin, we found that we had many things in common—we even shared the same star sign, Virgo. Sigrid fit me like a tailor-made coat, and she felt equally comfortable with me. I liked that feeling.

UNTAMED

Once Circus Williams went on the road again, I could not get Sigrid out of my mind. I called her often and invited her to meet me in the different towns in which we worked. The time we spent together was precious to me, and I found myself looking forward to her visits with a kind of schoolboy anticipation. She frequently drove to the various towns to see me, but her responsibilities at home with her daughter and work sometimes came between us and prevented her from being with me. It was terribly distracting for me to have to stay in touch with Sigrid to tell her where I was going to be, then worry about whether or not she was going to be able to join me there. I did not like to divide my attention that way—my focus always had been and still had to be on work.

There were other considerations for me as well. I wanted to be faithful to Sigrid, but our long-distance love affair was driving me mad. From one day to the next I did not know when I would see her again, and I decided that I had to make our relationship go one way or the other. It could no longer exist in a state of limbo. Either Sigrid was going to make a total commitment to me and I to her or we would have to go our separate ways.

I telephoned her and said I could not go on this way any longer. I told her that I could not promise I would have a relationship with her alone because I had too many romantic opportunities, and they were near and she was not. When I left Berlin, I had asked her to go with me. I had since asked her to live with me several times, but she always refused. I said that I was asking her to live with me one last time.

Sigrid packed her bags, bundled up Tina, gave the keys to her apartment and car to her sister, and joined me at Circus Williams. I did not discuss any of this with Carola or Jeanette. I believed I was obligated to discuss all circus business with them, but I did not feel I had to discuss pri-

vate matters with either of them, or get Carola's permission
to take another woman into my life. One day Sigrid arrived
at the circus, bags and daughter in hand. I was so happy to
see her that I ignored all the raised eyebrows, and there
were quite a few of those.

The circus is like a big family. Everyone knows everyone else's business, and it is difficult to have any privacy.
All of my colleagues at Circus Williams knew that Jeanette
and I had separated, and they did not seem dismayed by
my continued presence at the circus. It was common
knowledge how much I put into my work and that Carola
depended on me to keep the circus running and working. I
do not think that anyone thought I would leave Circus Williams simply because Jeanette and I were no longer living
as husband and wife. I do think, however, people were
shocked to see that I brought another woman into an environment shared by Jeanette.

But I was not about to alter my life to avoid Jeanette.
My attitude was cold, but it had to be. I did not have a
home or an apartment where I could bring a new wife or
girlfriend. I brought my home with me from town to town
in the form of my trailer, and if I was to take another woman
into my life, it had to be under those conditions. I was not
flaunting Sigrid in front of Jeanette, I was simply living my
life the only way my work would allow.

Carola and Jeanette were not exactly thrilled by Sigrid's presence, but I did not care, and by showing that attitude I defied either of them to complain about it. Bringing
Sigrid to live with me was the best thing I could have done
for myself. I had been having difficulty severing my emotional ties with Jeanette after we stopped living together
because I was around her all day, every day. Once I became involved with Sigrid, it was easy to reduce my relationship with Jeanette to a friendship. After Sigrid came to

live with me, I knew my marital ties to Jeanette were completely cut.

Since Sigrid was not one of our circus people, she had to learn about everything from scratch. Circus life is not easy, by any stretch of the imagination, and in those days it was far more difficult than it is today. For instance, we could not rely on a single doctor or dentist, but had to find one in whatever town we were working in if one of us had a problem. It was not easy to shop for anything, from food to clothing, nor was it easy to keep in touch with family and friends. Sigrid soon learned that most friends came from within the circus, as did any enemies a person created. Fortunately for me and Sigrid, she was well liked by other members of Circus Williams.

She quickly found out how unusual my life really was. She was terrified of some of the animals, but she realized that she had to get close to them if she wanted to be close to me and be a part of my family. Otherwise she would have had to stay on the outside, looking in. Sigrid really worked hard to fit into our environment. It was not easy for her. She was afraid of the horses, and a couple of times I yelled at her because she was so skittish around them. I was sorry anytime I yelled at her, but I could not understand the fuss she made. It annoyed and distracted me, and I did not have the patience to put up with it. Sigrid tolerated all of this and eventually got the hang of circus life—my life.

Although she approached this as something of an adventure, her parents were never excited about her relationship with me. Her father was especially displeased with our situation and often asked what she hoped to accomplish by living with a married man in a circus. The more she explained that my marriage to Jeanette was over, the more her father expressed his unhappiness. Sigrid's family was fairly wealthy and owned a very large Berlin company that manufactured paint and home-decorating materials as well as having a retail store. Her father hoped that his daughter would not marry beneath her station, and he was concerned about appearances. Sigrid was sensitive to her parents' feelings and tried to assure them that she and Tina were happy, healthy, and safe. Tina was five years old and an easygoing child who happily adapted to every situation. She and I got along very well, and that pleased me because I liked children.

Sigrid and I discussed marriage, but I was in no hurry to run to a judge. I was comfortable with our relationship the way it was. Her father, however, kept pressing Sigrid about her plans, so we decided to get married if he would make all the arrangements. The one personal detail I did have to deal with was a divorce. No one could do that for me, so I went ahead and made my break with Jeanette permanent.

It would have been difficult for me and Sigrid to be married in a religious ceremony because I was a baptized Catholic and she is a Protestant. So we decided to have a civil wedding. She kept in touch with her father while he made all the preparations, and while we were on tour in Italy, he told her that all the plans had been finalized.

This marriage was in stark contrast to my tremendous first wedding; extraordinarily simple was the way to describe my second. And private—we did not even tell my mother or Carola about it. We flew to Berlin between towns and shows and her sister, parents, and in-laws met us there. We were married on April 10, 1968, in a courthouse in Berlin, and we flew back to Italy that night after dinner. There was no time for a celebration or honeymoon, but Sigrid did not complain. She understood the time constraints of my life.

When we rejoined Circus Williams in Italy, and news of

our marriage leaked out, everyone was disappointed because we had not made a formal announcement and planned a party. Carola was upset that I had kept her in the dark because, she said, she was looking forward to meeting Sigrid's parents. I also think she was hurt because I had left her out of something so special in my life. I felt guilty later on that I had not told her myself. Jeanette was cold and indifferent when she heard the news.

My mother wished us well, but was hardly disappointed that she had not been invited to the wedding. She and I had grown farther and farther apart, and by that time I seldom even wrote to her. She had her own life and was only vaguely interested in what I was doing. I was very much separated from her physically and mentally.

I was not worried that Carola might fire me or change my position with the circus—that would have been foolish, considering how well it was doing. She expressed her displeasure with me because I had not told her of my marriage plans in advance, and then she dropped the subject. Eventually she even accepted Sigrid.

Someone once told me that the Chinese symbol for war is two women under one roof. Although Sigrid, Tina, and I had our own trailer, we lived close to Carola and Jeanette, and I still worked with Jeanette every day. Sigrid was smart and extremely tactful. She was aware of the delicacy of our situation and went out of her way to be civil and courteous to Jeanette and Carola. She also knew how much Carola meant to me, and because of that, Sigrid treated her as she would have treated a regular mother-in-law.

These conditions were difficult, but we made the best of it. Fortunately Sigrid was immersed in taking care of Tina and me, and that made the circus world a little easier to bear. I was not able to spend as much time with them as I would have liked, but I saw them during the day at mealtimes. Tina accepted me as a parent, was obedient and well behaved, and we enjoyed the time we had playing the roles of a daddy and his daughter. I felt self-conscious about having Sigrid and Jeanette so close to each other. I always felt as if I was in the middle of something that I could not quite define, because there was no open warfare. There were sparks, but never any explosions, so I just kept my head low and hoped that this fragile peace would last. Too much was happening around the circus for me to have to worry about any personal problems.

In 1967, a couple of months before Sigrid and I married, I was contacted by Trolle Rhodin, an old friend who had owned a circus in Sweden and now worked as the talent director for Ringling Brothers and Barnum & Bailey Circus in America. When Irvin Feld bought the Ringling operation, he told Trolle that he wanted to open a second troupe and create a Red Show and a Blue Show—two arms of the same large circus, working and touring simultaneously in different parts of the country. He asked Trolle to find the talent for the second show.

Trolle came to see me in Europe and said I was the only person he knew who could accomplish the spectacular things Mr. Feld wanted done. I was a hard sell. Although a job with the Ringling circus was the dream of circus performers the world over, I felt very secure about my position with Circus Williams. I liked security. I did not like rocking the boat, and even though my salary was not the greatest, at least I knew I could count on it every week. Circus Williams was doing exceptionally well, and I had no complaints. I had total creative freedom. I had taken our animals to great heights, and I felt there was no end to what I could do with them. And I knew I could count on Carola for anything I needed or wanted.

Trolle visited me several times and even brought eight-millimeter films of the Ringling circus and America for me to see. He knew that I wanted to go to America, and he tried to convince me that I was passing up the chance of a lifetime if I did not accept the job with Ringling. I had never been impressed by fancy talk and promises, and I turned Trolle down. Some of what he said sounded too good to be true, and besides, I could not leave Carola in the lurch.

Early in 1968 a determined Trolle returned to Europe with John Ringling North and Irvin Feld. He wanted them to see me perform, and they attended several of our shows. Mr. Feld was quite impressed by my work both as a trainer and a performer, and he invited me to go to America to see how the animals were handled there and look over the Ringling operation. Mr. Feld was not an easy man to turn down. I was very reluctant, but he persisted and said that I should at least go to America for one day to see how things were done. I agreed to do it because I was curious.

In the summer of 1968 I visited the United States for all of one day, but I had to take two extra days leave from Circus Williams for traveling. This was the first time I had ever been on an airplane, and I thought the plane trip was fantastic. In America I saw so many different things for the first time. And the big airports! I tried to stifle my excitement so that I would not appear to be silly, but I was truly overwhelmed.

I found that the Ringling circus was as grand an operation as I had heard. Everything seemed to be done with the utmost care, and after only one day I understood why Ringling had such a fine reputation. Still, I turned down the job. Circus Williams was my home, and I owed much to Carola.

When I returned to Germany, I felt exhilarated by what I had seen, but Carola was distraught over my absence and told me that if I ever left Circus Williams again, she would close it down. We had quite a heated discussion because she made me feel like a prisoner, but in the end Carola won, and I assured her that I would stay.

To describe Trolle as determined would be putting it mildly. He did not want to take no for an answer, so he tried a different tack. Shortly after I returned to Europe, he approached Carola with a deal that would involve leasing some of her acts, including me, to Ringling. Carola was familiar with that kind of business because it was the way most acts in Europe worked—from circus to circus, season to season, under contract. By the time Trolle suggested this to Carola, she had already had ample opportunity to think about Ringling's interest in me and the future of her circus.

His timing could not have been better because the climate at Circus Williams had become tense, made so indirectly by Jeanette. She had several suitors, and Carola was extremely and justifiably worried about what would happen to her circus if Jeanette married and her husband said he was taking over the family business. Carola and I had discussed this, and we knew this was a situation we would eventually be forced to confront.

Carola asked my advice about making a deal with Ringling. Trolle had left a contract with her to read, consider, and—he hoped—sign. She was torn between keeping Circus Williams intact in Germany and protecting her own interests. We talked about it at length; it was a difficult situation for her, and she was terribly troubled. Carola had been in the business fifty years, and if she leased her major acts to America, she would have to close Circus Williams. I reassured her that if she decided to keep Circus Williams working in Europe, I would stand behind her. I was as supportive as I could be and kept telling her, "You don't have to sign."

Trolle and Mr. Feld returned in the fall of 1968 with

some new proposals that called for Carola to lease Circus Williams to Ringling for five years and then sell it outright to them. After much deliberation and a lot of sleepless nights, Carola signed these contracts. It was a very emotional time for my stepmother. She cried because she would have to be away from the circus. Carola was old, but not that old, and she had not planned to retire yet. Even when Mr. Feld showed up with the contracts, I told Carola, "If you don't feel good about this, don't do it." Mr. Feld told her that any of our employees who wanted to go to America as part of Circus Williams would be welcome. As for Carola, her days of traveling with the circus were over. She decided to retire and stay in Cologne.

I never believed that this day would come. I felt very sad for Carola, and for myself, when she cried over what she had done. She had haunting regrets, but once she had signed the contract, we were committed and had to see it through. I felt strange about leaving this part of my life behind. Circus Williams had really provided me with the only home and family I had ever known. Even though we would be taking many of our troupe with us to America, it was hard to leave the life I had known in Europe. I wondered what on earth I would do if the job with Ringling did not work out and I were to find myself a man without a circus. I seemed to have no control over the changes that were taking place in my life, as if everything was predestined.

Before Mr. Feld returned to America, he wanted to know about the special talents of everyone with Circus Williams. We had to let him know who would be working for Ringling so that they could be included in the contracts. I told him about each performer and worker, then he asked if Sigrid could do anything. Without even asking her, I immediately said that my dear wife, who was so deathly afraid of horses, could work in the High School and "Liberty" acts.

There was no time to ask Sigrid if she wanted, or was even willing, to learn to do these things. It was a question of economics and giving the new boss what he wanted. I was certain I could teach her to work with the horses, so Sigrid was included in the Circus Williams contract, along with thirty-four other employees and Carola. Even though she would not be joining us in America, Carola would be paid for her leasing agreement out of the monies Ringling allocated for Circus Williams.

Sigrid was not amused by the commitment I had made on her behalf. Our lives became very rough as I raced against time to train her. She had to be able to do the work before we left for America, which meant I had only until the end of our season to teach her. Jeanette was also included in our new contract to work in the same horse acts. I worked it so that when we got to the Ringling Circus with its three rings, Sigrid would be in one ring, Jeanette, because of her position with Circus Williams as Carola's daughter, would be in the center with me assisting her, and Ingeborg Rhodin, Trolle's wife, would be in the third. This was difficult for Sigrid, especially when introductions were made and the three of us were presented as Sigrid Gebel, Gunther Gebel-Williams, and Jeanette Williams. I could not give Sigrid the Williams name because it was a special honor bestowed upon me and it was not within my power to pass it along to my wife. Everyone in the audience thought that Sigrid was my sister and Jeanette my wife.

The first thing I taught Sigrid was bareback riding. I believe that if she ever had a reason to hate me, this was it. Learning to ride with a saddle can be difficult enough, but riding bareback can be brutal, especially for a city girl who had never been close to a horse. Sigrid was then, and is still, truly afraid of horses. I had no patience with her discomfort and fears. It had to be done, and that was all

there was to it. It became a fait accompli when her name
went into that contract. In spite of her fears and frustra-
tions, Sigrid learned bareback riding. Teaching her was no
easy task. I felt sorry for her after some of our long teaching sessions, but I could not let my feelings get in the way
of the work that had to be done.

From bareback riding, Sigrid went to the High School
act and the "Liberty" horses. The former had to be presented with elegance, grace, and poise. There is nothing
driving about High School riding, but it requires the ability
to take a horse through difficult paces and make it look easy.
Working with the "Liberty" horses involves being able to
guide them through several different formations and tricks
with the aid of two whips, which are used to give the horses
direction. The horses must fall into single file behind each
other, then regroup in pairs and trios, then stop and form a
line and stand on their hind legs. Sigrid never liked any of
it, but she knew better than to waste my time, so she worked
hard and learned. She did so well that I created a kind of
ballet with the "Liberty" horses she presented, in which
they took up different positions that resembled dance steps.
Sigrid has always been proud and strong-willed, and that is
a good thing because as concerned as I was about not
breaking an animal's spirit, I did not worry about how hard
I worked my wife. Sigrid is smart, and she was determined
to come out of my training unscathed, without complaining,
and to prove to everyone that she could learn to present
the horses. While Sigrid worked, one of my working men
and some of the younger performers looked after Tina. Young
as she was, Tina learned to move around the circus without
fear and enjoyed watching the performers during rehearsals.

Sigrid learned to do everything well, but not without
tears. I was hard on her. I am a rough teacher. The moment I knew that she would have to perform in the circus,

I threw her onto a horse and made her practice for hours on end. She would wake up in tears at the start of each day because she knew what was ahead. In retrospect I feel very bad about the way I treated her, but at the time I could only look ahead to the challenges we faced and force Sigrid to go on. Many times I told her, "That is my name on the marquee. People know that I train these animals, and I want them presented my way. You will learn to do it my way." She did, and she turned out to be quite a trooper, with a very tough skin.

Sigrid did not squabble about going to America. She understood why we were making the move and prepared for it as earnestly as anyone else in the troupe. As long as we were together, Sigrid did not care what we had to do. We decided that it would be a good experience and an adventure to pack up everything, leave the past behind, go on the boat, and make a new life. After all, it was not like starting a new job in a strange place. We still had the same work. Her parents were not so happy that she and their granddaughter were leaving Germany, but they did not try to stop her. We seldom saw them while we were in Europe, and we knew we would see less of them now. The situation had not changed with my mother, sister, and I. We hardly ever saw each other. I periodically sent money to my mother, and I assured her that that would continue. She and I did not have a sad parting, but I was sad about leaving Carola behind, and I tried to convince her to live the rest of her life in America with me. It is difficult to change elderly people, and she refused to go with us. She had her old friends, brothers and sisters, and Holdy in Germany, and would not be alone. Carola and Jeanette were very close, but Jeanette wanted to work with the circus, and Carola would not stop her.

When we closed our show in Cologne, Carola was visibly upset, and I was sharing her pain. Big changes are never easy to make, and they are even more difficult when they involve something that affects your entire life. It was hard for me to do that last show in Germany, because I did not know if I would ever return again, or if I would return a failure. I put my emotions aside and moved ahead because it had to be done.

I had worked hard to place any animals we would not be taking with zoos and other circuses, and by the last day they all had homes. We closed up our winter quarters, loaded everything on a train in Bremerhaven, went to the boat, and began our trip to America.

On the way to the dock I thought about the thirty-five people and all the animals traveling with me. We had thirty-five horses, seventeen elephants including Congo, Suzie, Tetchie, Mary, Cheetah, and Rhanie (twelve from Circus Williams and five new ones that Mr. Feld had ordered), and eight tigers, including Bengal. We knew that if this venture did not work out, we could not turn around and go back because there was nothing to go back to, so from the beginning I convinced myself that it would work. I told myself that I was not leaving Circus Williams; we were all simply going to America. And that was true. My roots came with me. I only changed locations. (More than twenty years after we sailed from Germany, part of Circus Williams was still alive in me, my family, and the animals. In 1990, when I retired as a Ringling performer, we still had ten elephants from Circus Williams, whom I entrusted to my son, Mark.)

From the outset Mr. Feld was very helpful. He was an old-time promoter and knew what moving and mounting a show entailed. He did everything in his power to ensure a safe and comfortable passage for us. However, there is only so much anyone can do to make a container ship filled with elephants, horses, and tigers a pleasant place during an Atlantic crossing.

The trains in Bremerhaven were located close to the

dock, so I walked the animals from the railyard to the container ship, which had a large door at the rear where we would load our precious cargo. We had made it that far without incident, and I wanted to be certain that I could get the animals loaded without any problems. I told the captain that once I walked the elephants on board, I did not want the slightest bit of noise or disturbance that might spook them and make them run. I had to move seventeen elephants onto the ship and chain them in their places as quickly as possible. It only took about five minutes, but I was so relieved when it was over.

I was not a seasoned ocean traveler. I had never even spent time in a rowboat. This was another first for me, and one I surely could have done without. The seas were so bad for those two weeks during November that whenever anyone went on deck, they had to tie ropes around themselves so that they would not be washed overboard. I was not prepared for this kind of trip, and I was seasick from morning until night. I was not alone. A couple of horses did not feel well either, but at least they were not out in the cold and they had enough food. This was the first time our elephants had been on a ship, and they did surprisingly well, as did the tigers.

I had never been on a boat that size in my life, and I never want to see another one. For me to make a trip like that again someone would have to hit me over the head and drag me aboard. Sigrid, on the other hand, felt fine. She had spent a lot of time on the water with her father, who was an old navy man and always owned a boat. Tina was young and it did not seem to bother her, either, and most of the other circus people also fared well.

Everyone tried to make the best of it, and we thought we were going to make it without incident until one day a man from the circus yelled, "Man overboard!" I rushed to tell the captain, and then the fool who issued the cry said it was only a joke. I was furious that anyone would make a joke like that under such circumstances.

It was also no joking matter to shovel manure with the ship constantly rocking and my stomach moving with it. We had to haul it to the upper deck and throw it overboard. We did this countless times. And each time we did it, we had to tie those ropes around our chests so that we did not disappear over the side with the manure. But what the hell, it gave us something to do.

The voyage to America was nerve-racking and tiring, but when I saw the Statue of Liberty in New York harbor, I silently thanked God. I prayed that everything else would work out, and it did.

It was daytime when we arrived, and we glided right by the Statue of Liberty. It gave me a fantastic feeling, and I stood tall because I felt so proud. The ship sailed on to Elizabeth, New Jersey. We were not far from Newark Airport, and I watched in awe as every few minutes a plane landed or took off. My chest swelled and I thought, "We made it, and we made it good."

As soon as we docked, we hauled containers until everything was unloaded. All arrangements had been made ahead of time by Ringling, and trailers were on hand to pick up the horses, luggage, and props. The tigers were unloaded, transferred in their cages to trucks, and taken to the Ringling winter quarters in Venice, Florida. I had to unload the elephants, who had to be transported to the winter quarters by train. That was another experience.

After being on the ships for two weeks the elephants did not want to go on the train. Several spanking-new train cars had been sent for them, but they wanted no part of it. I coaxed fifteen elephants onto the trains, but two still refused. One of the holdouts was a favorite elephant of mine,

Tetchie. Long after I had gotten the other slowpoke onto the train, she stood strong. Tetchie did not want to do any more traveling. That was it for her. I talked a blue streak, but all my voice commands and pushing could not make her move. It took hours before I finally got Tetchie onto the train.

I sent my best workers with the elephants, then collected my family, and we began our trip to Florida. Two of the things I had brought with me from Germany were the custom trailer that Sigrid, Tina, and I called home, and my Mercedes sports car. I drove the trailer to Florida, and Sigrid drove the car. This was some experience, going to America for the first time and having to drive to Florida. I had never driven such a great distance. In Europe the distances between cities and towns are relatively short. Now I was faced with a few thousand miles in a trailer with German plates, and Sigrid following behind me with German plates. I made so many mistakes on the way to Florida that I felt ridiculous. In Washington, D.C., alone, I was lost for a couple of hours. I finally had to pay a taxi driver to lead us out of that city and back onto the freeway. It was a heck of a way to see the capital. I had little patience for this kind of situation because I hated to waste time. Later when I had to drive great distances, I made sure I was much better organized, and nothing like this happened to me again.

My first impressions of Americans were wonderful. Everyone I asked for directions was helpful, and this was a kind of indirect welcome for me. We arrived in the late fall, so the weather was pleasant. I tried to take in as much of the scenery as I could, because I wanted to remember this first American trip in great detail. I was delighted by the climate in Florida, especially since I had just come from a country where it is almost always winter. I was thrilled by the palm trees, colorful tropical flowers, and sun-bleached homes. In some ways I was almost like a schoolboy on his first spring break. Even though this was by no means a vacation, I was overjoyed to be where so many Americans fled when they had time off.

Once we were working with Ringling Brothers, my wife's work hours rivaled mine. Sigrid's day started early every morning, when she made breakfast for me and Tina. She then did whatever housework she could before getting Tina settled in with a sitter at the circus so that she could rehearse her acts. Sigrid rode the High School horses for two years and worked with the "Liberty" horses for almost fifteen years. She was also involved with me in all the production numbers and had to attend those rehearsals. Before we came to America, she became such a good performer and made such a beautiful appearance that I incorporated her into some of my elephant acts, so she had to be on hand for those practices too. Sigrid has lived a tough life.

In addition to her work with the circus, Sigrid cooked five meals a day for us—breakfast, lunch, dinner, something before the last show, and something after it—did the housework, took care of all our paperwork, shopped, took care of our clothing, helped create our costumes, raised Tina, and handled other things that came up within our family. She also had to handle all correspondence to friends and relatives overseas because I did not have the time or the inclination to write. She did this all without complaining, and I appreciated it more than I could say. I never had time even to listen to her problems. She had to stand on her own two feet. She knew what I expected of her, what I wanted in my life, what I liked, and what we needed as a family, and she took good care of us.

After twelve years Sigrid's circus work was reduced to only presenting the "Liberty" horses. She did not have to do the opening or the finale, so it was a little easier for her.

After fifteen years Ringling completely released her from her contract. Sigrid stopped performing in 1988 at the age of forty-three. Many of our fans were disappointed when she left the show because she is a good-looking woman and they enjoyed seeing her. But Sigrid had earned a break.

We had not even been married a year when we moved to America. Sigrid and I had the same time constraints on our marriage that Jeanette and I had endured. The difference was that when we got married, I was more mature and Sigrid was a woman, not a teenager. We were both better able to handle a life that was almost completely devoid of private time. But at least we lived together as a family.

Sigrid and I worked well together in everything we did. She never balked over anything or said, "That is not my job," or "That is your idea. You see it through." Tina also adjusted very well to her·new situation. Family life around the circus was unique because we worked so many hours a day and spent so much time on the road. There was no community playground or swimming pool where Tina could go to play and make friends. She found friends among the other performers' children and enjoyed being around the circus, but Sigrid and I were concerned about her education. I believed that I should give my children the same opportunities that Carola and Harry had given theirs and that they should have a proper education. I also felt strongly about this because my own education had been cut short.

Ringling did not have a teacher traveling with its shows, so Sigrid and I had to do some serious planning about how we were going to put Tina through school. Obviously we could not enroll her in the neighborhood grammar school and send her off to class every day. After our first year in America we made a painful decision; we brought Tina to Sigrid's parents in Berlin and enrolled her in a German grade school. At the time we had no friends or relatives in the

UNTAMED

United States on whom we could depend to take care of Tina while she attended school, and we were unfamiliar with American boarding schools. We knew that Tina would be safe with Sigrid's parents and that she would get a good education in Berlin.

This was the first time Sigrid had been separated from Tina. From the beginning it was hard for her, and I do not think it ever became easier. We believed we were doing the best thing for our daughter, so we did not feel guilty. I did feel bad about breaking up our little family. I had been so pleased that we were living and traveling together, and now, after only one year, we were apart. Sigrid and I found comfort in knowing that we would one day be reunited as a family and that Tina would be the better for the time she spent in Europe.

We had not been missing Tina long when a miracle happened in my life. During the first year that Tina was away at school, Sigrid conceived our son, Mark. I could hardly believe my ears when she came home one day from a visit to the doctor and told me that she was going to have our child. I still have the piece of paper on which the doctor outlined the things Sigrid should and should not do while she was pregnant.

I was ecstatic. I never dreamed that having a family could be so exciting. I never thought I would have a child of my own, much as I always wanted one. I wanted to be a proud father and to be able to do things for my children. One of my goals was to have a secure family. Once I got married, work stayed at the top of my list of priorities, not only because I loved my animals but because I knew that hard work would give me the means to take good care of a family. When Sigrid became pregnant, I was overjoyed. It was one of the few things that really meant something to me, something that no one in the world would be able to take away from me.

One of the greatest moments of my life, and a major turning point, took place on August 17, 1970, when my son, Mark, was born. Yet, despite my great anticipation of that event and the happiness it brought me, I could not stay with Sigrid during our son's birth. I did not leave the hospital because I had to work—Mark came into the world at night, after working hours. I left because I could not bear to see my wife suffer.

We were performing in Houston. The Ringling circus was booked there for two weeks, so as soon as we got into town, Sigrid found a doctor, because she was so close to her delivery date. She went into labor on the last night of our Houston engagement, while I was working, so she went to the hospital by herself, and I met her there about 6:00 P.M. I stayed with her for a short time, then went to a hotel, where I spent the night. Sigrid's mother had come to the United States with Tina to be close to her when she gave birth, so the three of us waited together for news from the doctor. I was delighted to see Tina again, but I was so worried about Sigrid that I could hardly enjoy our daughter's presence. I was grateful that my mother-in-law was there to help me look after her.

I did not take my place beside other husbands who were anxiously waiting at the hospital, because it was too scary for me. I was worried about my wife, but I could do nothing to lessen Sigrid's discomfort or ensure her safety. I was so nervous and felt so helpless that I did not want to know anything, hear anything, or see anything, so I drove far away from the hospital to the hotel. Sigrid was disappointed because I did not stay with her, and my actions surprised her mother, but I cannot stand to be inside hospitals for any reason because of the suffering they harbor.

When the doctor telephoned me to say that I had a son and that both he and Sigrid were fine, I could not believe it. To have a child of my own, and a son at that—what more could I have asked? I did not jump up and down to show that I was happy, but deep inside I felt an intense excitement. I had experienced so many disappointments in my lifetime that I was always reticent about showing any physical signs of emotion when I was glad or happy. However, I did not mind showing how relieved I was once I knew that Sigrid and the baby were all right.

Knowing that I had a son of my own felt very strange to me in the beginning. I felt that it was too much to hope that this could turn out to be good. I was so skeptical about having a child, and apprehensive because this was something completely new to me. Even when Mark was growing up and walking around, the thought of having a son of my own was at times overwhelming for me.

I was not afraid that I would not be a good father. I had dreamed of having children of my own upon whom I could shower love and attention. I do not know what made me so apprehensive. Perhaps it was because I knew how to take care of animals, but not children. This anxiety slightly colored the joy I felt about my son's birth, but I never regretted having him. I just did not know how to act toward him.

The circus train had left Houston on the night Mark was born. I stayed behind because of Sigrid and went to the hospital in the morning with my mother-in-law and Tina. I watched in awe as Sigrid cuddled Mark, but when she held him out for me to hold, I stepped back. I could not bring myself to touch him; I was afraid to because he seemed so fragile and tiny. I could not grasp the idea that this little person belonged to me. I was mystified by the whole thing.

Sigrid thought I was being silly and tried to talk me into holding Mark, but I was adamant. I had never held a human baby, and I was not ready or willing to start just yet. I was content to know that she and he were all right, that he had ten fingers, ten toes, and all the other essential parts, and that everything was in fine working order.

I was also pleased to see how well Sigrid looked. She had gained hardly any weight while carrying Mark, even though she stopped performing four months into her pregnancy. She chose to leave the show temporarily and have a replacement act take over for her because she worked in the middle of eight horses and was afraid that one of them might kick her and cause her to lose the baby. When she left the hospital a couple of days after giving birth, she was wearing a size-seven dress, the same as she wore before becoming pregnant, and she looked as beautiful as ever.

I could not linger at the hospital, because I had to take a plane to Salt Lake City to catch up with the circus. Sigrid, her mother, and Tina joined me two days later with Mark. I was so nervous when I was around Mark that I thought I would surely go to pieces if I spent too much time with him.

On the day Sigrid came home with our son, she and Tina forced me to hold him. Tina kept insisting that I do it, and finally Sigrid looked at me with a very stern face and declared in her strictest German fashion, "You did it, you take him," and then she handed him to me. Once Mark was in my arms, I was afraid to move, afraid even to breathe too deeply lest I hurt him. I sat perfectly still until Sigrid took him back.

Having Mark in our trailer was another scary experience for me because I did not know if we had to change our way of living to accommodate a baby. I am ordinarily fanatical about cleanliness, and Sigrid always kept our place immaculate, but I was not sure if that clean was clean enough for an infant. I was always bothering her about every little thing, because I was worried about the baby's environment. Sigrid was meticulous about the way she kept Mark, and I knew I had nothing to worry about, but still I was perpetually concerned about him. I could not help myself—I had never had anything to do with such a young child.

Sigrid often encouraged me to hold him, but I was afraid that he would break. I was used to knocking around with big, strong animals, hauling heavy equipment, and working with things that were meant to withstand a lot of pressure and rough treatment. I did not know how to handle something as soft and small as a baby. Even baby animals whom I had raised never seemed to need as much careful handling as a human baby. Many weeks passed before I became comfortable with handling my son.

One of my greatest fears, apart from thinking that Mark would break, was that he would cry all night and keep us awake. Fortunately Mark was a good baby, and he let us sleep. I believe this happened because he was contented. Sigrid was a great mother, and that pleased me. She had always been good with Tina, but I had never seen her with an infant. She was extremely attentive to Mark, and we never had any problems with him.

UNTAMED

Sigrid did everything when it came to taking care of Tina and Mark, and they grew to be good children. I never had to discipline them because they were unruly or out of control. My word was enough. I avoided hitting my children because I believed to do so was wrong, not because I was afraid of becoming like my father. I knew from the time I was a little boy that the things my father had done to his family were wrong. By the time Mark was born, my life was normal, and I was free from my father's influences. I did not approach fatherhood with the idea that I had to change in order to be good to my children. I knew that very little about me was a reflection of Max Gebel.

I think I turned out to be a pretty good father once I realized that Mark was sturdy and healthy and could withstand hugs and kisses. I may have been a bit strict with my children—they would say too strict—but I was always good to them. I never gave them family vacations or much leisure time, but our lives did not permit those luxuries, and we learned to be happy without them.

We were also fortunate in other ways. Many men and women have to count every penny they spend once they have children. Sigrid and I were lucky because we were able to cope with everything without feeling that we had to make great personal sacrifices. We did not have to worry about who was going to pay our rent, because we had our own trailer, and later our own circus-train car, another trailer, and a customized bus, all of which were homes on wheels. There was no phone bill to pay, no gas or electric bills. We only had to take care of our food, clothing, and certain medical bills. Somebody picked up the trash outside our door, somebody filled up our water tanks—all these things were taken care of by circus personnel. We always had electricity when we lived on the train because the generators were kept running. We had no concerns about anything. I never had to say, "Oh, my God, I don't know how I'm going to pay for this," or "We have to sacrifice this to pay that."

Living in a circus-train car was not a bad situation. The trailer we used when we first came to America had a bedroom, bathroom, kitchen, and living room. The train car Ringling bought for us was ninety feet long, and we furnished it as if it were a regular home. I covered the floors with carpeting and painted the walls, and Sigrid made curtains and selected all the furniture we bought. Mark lived with us and so did Tina after she returned to the United States. When she got older, Tina had her own state room. Life on the train also afforded me the luxury of not having to drive from one engagement to the next. For the first time in my life I could sleep late and have an entire day of rest whenever we were traveling great distances.

In Germany we had forty-foot trailers and circus wagons with partitions in the middle for two people, with all the necessities inside except running water. We did not have any running water in the circus business in Germany. There was a toilet wagon that everybody had to use. That was a little rough, especially when it was cold. When I was with Circus Williams, I did not have a shower in my state room, so I built a barrel and bought a large heater. I would turn on the heater, fill the barrel with hot water, and sit in it up to my shoulders. Other people in the circus used a water bucket for washing. In America we had showers in our living quarters.

When we first moved onto the train, I enjoyed having some leisure time, but I was never a person who could sleep for many hours, even if I needed the rest. I would sleep for only a short time and then get up and go to work. Living in the train car forced me to relax, because while we were traveling there was nothing else to do. I would sit idly around, thinking about all the things I could be doing if I were not stuck on a train. This made me uneasy.

UNTAMED

I was also forced to use regular dressing rooms, and that did not please me. I am especially particular about the towels and toiletries I use, so Sigrid had to make sure that she brought our own clean towels and my personal toiletries, including fresh soap, to every dressing room we were assigned. I would never use anything that had been used by somebody else. She would mockingly say that I was as fanatical about not being exposed to germs as Howard Hughes. The truth is, my becoming ill would have caused a particular type of chaos. No one else did the things I did, and no one could work as my stand-in. If I could not perform, half the acts in the circus would have had to be canceled. I had no choice but to keep myself healthy.

After ten years of living on the train, we decided to get another trailer that could be used for personal travel and as a dressing room. We planned to live on the train and use the trailer for changes, resting, and eating between shows. I also saw it as a means of escape and a way to get back on the road again. Driving for any length of time was not the best thing for me when I had to do twelve or thirteen shows a week, work hard around the circus and train the animals, conduct animal walks into and out of each town we visited, and raise and take down tents, but I did not look at the practical side of that matter. I had to have a place where I could go away for a while and not see or hear the things that normally filled my life. Although he bought the trailer for me, Irvin Feld was unhappy whenever I drove it, because he was concerned about my safety when I was tired. I did my best to allay his fears, because they were genuine and justified, but I had to have that special space.

I could escape from my work physically, but I could never escape from it mentally. Sometimes my family would travel by train while I drove to the next venue, and I would worry about them and everything else that was on the train. Often when I was traveling in the trailer, I found myself wondering if the things we started out with were going to show up in the next town. For years while working in Europe I oversaw the movement of every line and cage and was responsible for making certain that all of our equipment, baggage, people, and animals showed up at each new place. I did not lose that conditioning when I came to America.

After a few years of alternating between the trailer and the train, I got rid of the trailer and bought a bus. Sigrid and I had always dreamed about having a tour bus on which our entire family could travel and be comfortable, and we finally bought one, complete with a bedroom, bathroom, kitchen, living room, and enough open space for Mark to sack out with a sleeping bag and Tina to crash on the couch. We used the train car during our stays in each town and traveled between the cities on the bus, which I drove.

I never thought it was unfair for my family to have to live on the road year-round instead of in some pretty town in a house with a big green lawn and swimming pool. We owned a home in Florida that fit that bill, and we got to enjoy it a few weeks out of the year during our winter break. Knowing it was there was enough to keep us happy and content while living on the road. Sigrid had adjusted to life in the trailer and on the train very well, because even though she had lived in a large house when she was a girl, she had spent weekends on a boat and knew how to live in small quarters. It did not matter where we lived so long as we were together as a family.

We actually did not have to travel by train, trailer, or bus. Mr. Feld had given us the option of flying and staying in hotels. He gave us many opportunities to change our lifestyle and do things differently, but I turned all of them down. I wanted to stay as close to the animals as possible, and I also wanted my family to feel that even if they were not living in a regular house, they at least had someplace to call home. They would not have felt that way living in hotel rooms.

Because we were fortunate enough to have this assortment of living accommodations on the road, we were always able to entertain guests. Carola came to the United States and stayed with us for several months each year; Sigrid's mother visited as often as possible, but her father never came to America because of his fear of flying. My mother and my sister, Rita, and her daughter even came to see us several times. They were interested in seeing America, and when they traveled with us, they saw many different places. Visits with my mother and sister were always strained. I hardly knew Rita after being separated from her for so many years, and we had little in common, but she was still my sister and I was glad to see her, even if there was little warmth between us. We spent time together over meals, sometimes talking about old friends or places in Germany, but we did not discuss our childhood. Most of our conversations were extremely superficial. Since Carola's regular visits were so lengthy, we treated her to the luxury of her own trailer. It made her feel important, which she was to us, and also ensured our privacy as a family. Everyone else who came to visit had to share quarters with the rest of us.

In addition to being able to entertain foreign guests when we lived on the train, we actually got to meet many people in each town we visited because folks would come to our train car to say hello or bring goodies and gifts. That is how we got to know a couple named Chavis, who became two of our dearest friends.

We first met Martha and Willard Chavis when they dropped by to say hello while we were doing a show in Columbia, South Carolina, near their home. They had seen the performance and then gave us a taste of genuine southern hospitality by bringing a homemade cake to our train car. My mother was visiting us at the time, and I think she was somewhat impressed by the attention and affection given us by strangers. I always tried to be cordial and graciously accepted the Chavis's gift, but I hesitated when the time came to taste it. Not that it did not look and smell delicious. It did. It was just that I was always concerned about eating anything that came from someone I did not know, because there is no way of telling what a stranger might do. I worried that I might be poisoned or made ill by something that came from a less-than-stable person.

I waited until my mother ate a piece of the Chavis's cake, then let a couple of hours pass to see if anything happened to her, before I ate a piece. I never told this to her, because I am certain she would have been furious and offended. I did the same thing until the day I retired. If somebody brought a cake or something else to eat, I gave it first to my grooms. They ate anything anyway.

In curious ways like that, I was always afraid that something was going to happen to me. There I was, messing around with tigers and elephants every day of my life, worrying about being poisoned or done in through some other offbeat means. Once, when Ringling was in Little Rock, Arkansas, circus workers were driving animal cages down a hill and suddenly the vehicles started moving too fast and the cages slipped over. The safeties on the doors opened, and two lions from a hired act escaped. Before we had a chance to stop them, both cats took off into a heavily wooded area behind a nearby fairgrounds building. We quickly called the police and they brought in helicopters to help.

I could not stand by while other people went after these dangerous creatures, so I picked up the biggest stick I could find, which was not very big, rounded up some of my working men, and went out in search of the lions. I led our party into the woods through some low brush and secondary growth. The grass in that area was high, and I suddenly thought that maybe there were snakes out there. I reckoned that if I was the first one to disturb them, I would be bitten. I turned around and asked one of my workers, an obliging man named John, who was walking directly behind me, if he would mind walking in front of me. He willingly traded places with me. After a while I thought, "Wait a minute. Maybe John is going to disturb the snakes, but they will pass on him and bite me because I'm right behind him." I tapped him on the shoulder and said, "John, go behind me." He heaved a sigh and complained, "Boss, please make up your mind." He went behind me again, and I thought, "Good. I don't want to be bitten by a goddamn snake." There I was, looking for two lions with a little stick, and I was scared to death that I would be bitten by a snake.

There were no snakes, or at least none that bit any of us. We finally found the lions, but the police had to shoot them. We would never have been able to capture and return them without someone being hurt or killed.

Even today I think back on that and wonder how I could have gone after lions with only a small stick. If I had found one of them, what would I have done? I would have hit the lion on the head, the stick would have broken, and I would have been left with nothing. So stupid. No gun, no knife, no nothing. And I was only afraid of the snakes, not the lions. This has been the story of my life. I never had the idea that something would happen to me when I was dealing with the animals, only with cakes or snakes. Now I carry a gun all the time, but not to protect myself against animals, to protect myself against people.

Although most of our experiences while living on the train were pleasant, there were some fans who gave us a real start. One was a young woman who seemed to latch onto us and would not let go. We returned to the train late one night after a show and found this girl, who could not have been more than eighteen or nineteen years old, sitting on the steps of our car. It was raining and cold, and even though I felt sorry for her, I had to ask her to go away. She just sat there. After telling her to leave several times I telephoned the police. Before they took her away, I gave them ten dollars to give to her because she looked so down and out. The police drove her to the stationhouse just to get her away from the circus and then told her to go home. She turned up after this in several towns where we were performing, always hanging around our train car. I was not so concerned for my own well-being as I was for that of my wife and children. I kept calling the police, hoping to dissuade her from coming back. The police would take her away, but she would be back soon after. Then, as suddenly as she had shown up, she dropped out of sight and we never saw her again. Experiences like that can give you the creeps.

While we were living out our adventures and misadventures in America, Tina was going to school in Germany. Although her grandparents were very good to her, Tina often wrote us long, tearful letters saying that she wanted to be with us and her brother. I, perhaps better than Sigrid, understood Tina's desire to be with her family. I felt guilty about making her stay in Germany, but I did not see any alternative. She had to have an education, and we could not give it to her on the road.

Tina spent every summer with us for five years, and it was always sad when she had to go away again. We visited her in Germany during our winter breaks, but this was too little to make her happy. Sigrid telephoned Tina often and tried to console her with assurances that as soon as she graduated, she would be home with us for good. Tina, how-

UNTAMED

ever, got her wish sooner than any of us anticipated. While we were visiting her and her grandparents one Christmas, Sigrid noticed a change in her father's health. She told me that she believed he was seriously ill and that Tina should come home with us.

Tina had been especially homesick that year. We were playing with her one day when she suddenly burst into tears because she knew we would be leaving Berlin without her. We were so upset by this that we finally said she did not have to stay in Germany if she felt that bad about being away from us. It was the best Christmas gift we could have given her. Later we sadly discovered that Sigrid had been right about her father being ill, and it would have been a tremendous burden if he and his wife had had to care for Tina under such difficult circumstances.

As a present that year for Christmas Tina's grandparents had given her a new bicycle. Even though we wanted her to be able to enjoy it, we couldn't bring it back with us, and Tina had to leave it behind. She was unhappy about that, but she was still glad to be going home with us. When I think back, I am surprised that I was not more sympathetic to her cause and didn't find a way to lug the bicycle back on the plane.

By this time Tina was eleven years old, and we had to figure out what to do about her schooling. We were determined that she should be well educated, no matter what it took to accomplish that. She was already fluent in German, and we wanted her to learn English equally well. Before leaving Berlin we decided that the best way for Tina to continue her education would be with a private tutor. Because we were on the road all year, we did not have the contacts other parents develop in their communities and consequently did not know how to hire an American teacher. We solved this dilemma by bringing a teacher from Germany back to America with us. We paid him to work exclusively with Tina, not any of the other children at the circus.

One might have thought that Tina would have suffered a bit of culture shock when she came back to the States after being away for five years, but she did not. Sigrid and I were always amazed by her ability to adjust to different situations and environments with little or no effort. She was happy because she had been reunited with us, and it was easy for her to continue her studies because her lessons were taught in German. The teacher held classes in our train car, and Tina learned well and was not at all distracted by her colorful surroundings. She became reacquainted with English through our circus friends.

Just when we thought we had everything on the right track, Tina's teacher had to return to Germany because he had been in the United States on a limited visa, which expired after one year. Sigrid and I were at our wits' end over this and did not know where to turn. We had never imposed on anyone for anything. We broke that custom when it came to getting Tina into a regular school.

Martha and Willard Chavis had become good friends. We liked and trusted them, and we respected them for being God-fearing, family-oriented people. They repeatedly told us that if we ever needed anything, we should let them know. Now we thought of them as we planned the next stage of Tina's education. Sigrid and I discussed the possibility of enrolling our daughter in school in South Carolina under the guardianship of Mr. and Mrs. Chavis. It would mean sending her away again, but at least she would be in the United States, and we would be able to see her more often than when she was living in Europe.

Sigrid telephoned Martha and asked if she and her husband would allow Tina to live with them and their children

UNTAMED

while she attended school in Columbia, South Carolina. Martha gave us a resounding yes, and she and Willard took Tina in as a daughter.

We thought Tina was going to balk at having to leave us again, but instead she willingly, even happily, went to live with the Chavis family. There were no tears, no pleas for a parental pardon. To our great surprise, because she had been so tearful about being away from us when she was in Germany, Tina readily embraced the Chavis family and went about the business of leading a normal life. I suppose that, for a child, being away from one's family in the same country is more reassuring than being on another continent. She went to a regular public school, with typical American children, and learned to speak, read, and write English perfectly. Tina was and still is an easygoing girl. She is tall and thin with a lovely face, which only enhances her inner charms. As glad as we are that she is such a pleasant person, Sigrid and I have been taken aback at times by how fast she would attach herself to someone else and seem not to worry about leaving us behind. When Tina was a child, if she made a new friend, she would have been happy to go away with that person the same day. Mark would not leave us for a second for anyone in the world, but Tina would.

Time passed quickly and we were gratified by our daughter's progress. We were also pleased that she fit in so well and made so many friends. Then, only two years after Tina went to South Carolina, Mark turned school age, and we were faced with the problem of what to do about his education.

Mark had to be treated differently than Tina because he had a totally different personality. She could go anywhere and be happy. Mark was so close to us that we could not send him away. He would have been heartbroken and a bad student if going to school meant being away from home.

We knew that we had to do something different for him. The question was what?

Mark had also shown a tremendous interest in the circus and had been performing in small acts that I had built around him since he was two years old. He regularly helped me with the animals, and I was afraid that if we sent him away, he would lose his interest in these things. You cannot send a child away for twelve years and expect such interests to stay alive. Even if they did, on his return he would have had to learn from scratch what he would have learned so easily by growing up around the circus.

We decided that the only way to educate Mark was with a tutor, but we wanted this one to be an American. I discussed it with Irvin Feld, and he agreed to hire a teacher to travel with the Ringling circus if we could find someone who was qualified and did not mind living on the road. As before, we were faced with the problem of hiring the right teacher, but this time a friend came to our aid. Over the years we had made another wonderful and trusted friend, Arthur Eve, a retired Air Force colonel who lived next door to our home in Venice, Florida. Arthur could work his way through red tape and bureaucracy faster than anyone I knew, and when he heard that we were looking for a teacher, he posted a notice at the local school board and assured us that we would get a response.

Had I not seen it for myself, I would never have believed that so many teachers were interested in joining the circus. The response was overwhelming. Arthur helped us interview one hundred, from whom we chose three possibilities, and then Arthur told us that of all of them, Bob Grote was the man for the job. Bob was from New York, but his mother lived in Venice, where he had been visiting. Sigrid and I were glad that we took Arthur's advice, because we could not have made a better choice.

UNTAMED

Bob turned out to be great for our children. We brought Tina back from South Carolina, and she and Mark were tutored together. Every morning Bob came to our train car and held classes that were specifically designed for each of our children's levels. His teaching rivaled the kind of education Tina and Mark would have received in a private school. He also enjoyed all the traveling, and that made life easy for all of us. Tina completed her high school education under his tutelage, and throughout his ten years of schooling with Bob, Mark was six to eight months ahead of children in conventional schools. Our greatest concern was to have our children with us and to educate them so that they could have the same opportunities as people outside the circus. Our efforts paid off.

Knowing we had a teacher who was secure in his work, happy with his life, and good at what he did made our lives a lot easier. We did not have to travel to see our children or worry about how and when they were going to go to school. That freed our minds for other things and gave me one less distraction. Mark studied with Bob through his sophomore year of high school, when Bob decided that he wanted to stop living on the road and settle down. We then hired another teacher named Jim Boyd. Mark graduated from high school, but decided not to go to college. We told him he could do anything he wanted, but he wanted to work for the circus. I could not argue with that decision if it was what he really wanted to do.

Tina also decided to work for the circus instead of going to college, and she started to do so as soon as she returned from South Carolina, before she had even finished her high school education. At the age of thirteen she set her sights on becoming a showgirl. I teased her about it, and Sigrid protested that Tina looked too much like a little girl to be a showgirl. But she was cute and agile, and I thought she should be given a chance if that was what she wanted. As soon as she expressed a desire to work, I spoke with Kenneth Feld, who had succeeded his father as owner of the circus, and he was nice enough to hire her. We gave her a costume befitting her age and then went about the business of teaching her.

Tina learned, as the rest of us had, to pack an enormous amount of work into twenty-four hours. She went to classes in the morning, studied her schoolwork, practiced her acts, then did two shows each day. This was not easy for a teenager. It entailed a lot of responsibility. She was expected to be prompt at all times and do everything that was required of her without any excuses. Tina learned to do the show numbers perfectly. She then became an aerial dancer, graduated to acts with horses and elephants, and took over a dog act with Russian wolfhounds from some fellow performers who were giving it up.

Tina had the same demanding teacher as her mother. I started her out with acrobatics and soon discovered that she was a terrible student. She yelled and cried so hard while I was teaching her that I thought one of us would surely go mad. I often yelled at her when she did not do things correctly after I had shown her a sufficient number of times, but I knew a loud voice would not sour her on the work if she really wanted to do it. I was often yelled at as a child, and that did not prevent me from learning and doing things right. She was (and is) extremely intelligent, but was always afraid that she was going to get hurt. One day while I was trying to teach her some new acrobatics, she screamed so loudly that everyone in the circus came running over to where we were working because they thought something terrible had happened to her. I could never figure out why she screamed like that.

After years of performing in these different areas, Tina

chose to work almost exclusively with Russian wolfhounds and elephants, to appear in the spectacular opening and finale, and to teach other women to be aerial dancers. She's a good teacher and has a lot more patience with her students than I ever had.

We did not push Tina into a circus job. Actually she was not incredibly ambitious about doing any kind of work, which is why we were initially surprised when she said she wanted to be a showgirl. She was very low-key about it, and I was glad that she did not want to be a famous trapeze artist. That type of work takes a lot more ambition and passion than Tina displayed. It is also harder to learn, and I could not imagine myself teaching Tina to be a trapeze artist after what I went through just to teach her some acrobatics. She was such a tough student!

Tina did not want to be a star. She just wanted to work. That pleased me beyond words, and I was glad to let her do whatever she wanted. If she had wanted to be a circus star, we would have had to push her hard to get her to practice many long hours every day. Mr. Feld hired her the first day she said she wanted the job, and she has worked ever since. She has been a busy girl with little private time, but she has done herself and her parents proud. She has been able to grow at the circus and has the opportunity to do other things within the Ringling organization. Tina did not make a bad choice when she was thirteen.

Unlike our daughter, who had spent so many years away from home because of school, Mark has been in show business from the first day he could walk. He looks like a performer, tall and thin with bright, chestnut-colored hair, the same fine features as his mother, and a commanding, broad stride. We never pushed him into the circus business either. He just took to it and assumed his place with the attitude that he belonged there. It gave me such joy to see this little toddler following behind me trying to imitate everything I did. He did not stand any higher than my knee when he tried to take a broom from my hand so that he could sweep up the way he saw me doing it.

From the time he was old enough to understand us, we told Mark that we wanted him to have normal relationships with the circus and the outside world. I encouraged him to dream. We taught him that he could do anything he wanted to if he had the education and the willpower. In the early years, when we discussed careers and ambitions, he would say, "We will see what happens," but later, when he became a teenager, he told me that he wanted to stay with the circus.

Mark worked with me for eighteen years, and in that time he did anything that was asked of him and was always on hand when he was needed. I could not be prouder of him. In a small way I believe I know how Harry Williams felt when he squared his shoulders, swelled his chest, and watched me work. Mark learned the business the way I learned it, from the ground up and by watching. He was my little shadow from his earliest years, and his circus education began in much the same way as mine: cleaning up after the animals; feeding, grooming, and exercising them; and being my helper during practices. When he grew older, he became one of my watchers outside the tiger cage.

Mark learned to train the elephants in my style, primarily with voice commands. They all know him. Most of the elephants grew up with him, and he has learned to communicate with them and get their cooperation. I have never let my son work with the tigers. If the day ever comes when he expresses an interest in training them, I will teach him. He already knows my commands because he watched me work for many years.

I think I always knew Mark would choose the circus,

and perhaps I secretly hoped for that. When he was a little boy, he had tiny toy animals and a toy circus, and he would sit for hours playing with the animals, making believe he was a trainer and creating his own acts. I would look at him and think of myself playing with my little horse and buggy. At least my son could dream when he played and know that those dreams had a fighting chance of coming true.

As he was growing up, I stepped back many times and let Mark do things with the animals so that I could see how he interacted with them and if he knew how to work with them. As long as he wanted to do the work and did things correctly, I let him. I knew that he had to have the opportunity to put into practice what he had learned by watching me.

The first time Mark performed was in an elephant act that I presented on a Saint Petersburg, Florida, television show. He was responsible for bringing me a loaf of bread, which would be used to reward the animals, and he was also supposed to put his head under an elephant's foot when the animal lifted its leg on cue. I'll never forget it. Mark was only two years old and looked so adorable in a tiny costume that Sigrid had made for him. He and I had rehearsed his part over and over again, and he always did it in practice. At showtime he suddenly did not want to do it anymore. He refused to do anything that he had rehearsed. I tried to bribe him into doing his part by telling him he would get cake and chocolate afterward, but he still would not do it. Even though he had suddenly become a reluctant performer, people were so crazy about him that I kept him in the act.

Years after his first "performance," when Mark took an elephant out for the first time, I stepped back so that he would be in charge and the elephant would respect him and not look to me for commands. Once I saw that Mark knew what he was doing, I gave him more and more time with the elephants, and then the horses. The only time I ever stepped in was when I saw Mark trying to be too rough with the animals. Young men often believe that they have to be tough guys to be in control. They do not have enough patience, and expect things too quickly. A person becomes a much better animal trainer as he grows older. There is no such thing as a good, very young animal trainer.

Sigrid, Tina, Mark, and I worked together for a long time. I believe this is one of the reasons why our family is so close. Everyone has their share of work to do, and they do it. No one ever tried to get out of work by complaining or whining that something was not his or her job. We all invested parts of our own lives into each other's lives. We have worked and struggled together, so everything we own belongs to all of us.

I never dreamed it could be like this. I never even thought I would have my own family. I was happy to have Tina, but when Mark was born, my own son, who ended up interested enough in what I was doing to want to continue in my work—this had to be the reward for the countless empty nights I spent without a family.

10

Jeanette began seeing other men soon after our breakup and conceived a daughter, her first and only child. When we came to America, she was all alone and her baby was only one year old. I tried to help both of them and treated her daughter as if I were her uncle. It was pretty difficult for Jeanette to adjust to such a big move and manage a job and a child on her own. She depended on me to give her a lot of assistance. I was happy to help her, but it was tough for Sigrid because we had to live almost in a triangle. Jeanette was constantly looking for advice and favors. My marriage was not damaged by this because Sigrid was very secure about our relationship. But still it was not easy for her having to share what little free time I had with my ex-wife. Our marriage was strained, but Sigrid took things one day at a time, otherwise the situation with Jeanette could have destroyed us.

My wife and I never argued over this, but I knew it was hard for her to accept Jeanette's constant presence in our lives. Once Sigrid asked me how long I was going to look after Jeanette, and the only answer I could give her was that I did not know. Jeanette did not seem to feel guilty about expecting me to do so much for her, and I sometimes wondered if she even cared what my wife thought. I was always happy when Jeanette found a romantic interest, because I could back away and put some time into my own marriage.

I am certain that Sigrid was brought to tears many times by the stresses placed on our marriage, but she never shouted at me or demanded that I ignore Jeanette. She knew I could not have done that. Before we came to America, Carola made me promise to take care of her daughter for as long as possible. She pleaded that Jeanette did not know anyone here and would have no one to rely on without me. Carola had cried because we were leaving; I could not go away without giving her my word that I would look after her daughter.

Jeanette worked with us in Ringling's Red Show. Both she and Sigrid rode the High School horses, handled the "Liberty" horses, and worked in all the production numbers that included horses. Working with Jeanette was not easy for Sigrid, either. She really deserved a break from the intensity of Jeanette's presence, but she could not even escape it at work.

Some people might think me a fool for risking my marriage to fulfill a promise to an old woman. After all, Carola was a continent away. Those same people might say I was a miserable bastard, unfair and unfeeling, for having Sigrid work with my ex-wife, and then subjecting her to Jeanette's personal woes. But Sigrid knew that I had been asked to look after Jeanette, and she also knew that once I gave my word, I would not go back on it.

If I have been anything in my life, I have been true to my word, responsible, and reliable. I am very proud of that. A man or woman does not earn a good reputation if he or she is deceitful and dishonorable. I may have done things that stretched certain rules or moral boundaries, but no one ever said of me, "Don't trust him. He's a liar," or, "You can't count on him."

I have always felt an obligation to people who were good to me and who helped me survive. I could not suddenly change the way I had conducted myself since I was a boy and lie to Carola. Nor could I go back on my word when what she asked was so small compared with what she had given me during my lifetime.

I believe that even if my marriage had reached a critical point because of Jeanette's demands, I would not have asked Carola to release me from my promise. I owed her too much. I think Jeanette knew this and took advantage of my devotion to her mother.

If Sigrid had been a different kind of woman, I probably would have ended up divorced a second time. But she knew how to protect her interests because she knew me. She was keenly aware that I had no patience for distractions. To me Jeanette's never-ending problems fit into that category. Sigrid knew that the best thing she could do was to tolerate Jeanette's interruptions in silence, trusting that sooner or later they would pass. She also understood why I volunteered her to work in the circus. It was a question of economics—with her working we could count on two paychecks each week. I was in a different position than I had been in the past and had to think of financial security.

My ability to focus 100 percent of my thoughts and energies on my work makes me sometimes appear callous and insensitive, but I am neither. People who think me cold do not understand the demanding nature of my work and that anything short of my full attention can be detrimental to me and the animals. I have learned to distance and even divorce myself from my emotions, and that has probably saved my life on more than one occasion. No one who is emotionally distraught can go into a cage filled with tigers or leopards and expect everything to go smoothly. I have also learned to distance myself from other people's emotions and things that are beyond my control. It is a sad waste of time to get bogged down in things we cannot change. How could I go into a cage filled with tigers and come out in one piece if I was worried about whether or not Jeanette was going to show up at my house that night, or if Sigrid was going to be upset over something that had happened to her during the day?

I had to be able to tune people out. That did not mean that I did not care about them or was insensitive to their problems. When I turned a deaf ear to someone, whether it was Sigrid or one of my workers, I felt bad about it deep inside and went back later to find out what was bothering the person. I did not want to ignore other people, but there were times when I simply had to.

I felt sorry for Sigrid, but if I was going to be able to work safely and at peak capacity every day, I could not openly worry about how she felt about anything. I am certain that she privately spilled more than a few tears during those days, and I am sorry that I could not be there to dry them. I have tried to make up for that by being a good provider and, now that I am no longer performing, spending more time with her and being more attentive to her needs.

I have never done anything deliberately to hurt anyone. Since I was a little boy, I have had deep feelings for other people, even though I am not very trusting of people in general, and I have always been remorseful if I did something that hurt someone. Once, during the war, some of the other boys and I built our own bunker behind the building in which I lived. We dug big holes, then put wood and sand on top of them. It may not have been good enough to withstand a bomb, but we built it anyway. While we were digging and moving away the sand, I accidentally threw some of it into one of my friend's eyes. He cried out with pain and furiously rubbed his eyes and face. I was so upset by what I had done that I would not go away until this boy threw sand into my eyes and I felt the same pain that he had. I am very concerned when something happens to somebody and it is my fault. This has always stayed in my mind, and I tried to teach my children not to do anything to anybody that they would not want done to themselves.

I am a sensitive man, and I believe my sensitivity served me well in dealing with the animals. It helped me to understand creatures who could not communicate with me through words. I had to be perceptive and sensitive enough to understand what they were telling me by their actions or inactivity, and this enabled me to step inside their skins and really feel what my animals felt. That was the secret of my success. I reached deep inside, touched their spirits, and tried to become one of them. I could feel them doing the same to me. Nothing else was needed once we understood each other's essence.

Because I am so sensitive, it is easy for people to hurt my feelings or make me feel guilty. I am slow to anger under normal conditions, but easy to annoy. I do not hold a grudge. Once I speak my piece, the matter is closed, and I am ready to make a fresh start. However, I have never kept anyone in my employ whose deliberate actions caused an animal to be hurt. If someone does something stupid or careless involving the animals, then I become explosive. I have no patience for stupidity and cannot bear the thought of an animal being hurt because of it.

My lack of patience in general hampered me as a teacher—especially with Sigrid. She acted childish sometimes, and that annoyed me greatly. She was scared whenever I tried to get her to do anything new or different with the horses. Even though I was there to protect her, she was still frightened, and that drove me to distraction. I would become so frustrated with her that I would throw my arms in the air and rant and rave until I was red in the face. Once I physically pushed her during a show because I was displeased by what she was doing, and she fell on her butt. It was very embarrassing for both of us. I sometimes let the excitable part of my personality get the best of me, and I should not have allowed that to happen. It really could have messed up everything forever between me and Sigrid.

Fortunately for both of us it did not take long for Sigrid to learn to work with the horses. All of our friends and co-workers saw how hard I was on Sigrid, but nobody dared say anything to me about it.

Sigrid was, and is, the most agreeable woman I have ever met. She never complained, never argued, and I always apologized when I mistreated her. I felt even more guilty about my actions because Sigrid never said anything about them. She could have told me to drop dead, but she never displayed any hostility toward me. We rarely fought, and I believe that is what held our marriage together. Our children never saw or heard us fight because Sigrid never answered back. I also let her do whatever she wanted to do. If I did not like something, I changed it, but Sigrid was always able to make her own decisions and follow through.

Several months after we arrived in America, Jeanette met and married an aerialist employed by Ringling, and she and her husband continued to work with us in the Red Show for one season, which is two years. He was exceedingly competitive with me, and during the season he told Mr. Feld that he would quit if I was not fired. Mr. Feld was a very perceptive man. Instead of firing him, he sent Jeanette and her husband to work in the Blue Show, while Sigrid and

UNTAMED

I stayed with the Red Show. When this happened, we were finally relieved of some of the pressure that had been put on us by my ex-wife.

With Jeanette involved in her new life, I was able to pay more attention to my own family, and I focused on my role as a father, giving Mark as much of my free time as I could. I was strict with Mark in a different way than I had been with Tina. I always offered explanations. He was accustomed to hearing "You do this because . . ." or "You never do that because . . ." or "Don't you ever do that again, and here is the reason why. . . ."

Mark displayed such an affinity for the animals that I felt obliged to help him learn to handle and train them. Molding someone to be an animal trainer is different from teaching a person acrobatics or to present an act that has already been trained. It requires a different disposition, a different attitude. Mark was always very enthusiastic about everything dealing with the animals and not at all squeamish about anything. He would sit for hours just watching me, and after practice he would ask questions and we would discuss the things he had seen that day. He had to learn that our first priority was always to make sure that nobody got hurt—not animals or people—and for that reason one could never be too careful. I had more patience teaching him than I had with Sigrid and Tina.

While Mark was learning to be a good trainer, he was also learning the art of surviving in an unforgiving business. There is practically no margin for error in animal training, and if one does make mistakes, they follow him throughout his career. Audiences can be unforgiving because they remember the mistakes more than the overall act, and this can ruin a performer's ability to attract ticket buyers.

Mark handles the elephants and horses with great ease and precision, and that is because I trained him to know how to give an animal berth so that he can see it move. As long as a trainer can watch his animals while they work, he will increase their safety and be able to head off many problems. Some animals can easily sit up, while others have poor balance and find it difficult to sit on their haunches. Mark knows never to ask any creature to do something outside of its natural abilities. When a trainer approaches his work with that attitude, he and his charges will work well together. He also respects those with whom he works.

Respect is a critical factor in our business. For me it started with the way workers addressed me. I was taught that showing respect for an elder or someone in a position of authority started with my addressing that person by his or her last name. I therefore never allowed people who worked with me to call me by my first name, regardless of how long we had been associated. I told them if they did not want to call me Mr. Williams, the only other options were to call me "Boss" or "sir."

I never said this immediately. I waited to see if the person was going to stay, or until the first time he called me Gunther. Then I would say, "You do not call me Gunther. I respect people and I want respect from them." If someone had trouble with that, they did not have a job with me. Most of my working men opted to call me "Boss." I tried to set a good example for them. When others were around, I never called Kenneth Feld, the owner of the Ringling circus, by his first name, although I am older than he is. I demanded that same kind of respect from my workers.

I always expected people to be on time for work, but I never put anybody down for being late if they had a good reason. Very often young fellows got to work late, but I did not chew them out if they were apologetic and had a rational explanation. If they strolled in late without a good reason, they heard it from me. Often the young people would get tears in their eyes when I was angry with them. I had to be careful about how and where I approached them so as not to embarrass them by making them cry.

Unpleasant incidents with my working men were rare, and that made life easier for all of us. I did not like to work in a strained and tense atmosphere. It wasn't that way inside the tigers' cage and I didn't want it to be that way outside. I hoped that everyone would enjoy their work because people are more productive and certainly happier when they like what they are doing for most of their waking hours. After so many years I had learned how to evoke the right attitude from just about everybody, and we all worked pretty well together. I have tried to impress this upon my son.

I changed the lives of many of the people with whom I worked. They often joined the circus with the idea that it was easy work for lazy men. If they were around long enough, they quickly learned that the circus involves hard work and long hours and that there was no place in our ranks for anyone who did not carry his own load. I tried to instill in the young people the importance of a work ethic and the idea that real life comes with certain responsibilities and realities. One of those realities is that you only become somebody when you have a job and you make it your first priority. You cannot have a girlfriend or a family unless you have a job. Over and over I told young people, "First the work and the money, then everything else."

Through the years I put up with a lot of silliness and strange quirks from the people who worked for me. I think that if any of them was asked what it was about me that confounded them the most, he or she would say that it was the way I constantly changed my mind. As I said earlier, I was always trying to find better ways of doing things, and as soon as I did, I would tell my men to disregard my previous instructions.

I was not very demanding unless I was really upset and I had to yell at somebody. Otherwise I just looked for the right solutions. I tried to be a perfectionist in everything I did, but many things for the animals could not be perfect because they are affected by so many different conditions. If we were going to do the best possible things for them, we had to be flexible and open to many situations. Piccolo complained for almost thirty years about the way I change my mind, but he still did whatever I asked of him.

When it came to my work, I always had to be on the mark in my timing. Timing was important in presenting the animals and in accomplishing my daily tasks efficiently. Who cared if I arrived at Tampa (where we kept our animals in alternate years when the Blue Show was rehearsing in Venice) at 9:00 A.M. or 10:00 A.M.? Who cared? I cared. I wanted to be there at the same time every day so that my workers could count on me. I never liked to be kept waiting, and I tried never to keep anybody waiting for me.

It was important for me to strive for perfection in my work because I knew it could mean my life. An animal trainer has to do the right thing every time and take the right steps every day. The tigers have to be worked with such precision that there is no chance of them doing something unplanned. It is tough to achieve that kind of perfection in a business where no two days are alike—where each day is influenced by everything from weather to a tiger's ingrown toenail.

Total concentration and the message that I was in control enabled me to work with the tigers on their level. They respect authority when it exceeds their own. The animal kingdom operates on the principle of survival of the fittest. As long as I was able to muster that intense concentration and authority, I was not a man when I entered their cage but a tiger—the tiger that was in control.

Not only did I have to be in charge of numerous wild

animals and some thirty workers every day, I had to over-see travel, work, and rehearsal schedules and do all of my other duties. When a person must exercise that kind of control for sixteen to eighteen hours a day and sometimes more, it is difficult to disconnect that part of the personality when he or she finally gets home. It is no wonder that I developed high blood pressure. I do not smoke, and I have not gained a single pound in the last thirty years—my waistline is still thirty inches—but in that time the stress in my life has been constant.

I have been accused of being somewhat dictatorial with my family, but it is difficult to be a member of the gang when you are accustomed to being in charge. Just as I command respect from my animals, I command a certain amount of it at home, but I try always to give respect in return.

I cherish my wife and children and truly appreciate them. When I was a young boy, always alone, my heart ached to have a family it could embrace. The only sense of togetherness I got was from the circus. The circus helped fill a terrible gap in my life, and I could never give it up.

My family is my Achilles heel. There is nothing I would not give them, nothing I would not do for them, and their security is always foremost in my mind. I know that I am overly protective of them. When my children are not at home and no neighbors or friends are there, it is very unsettling for me. I am always looking for everybody, and if Sigrid is home, I repeatedly ask her where the children are and when they will return. I do this even though they are old enough to be out on their own and make their own living.

I am frightened that one day Sigrid and I will be alone. I hope I have not been too tough on her and that she is not hurt by my need to have a lot of people around me. I have to keep going back to the circus to have that family around me and that sense of togetherness. It is very important to me.

Some of the things that have meant the most to me in my life have been intangible. I could never show anyone what it meant to be taken into a stranger's family and made to feel that I belonged, or how it felt to have friends who made sure I had a full belly and a place to rest my head wherever I traveled. Those things have no actual material value, yet they are priceless to me. That is how I feel about being an American.

When Trolle Rhodin asked me to come to America, I was almost afraid to believe the offer was real. Apart from all the other considerations that colored my thinking, I found it hard to believe that something I had dreamed about for so long was being handed to me. It was thrilled to have achieved such status as a performer that Ringling Brothers and Barnum & Bailey Circus wanted me. The highlight of many circus performers' lives is working for Ringling. Wherever a circus performer goes for a job, the first thing he or she is asked is if they have ever worked for Ringling.

Before they set their sights on Circus Williams, I do not believe the owners of the Ringling circus or any other circus in the world had ever hired an entire company for anything. They had hired individual acts, as all the circuses did historically, but it was virtually unheard of for a circus to hire another complete circus. We were hired directly for a new opening show. When we got to America, we only had to hire a couple of performers and the show was open.

Knowing that I was bound by a contract that told me exactly what I was going to be doing for five years was scary in one respect and reassuring in another. It was frightening to think that whether I liked working for Ringling or not, I had that job for five years, but at least the contract offered security for that length of time. After one season with Ringling I decided that I liked it here and knew that I never wanted to live in Germany again. During our first year in the United States Carola came to visit us, and when we told her how happy we were, she signed another five-year contract with Ringling.

As soon as Sigrid and I knew that we were going to be working in America for at least the length of our contracts, we took the money we had saved and bought a couple of lots in Venice, Florida, not far from the Ringling circus's winter quarters. We built a house on that land in an attempt to settle down a bit, even if that only meant a place to keep our personal belongings, and I wanted to establish roots in America.

When we first arrived, in order to work in this country, all of the Circus Williams people had to have work visas. After being in the United States for five years, we were allowed to apply for green cards, working permits issued to foreigners by the Immigration and Naturalization Service. I was proud to carry my green card because it made me feel like an American citizen, even if I did not have the right to vote. In my heart I knew that it was not the real thing, but at that time a person had to stay in this country without

UNTAMED

leaving for five years before he or she could apply for citizenship.

I had hesitated to apply because I did not know if we were going to have to go back to Germany when our contract with Ringling expired. Once we signed our second five-year contract, I submitted citizenship papers. I wanted to be a complete part of this country and did everything I was supposed to do to prepare for it.

The toughest conditions I had to meet were learning to read and write English and memorizing history and civics in preparation for a written test given by the government. I had to learn all those things in what little time I had after each show. I did not know what kinds of questions would be asked when I was tested, so I figured I had to learn a lot. I would come in from work bleary-eyed and sit over my books trying to decipher the English words until my eyelids closed from exhaustion. Mark tutored me every night and I got a lot of help from Sigrid and some friends at the circus, but I was very impatient.

I was determined to take the citizenship test as soon as possible. I had to take it in the state of Florida because my permanent residence was there. While I was playing in Tampa in 1976 an opportunity arose for me to go to the local immigration office to sign up for the test, so I did it. On the appointed day, I was in New York, but I had a day off, so I flew to Florida. After all that I failed the test. This had to be one of the biggest letdowns of my life. I flunked because my writing was so bad.

Not only was I disappointed, because I was looking forward to becoming a citizen, but I did not know when I would have the time to take the test again or how on earth I would find enough hours in each day to study harder than I had and practice my writing. I remained undaunted, however, and forged ahead, determined that I was going to become a citizen in 1976 during America's bicentennial celebration. The last chance to take the test that year came while we were appearing in Philadelphia. The test was being given in Miami, so I headed for southern climes with my application papers in hand.

This time I got lucky. One of the men at the Miami immigration office was a fan of mine, and he treated me very nicely. He looked over my papers and said, "Gunther, I see there is a concern here over your writing. What can you write?" He pushed a piece of paper and pencil in my direction so that I could show him what I could do. In my eagerness I wrote any words I could think of—*red, blue, green, cat,* any word I knew. The man looked at my scrawl with a mixture of amusement and curiosity and said, "Okay, but this makes no sense. Can you write anything that makes sense?" I was scared to death that I would mess up a second time and have to go through the entire procedure all over again. I took a deep breath, tightened my grip on the pencil, and wrote, "I am an animal trainer in a circus." He looked at it, smiled, and said, "Okay, you're an American."

This was a really happy time for me. I was sworn in during the winter of 1976 at a ceremony in Florida. My sister, her husband, and their daughter had planned to visit us long before I knew when I was going to become a citizen, and it just happened that their trip coincided with my swearing-in. They attended the ceremony, as did Sigrid's mother and aunt, who visited us every winter. It was a proud moment for me. I felt so good, but while I was sitting in the hall waiting to take the oath of citizenship, I thought that it was too bad that I could not have shown my love for this country by doing something for it when it was in trouble. I would have been proud to fight, even lay down my life for America.

Soon after I became a citizen, I received this letter:

UNTAMED

Dear Fellow American:

I congratulate you on becoming a citizen of our great nation.

Of very special importance is the fact that while many of us are citizens by birth, you have by choice selected America as your new land. The citizenship you have acquired today brings you even greater guarantees of freedom, human dignity, security, equality and opportunity than those offered in the past. Your new citizenship gives you the right and also the responsibility to take part in the business of our government. I know you will hold strongly to these new rights and responsibilities and exercise them at every opportunity.

America has been blessed with almost boundless natural resources and wealth. Yet, its greatest asset continues to be its people. Our founding fathers had great faith in the worth of the individual. They believed that people from everywhere who loved freedom and justice should be entitled to enjoy these rich blessings. Thus they provided in the Constitution for the naturalization of such persons.

Naturalized citizens from all lands have made significant contributions to the betterment of our nation. I am sure that you will follow in this tradition and firmly resolve to do your part in making America an even more wonderful place in which to live.

Sincerely,

Jimmy Carter

Since the day I became a citizen, I have lived with the idea that through my work I have been giving something back to this wonderful country. I do the best I can and have tried to make America as proud to have me as I am to have it as my home.

Mark was actually the first member of our family to become an American when he was born here. Tina became a citizen in 1981. Sigrid was the last member of our family to give up her German citizenship. We held off on her naturalization because her parents owned a business in Germany and we did not know what complications might evolve when they died. In 1984, after both of her parents had passed away and the family business was dissolved, Sigrid became an American too. By then, we had already been here sixteen years.

When we first came to America, I was taken by how much easier it was to live here, because it was the biggest place I had ever seen. It was not crowded, and everything was spread out. Everyone was nice to me, and people helped me whenever possible. I cannot remember having any concerns about living here in those early years. My concerns started later on with the heat. I never felt anything so hot in my life as when we were in Texas and Arizona. I was always concerned about caring for the animals in that kind of weather. They handle cold much better than heat. Temperature is a big concern in a country where there are so many different climates. It was always difficult to keep conditions warm enough or cool enough so that none of the animals would die.

I had my share of problems with American police, usually because they did not understand how the animals had to be handled when they were being brought from the train yards to wherever we were performing, or because I was speeding or gave someone lip. I was never arrested, but I came damn close to it in Indianapolis. A police officer went so far as to handcuff me and make me sit in the back of his patrol car.

UNTAMED

It all started when we were on an animal walk from our venue to the trains. One police car had been assigned to move through the streets with us, and the officer in that car wanted us to stop the walk and wait for another police car because he did not think we had enough police protection. I said we would stop the walk if he could tell me how long we would have to wait. When I am moving so many animals through the streets, everything is business. I do not have the mind or patience to worry about the tone of my voice. The officer took exception to the way I spoke to him and told me, "As long as I want." He got gruff with me, and I treated him the same way. It escalated until he handcuffed me and made me sit in the car. I had to stay in his car until a lieutenant arrived, who then apologized for what had been done to me.

What the police had failed to realize was that they could not leave me standing in the streets for an extended period of time with twenty elephants and thirty horses. This happened to me several times in different places. Those police officers would have been singing a different tune if they had had to worry about controlling a bunch of wild elephants or hysterical horses.

Trouble with the police may have followed me from Europe to America, but that did not bother me. I was used to it. I cared more about what people in general thought of me, and I never had trouble making friends—that is, when I had the time to spend with people.

The only time I really had to work on friendships outside the circus was during our winter breaks in Florida. The first year we had our home in Venice, I was on the beach thinking about how I was going to manage the house while I was on the road. I had been wishing I had a good neighbor or friend upon whom I could rely to help me when I was away, but I did not know anyone in the community. As if in answer to my prayers, I met Arthur Eve on the beach that day. Arthur had been stationed in Germany for many years, and we found a great deal to talk about. It was an easy and immediate friendship. Arthur turned out to be one of those rare friends who will do anything for you and never ask anything in return. The better I got to know him over the years, the more I realized that he is one of the most wonderful people I have ever met.

I told Arthur about my concerns, and he offered to look after our home most of the year while we were on tour. I came to care about him and depend on him so much that I often said, "Arthur, if you ever find yourself at death's door, call me and I will pull you back again." Arthur is my best friend.

Another colonel came into my life some years later, a face from out of my and Harry Williams's past. We were appearing in Tulsa when Leslie C. Wood, a lieutenant colonel retired from the U.S. Army Cavalry, came to our dressing room and introduced himself. I remembered him from almost forty years before, when he was stationed in Germany and in charge of postwar entertainment for the American soldiers. He was Harry's friend, and they sometimes socialized when Circus Williams was in Cologne. When he came to see me at the Ringling circus, Lieutenant Colonel Wood gave me a cavalry mouthpiece for one of my horses and three small pieces of brass that are more precious to me than gold: the crossed swords of the 29th Cavalry, an officer's star, and the initials "U.S." Inscribed on the card that accompanied these gifts was this message:

To Gunther, who, if circumstances and timing had been different, would probably have been a general in the U.S. Horse Cavalry!—Woody

After Lieutenant Colonel Wood and I became reacquainted, we saw each other every year when the Ringling circus went to Tulsa. I have such great memories of great people! The friends I had before I became famous remained my friends afterward. I did nothing to change my personality after coming to America. But my looks were something else.

In the 1960s, in Germany, I had let my hair grow a little longer than I had worn it in the early part of my career, and I had long sideburns. Before my first American performance in January 1969, I let my hair grow longer so that at one point it grazed my shoulders. I wanted a different look. My blond hair became my trademark, and I was actually known as "the blond animal trainer."

Once I started working for Ringling, I went from long muttonchop sideburns, a short beard, and the traditional circus costumes and uniforms of Europe to modern hairstyles and fancy, abbreviated costumes. Sigrid started changing my look by playing around with my hair, but Irvin Feld completed the task by altering the rest of my appearance. Since I was a hot new property in America, he was splashing my name all over billboards from New York to San Francisco, creating a lot of excitement about the "blond animal trainer." Irvin wanted me to have a tremendous visual impact on people even before they saw me step into a cage or command three rings of elephants, so he put me into tights and short sleeves and created an entirely new image for me. I was not built badly, so I could wear the costumes he ordered. After twenty-three years with Ringling, I was still walking around in tights and short jackets, and I still had my hair.

Although I am only five feet four inches tall, I look much taller when I perform. I attribute that to my costumes. The new look did not change the way I felt about myself as a performer, but it helped me to be physically more comfortable. When I had worked in Europe during the summer months, I would feel like I was going to die in my heavy button-down costumes and closed uniforms with jackets. When Irvin changed the way I dressed, it was a relief to have lighter costumes.

I was open to all of these changes. I have always been a person to say yes first. I never rejected a good idea before trying it out. If something had to be done that was better for the show, better for the animals, I was absolutely agreeable.

Apart from making some cosmetic changes, the only real adjustment I had to make to perform for Ringling was to spread out all of the acts, because the Ringling circus was bigger than Circus Williams. I was able to do this because I was confident and comfortable with myself. As a person grows older, he or she becomes a much freer performer, and the freer you are, the better you perform and the more able you are to adapt to different situations. When a performer loosens up like that, he or she can make something difficult appear to be easy. That is the secret of a good performer.

I changed the elephant act for Ringling because I had to integrate five new elephants into it. The tiger act was ready before we came here, but it was really something new and different for me because I had only performed it a couple of days before we left Cologne. I had eight tigers in that act when I started presenting it here in January 1969. I had purchased them in Germany to build up the cat act I had created for Circus Williams. By the time I got to America, my old friend Charley Baumann had already been working for Ringling for years with twelve tigers and he had introduced the gentler European style of training I mentioned earlier. In that respect he had been priming circus fans for some of what they were going to get from the blond man who called himself an "animal trainer, not an animal tamer."

Americans were used to seeing people like Clyde Beatty and Frank Buck work with wild animals. Beatty was the best-known animal trainer of his time, and he worked with many lions and tigers in the cage and risked his life so many times just to be different from everybody else. I respected his work because I knew how dangerous and difficult it was, but I never tried to be like him. I never wanted to have the feeling that every time I took my butt into a cage, I was in danger. I had the same kinds of animals as he did, but I worked differently with them.

I think Americans were ready for this change, because my reception here was good. The circus had put out a lot of advance publicity on me, but even though fans were receptive, it was not easy for me to perform here the first couple of weeks. I was a newcomer, and the environment was new, so I was not relaxed and did not feel free. Audiences in Germany and other parts of Europe knew me. We were like old friends, and I was comfortable when I worked before them. In America I had to make a conscious effort to relax, something I had not done since I was a child working under Harry's direction. As I became more familiar with this country and my surroundings at the Ringling circus, I gradually became more relaxed.

Many of the performers who came over to Ringling from Circus Williams left after a few years because they found it trying to have to create different acts for each season. Because I had been doing that in my own individual acts—a first in Ringling's history—when Mr. Feld saw how successful it was, he wanted it done by everybody. Before I came to the Ringling circus, everybody had an act that was hired for one or two years, then the act moved on to a different circus or carnival and another took its place. Many of the other Circus Williams performers did not want to go through so much trouble. They knew they could have the same act in Europe for twenty years and just travel around with it. I also introduced backup training to Ringling—training more than one animal for a particular job, thereby ensuring the life of the act in the event an animal became ill or died.

The circus had created so much excitement about me that there were requests for interviews from the press and television people everywhere I went. I did not give many interviews when I first came to America because my English was so poor and I had difficulty understanding reporters' questions. I was somewhat flustered when we came to New York City and I was told by the circus's publicity people that I was booked on the Johnny Carson show. I may have been here only a short time, but I knew who Johnny Carson was and how important an appearance on his show could be for a performer. I believe I was the first circus performer to actually sit on Carson's panel, not just to juggle for a couple of minutes, say "Hi" and "Good-bye," and then be whisked off the set.

I became less concerned about trying to speak to Johnny Carson in front of millions of Americans once I found out what they wanted me to do for his show. I was asked to bring a tiger from my act onto Carson's set. I was worried about that because no one can ever predict what will happen with a wild animal. My tigers were not trained for something like that. There is no such thing as a stage-trained tiger. I wanted to oblige everyone, so I agreed to take a tiger with me, despite my great reservations about it. I chose the one I had known the longest and trusted the most—Bengal.

At that time Carson's show was broadcast from New York City. With the help of some of my working men from the circus, we loaded the caged Bengal into a truck and brought him from Madison Square Garden, where the circus was appearing, to the television studio further uptown.

Everything went smoothly until we arrived at the building in which the studio was located and the elevator operator refused to get into the elevator car with Bengal. All the guy had to do was push a button to take us to the studio level, but he would not do it, even though the tiger was caged.

I was furious and wanted to push the button in the elevator myself, but because of some ridiculous regulations, no one except authorized personnel was allowed to operate it. We had a big argument over who was going to push the button. There I was, becoming angrier by the minute, trying to communicate in a desperate mixture of German and bad English with people who did not understand what it was like to be standing around with a five hundred-pound tiger who was not having a good time. Someone finally found a supervisor who was not afraid to ride the elevator with me and my friend, and he pushed the button.

Once I got Bengal safely into the studio, the rest should have been a piece of cake, but it was more like a pie in the face. Carson and I talked on the air, but it was difficult for me to understand him. He asked me many things, and because my English was so bad, I gave him answers that had nothing to do with the questions. Each time I answered incorrectly, Carson would say, "No, no," and everyone in the audience laughed. My own sense of humor, and Carson's patience and quick wit, got me through that part of the show. When I brought Bengal onto the set, Carson was quite effective. Although everything was staged, he made things that were harmless look frightening. Whenever Bengal opened his mouth, Carson would jump back as if he were in danger. He even pretended to give the tiger commands. Despite the glitches, it was a successful beginning for me, and great publicity for the circus.

Throughout my career I made five appearances on the Carson show, each time with a different animal. I introduced Carson to leopards, elephants, horses, and tigers. Once I brought along two adorable small tigers, and for another appearance I brought a large African elephant onto the stage and Carson sat on him. Of course over the years my English improved enough for me to understand and answer questions, but I think the most fun Carson had with me was when I did not understand a word he was saying.

Publicity swirled around me even before I came to America. Because of my reputation with Circus Williams I was a hero figure for many people, young and old. The same thing happened here over the years. I am pleased that people think of me that way, but all I am doing is a job.

I suppose John Wayne was my greatest hero. I thought he was the bravest and most dynamic man who ever lived. In my younger years every movie star who presented a strong and courageous image was a hero to me. I have had the chance to come close to many of them and find out what they are like in real life, and I admire them still.

But as I grew older, the people I accepted as heroes changed slightly, from movie stars to men and women who devote their lives to saving others or making the world a better place to live. Audie Murphy was one of the greatest World War II heroes in America, and I greatly admire what he did for this country and that he saved so many lives. He won a Congressional Medal of Honor and other decorations for bravery under fire in Europe and saving the lives of many of the soldiers in his platoon. I admire people like that. Dr. Denton Cooley, a pioneering heart surgeon, is also one of my heroes. A newspaper once quoted me as saying that, and Dr. Cooley found out about it. In 1984 he invited me to visit him at the Texas Heart Institute in Houston, and I watched a couple of heart operations. This was one of the most exciting events of my life.

I have had quite a number of experiences with celebrities, either because we attended the same parties or because they attended a circus performance and came backstage to see me afterward. I met Bob Hope, Barbra Streisand, Larry Hagman, Patrick Duffy, Robert Wagner, and Natalie Wood—so many celebrities that it is hard to recall all the names. Everybody has been so nice to me, and we have a mutual respect for each other as performers.

Robert Wagner and Natalie Wood actually offered us the key to their home in California so that we could use it whenever we were there. Actors and actresses understand what it is like to live on the road for most of the year, and I thought that was such a kind and insightful gesture. We had so many invitations like that, but we hate to bother anybody.

One of the few entertainers with whom we have developed a relationship is Barbara Mandrell. She is one of the small group of really close friends our family has. We met Barbara when she came to see the circus. She later hosted Ringling's Blue Show, then our show. Our family was invited to her home the next time we played in Nashville, and Barbara got up early in the morning and cooked for us. She has an incredibly full schedule, too, and I was really touched by her efforts on our behalf.

I met Princess Grace at Madison Square Garden during the circus intermission, and later on we had dinner together and I met Prince Rainier. I also got to meet Elvis Presley. His agent, Colonel Tom Parker, invited us to see Elvis's show in Vegas, and before the show he brought us into Elvis's dressing room. Elvis signed a picture for me and later announced that I was in the audience. Someone had a recorder that night and he taped Elvis and gave me the cassette. That is one of my treasures.

I never got to meet John Wayne, but I almost made a movie with him. He made only one circus movie, *Circus*

World, which was filmed in Spain in 1964. People from Hollywood showed up in Germany looking to hire a circus that would go to Spain and work on the movie until it was completed. They approached Circus Williams in the middle of the year, when our season was in full swing, and we could not fire all of our contract performers so that we could make a movie. Franz Althoff ended up working on the film.

Even though I did not get to work in a movie with John Wayne, I did appear in two European films. In 1958 I starred in a German movie called *Rivals of the Ring.* It was a long circus film, and I had quite a number of lines and appeared in many scenes. The other was an Italian film, in which I did not have a speaking part and only doubled as an animal trainer. I appeared in one tiger-fight scene. They were fun to do and, more than offering a bit of diversion for me, they reflected the popularity and reputation I was enjoying in Europe.

I appeared in quite a number of newspaper and magazine ads for various companies, including Esso, while I was working in Germany. I also appeared on a number of television commercials once the home box became popular among advertisers. When I came to the United States, I continued to get print and television work.

I did a few commercials for illustrated books and some other things, but the biggest commercial contract I ever had was for the American Express card. The first commercials I made for American Express were filmed in Knoxville, where the Ringling circus was appearing. The idea the producers had for one of the spots was that I was traveling with a suitcase and a tiger. It would have been nice if someone had let me in on this, but no one told me that I was supposed to appear with a tiger, so I did not rehearse an animal for the commercial. I never liked to do anything that was not planned, because that is how accidents can happen, but the job had to get done, so I agreed to bring a tiger onto the set.

We did that commercial in the morning, and I was relieved that everything went smoothly and that the filming had gone so quickly. That afternoon we filmed another commercial featuring me and my favorite leopard, Kenny, the one whom I regularly draped over my shoulders.

After my doing so many performances with Kenny, he was accustomed to working with me, and I felt comfortable about working with him. I thought that doing a commercial in which I had to carry Kenny on my shoulders was going to be a snap, but I was wrong. That leopard gave me so many problems that day that I was beside myself. He was like a totally different animal. He was cantankerous and stubborn, and much meaner than he normally was around me.

Nothing about that commercial was easy. I had a long speech and I had to look like a businessman in a suit, button-down shirt, and tie. At one point in the commercial I was supposed to hoist Kenny onto my shoulders, hold an American Express card in one hand, and say, "It's easier to carry this [the card], than this [the leopard]." The camera was supposed to pan from the card to the leopard as I said my line. Animals are very much like people, and when they are doing something that does not interest them, they become bored and want to extricate themselves from the situation. The commercial was so long that by the time I got to that line, Kenny was bored and tried to jump down from my shoulders. We had to do it over and over and over again, and the more we repeated ourselves, the more ornery Kenny became.

Kenny weighed about seventy-five pounds, but by the time we were midway through that commercial session, he felt more like one hundred pounds of dead weight. I was sweating so much in that suit that my underwear was actually sticking to my skin. I was concerned about Kenny because I had worked with him long enough to recognize a problem in the making. I knew he was going to do something, I just didn't know what or when. I knew when he bit my hand.

I had been trying to get him to stay on my shoulders, and he didn't want any part of it, so he delivered that message in very graphic terms. I had to put Kenny in his cage, leave the set immediately, and go to a hospital so that I would not get an infection. After I was treated, I returned to the set to finish the taping.

I actually looked surprisingly good in that commercial. No one watching it on television would know how profusely I had been sweating or that I had been hurt and had holes in my hand from where the leopard had bitten me. It could have been worse, and I certainly had been hurt more seriously in the past. Sigrid was very concerned about what had happened, but I brushed it off. I always told her, "You will know I am badly hurt when you see me carrying my head under my arm."

The problem with Kenny illustrated something that was prevalent on every commercial and film set on which I had worked. People have no idea what it takes to handle a wild animal. Animals that appear in movies are often specially trained to do many things, including letting someone pet them for more than a few moments. Our animals are only trained to perform in the show. They do not like to be handled for long periods of time or moved around from one place to another like a sack of potatoes. They are also unpredictable and cannot be made to do special things for the camera on cue unless they have practiced over and over again. Even then there is no guarantee that they will do what someone wants them to do.

UNTAMED

The commercial with Kenny was shown for the first time during a Super Bowl game, and I got a great deal of exposure from it. Despite the problems I had experienced with the leopard, that commercial was a good thing to do. America was good, Ringling was good, my whole life was good.

At Ringling Brothers and Barnum & Bailey circus winter quarters in Venice, Florida, I taught a tiger named Lucky to stand on its hind legs, then jump into the air to retrieve a treat of meat held at the end of a stick. Some tigers have great balance, and others have all they can do to sit up.
Courtesy TOPIX/Jack Briggs

Tetchie got a chance to show off at the Ringling winter quarters in 1970. That's me, resting on her elbow.

I made animal training history when I built an act around twenty-two leopards and mountain lions. Leopards were the most difficult animals I ever trained.

Training leopards was one of the greatest challenges of my life. Here a panther received a reward for sitting on a ball. This was a major achievement for him.
Courtesy Sam Siegel/Metropolitan Photo Service, Inc.

Here I am giving verbal instructions to tigers Madras, Siros, King, and India. Verbal commands became my principal method of training while I was working in Germany with Circus Williams.

I displayed bareback riding skills during the 1970 opening act for Ringling.

Christmas in 1974 with Tina (partially hidden), Mark, and Sigrid
Courtesy Tamara Chow

Dickie arrived at Ringling as a baby and was raised by me and Sigrid.

A performing family—Mark, Tina, Sigrid, and me in Greensboro, North Carolina, 1978

Getting leopards to jump through a ring of fire was difficult because most cats are afraid of fire. I had to find the right animal for every job, and in this case it meant finding the leopard who was not afraid of flames.
Courtesy P. F. Bentley

Tina does a split while Nellie stands on her hind legs in this 1982 photograph. When Tina decided that she wanted to be a showgirl, the first thing I taught her was acrobatics.

In 1984 Mark performed aboard two elephants while I gave the animals verbal commands from the ground.

Leopards are among the world's most vicious animals, yet I had very warm relationships with some of them, which led to moments like this and shared hugs with Kenny.

I stood beside King Tusk before performing in Austin in 1988. This elephant, who had been trained by someone else, almost killed me earlier in the year in Kansas City.

Courtesy Neil Leifer

A pensive moment around the elephants during my farewell tour in 1989.
Photograph by Eric Luse. Copyright © *San Francisco Chronicle*.
Reprinted by permission.

Gunther Gebel-Williams and Kenny
Courtesy Mario Algaze

CHAPTER
12

Carola became further and further removed from Circus Williams the longer it remained in America. Over the years her circus had become less of an independent entity and more of an integral part of the Ringling Brothers and Barnum & Bailey Circus. Even though she spent several months with us each year, Carola had actually been reduced to a tourist. She was no longer actively running the company and had nothing to say about the work we did. With all of us so far from Cologne, and operating under the auspices of another circus, it was as if Circus Williams did not exist for her anymore. All Carola did was put her signature on the contracts and collect a paycheck. She slowly lost her grip on Circus Williams, and after several seasons she relinquished ownership of it and sold all of its animals and equipment to Ringling.

This was a sad time for her because the circus had been her life. She had given it everything, including her beloved Harry, and it even indirectly claimed the life of one of her sons. But Circus Williams had also given her much in return, including a comfortable, full, and exciting life. Carola had been born into a circus family and had never been involved with any other type of business. She could have grown old at her circus if she had kept us in Germany, but there was no way to turn back time.

I felt sorry for Carola, but at least she was comfortable in her senior years and did not have to rely on anyone for monetary support. There were many people, myself included, who would have seen to Carola's needs for the rest of her life, but she was a proud woman who had survived many hard times through her ingenuity and strength and she did not want to depend on anyone for anything. She placed a high value on her independence, and the deals she made with Ringling guaranteed that she would be financially secure until she died.

Although I was sensitive to the effects these changes had on my stepmother, I could not allow myself to become paralyzed by her emotional upheaval. My number-one priority had to be my own future and my family's security. Once Carola was out of our business picture and the Circus Williams as we had known it no longer existed, I had to deal directly with Irvin Feld—a task that was not at all unpleasant.

I enjoyed living and working in America, and I was very satisfied with Ringling Brothers and Barnum & Bailey Circus. Irvin was easy to work for, and he loved and understood the circus. That was important to me, because it meant he also understood my work and would not question every little thing I did. When the second Circus Williams contract expired, I happily signed my own ten-year contract with him. This was the first time in my life that I was able to put my signature on a contract that would determine my future. Until then someone else had always done it for me, whether I approved or not.

Irvin Feld was a reasonable man who elicited a great

deal of cooperation and trust from his employees, but he was by no means a pushover. He was a tough negotiator who knew what he wanted and how to get it. Yet there was a childlike quality about him that was most endearing. Irvin worked hard, and he enjoyed the fruits of his labor on weekends when he traveled to wherever his circus was performing so that he could watch the acts and visit with his employees.

Irvin was the kind of person whose door was always open to everyone, from the guy who shoveled behind the horses to the stars around whom the circus built its shows. After a performance he would find a comfortable seat in a tent or office, and there he would sit, smoking his cigars and listening to everyone's problems. He did not always come up with a solution, but he listened and was sympathetic, and sometimes that meant more to people than walking away with answers. He was widely loved and admired by all who worked for the circus, and respected by business associates as the man whose word was good as gold.

Obviously I, too, had a great deal of respect for Irvin, and he did everything possible over the years to make me happy. I understood the visions he had for the circus, visions of spectacular, breathtaking shows that would advance Ringling's reputation as the "greatest show on earth"—the same kind of visions I had had for Circus Williams. He wanted acts that people would talk about long after they had left the circus and returned to their workaday worlds. He wanted bigger, newer, and better shows every season so that people would have a reason to see the circus whenever it came to their town.

I believed I could help Irvin realize his dreams for the Ringling circus by creating show-stopping acts that utilized a wide assortment of animals, including leopards, panthers, and mountain lions, as well as unique props. I worked for his company as if it were my own, the same way I had worked for Circus Williams, the only way I knew how. I believe the only way to realize success and maintain it is to treat the company you work for as if you owned it. Then you care more about everything and take a more sincere interest in your work. My attitude made Irvin trust me enough to give me the freedom to function as if I did own the circus. I could do anything that was necessary for the animals and the success of my acts without worrying about costs or other restrictions.

In return for Irvin's support I gave him the most sensational animal acts that had ever been seen. Every season I created new and different acts filled with drama and excitement. I trained every kind of animal, from a slew of leopards to a giraffe named Dickie, and presented all of them myself.

Well before we closed the decade of the 1970s, I was the world's most famous animal trainer. I had a huge following. With each season the printed word told of the new animal acts I had created, and from Japan to Russia to America people shared in the excitement.

In the United States people who had seen me perform during their teenage years were now bringing their children, and I was developing a whole new generation of fans. I felt even more responsibility toward the people who came to the circus with the hope of seeing things they had never dreamed possible. I found myself in something of a quandary because I had to best myself each season.

It did not take long for me to recognize that American circus audiences are not very different from their European counterparts, so one winter, while I was planning the opening number for the next season, I decided to revive the chariot act. I had not performed that act since I was a teenager, when Carola, worried that I would be killed, as Harry had been, threatened to throw me out of the circus if I did not give it up.

We were working at the Bouglione circus in France when I took my last fall from the Roman chariot and Carola canceled the act. She said she would never give me another chariot, and in so doing she would be able to sleep peacefully at night knowing that nothing would happen to me.

I had promised Carola that I would never do the chariot act again for Circus Williams, but I had not promised that I would not do it for Ringling. That may have been stretching things a bit, but that act had never been done in the United States, and I was sure audiences here would love it. Time had dulled my memory of the pain and deceived me into believing that it could be done without incident.

Since I was now more experienced, and no longer a small young boy who could not even maintain his balance in the chariot, I felt more secure about presenting the act. I believed that with a different setting and new equipment I could avoid the problems we had experienced in the past.

The chariot act had never been easy to organize, and I faced a new set of problems when I mounted it for Ringling. In Europe we had presented the act on a surface that looked like a racetrack drawn around a stage. In the United States it had to be presented in one of our three rings, which forced me to eliminate the stage. I was happy to comply, because the chariots had always hit the stage, which caused them to turn over.

There were a lot of guy lines, which are part of the rigging used for aerial acts and lights, coming down around the rings, so the new chariot could not be raised very high. If one of those lines got in the way of a man in a chariot being pulled by racing horses, he could lose his head. This made it difficult to design equipment for the act. I figured on using only one chariot, which I would race into and around the ring as an opening for the show. I decided not to use the traditional Roman chariot, but to design a new, ornate vehicle that was low to the ground and sat on wheels like a normal float. It was visually more appealing, and I believed it would be more stable.

We were already working on the new show when the chariot was delivered to our winter quarters. It had been crafted with the same whimsical feeling as merry-go-round animals, and it had a large tiger's head at the front of it. I was pleased with it and did not think twice about the tiger that the makers had incorporated into its design.

I trained several horses on this chariot without incident, which lulled me into a sense of security and made me certain I would use it in the new show. But before we opened the season, that cursed act blew up again. During practice one day I hooked the horses up to the chariot, and while they were running, they turned around for some reason, saw the tiger's head coming up behind them, and went wild. It was my mistake. The horses are normally crazy and like to run fast, which increased the danger of the chariot act. When they thought an actual tiger was after them, they really took off. Had I realized the tiger's head was going to spook the horses, I would have covered their eyes so that they could only see what was in front of them.

The horses ran over my helper, Piccolo, who was standing near the ring, and Sigrid, who had been watching me practice, had to run out of the way to avoid being hurt. One horse broke away from the chariot and ran into the arena, and workers and performers had to scatter. Piccolo's head was injured, but fortunately no one was badly hurt. I immediately canceled the entire act.

Every time we had done it in Europe, there was trouble, and I could see that history was going to repeat itself here. Like a child who was planning on being disobedient, I had not told Carola that I was going to revive the act, because I knew she would have said, "Do not do it." Afterward I never told her about the incident with the new chariot, because she would have scolded, "I told you to never use that act again." She had been right all along. I had learned my lesson. The new chariot is now on display at Ringling's world headquarters in Vienna, Virginia.

I told Irvin why I had changed my mind about the act, and he did not question my judgment. He knew I did not make offhand decisions and that if I had changed my mind, it was with good cause. He never lamented the money that had been spent and lost on the chariot, or the time that had been invested in trying to revive the act. He just waited to see what else I was going to cook up, and I never let him down.

From the beginning I felt very good about Irvin Feld. In many ways he was quite a different man from Harry Williams, but in terms of his generosity, kindness, and passion for the circus, he ranked right up there with the man I had called my stepfather. Irvin had not been raised in the circus, he just loved it. And he had the kind of business history that made him the perfect circus owner.

Born and raised in Maryland, Irvin moved to Washington, D.C., as a young man and opened a small drugstore. It evolved into a record store, then a chain of four record stores. He became heavily involved with music and performers and went into the personal-management business. He packaged rock 'n' roll shows and discovered and managed Paul Anka for the first ten years of his career. Irvin even owned his own record company, called Super-Disc, which was the first independent label to have a million-seller single.

In the early 1950s Irvin toured the country with rock 'n' roll shows that featured such performers as Bill Haley and the Comets, Chuck Berry, and The Platters. He knew where all the arenas were and had great contacts all over the country. In 1957 Irvin began promoting the Ringling Brothers and Barnum & Bailey Circus. The circus had gone broke the year before and folded the big top forever. The Ringling operation was in serious trouble, and Irvin turned to his rock 'n' roll background to save it. He believed the circus could cut some of its enormous costs and recover completely if it started playing arenas, which generally booked only concerts. Irvin's idea was right on target, and for the next ten years, under his promotional guidance, the circus came back stronger than ever. Then John Ringling North, the majority owner of the circus at that time, left the United States to live in Switzerland, and the show started going downhill. Such a complicated operation could not be run by absentee management.

Irvin felt he had only two choices: stop promoting the circus or buy it. He teamed up with his brother Israel, and after a year they had raised enough money from a partner, Judge Roy Hofheinz, the former mayor of Houston, and the Wells Fargo Bank, to buy the Ringling operation. The deal was consummated on November 11, 1967, and Irvin was given free rein to run the circus as he saw fit.

In 1970 the Felds approached Mattel, the toy manufacturers, with a concept for a Saturday-morning television show, but they inadvertently opened the door for the sale of the circus. Judge Hofheinz, who held about two-thirds of the Ringling stock, had suffered a stroke that year, and his health was in question. This set up conditions under which he could have sold his stock in the circus, and Irvin could have lost the vote of confidence that enabled him to run the show. Mattel pursued the purchase of the circus, and by February 1971 all of the principals agreed to sell.

The Felds had no equity ownership in the circus, but

they had been given Mattel stock and employment contracts to operate it. Just before it was sold to Mattel, Irvin's son, Kenneth, graduated from college, and he spent the next two years traveling with his father to learn the circus business. Irvin communicated his enthusiasm for this highly specialized work to his son, whose own enthusiasm Irvin appreciated and needed, especially after he lost his lifelong partner and brother, Israel, in 1972.

It was business as usual for all of us under Mattel's ownership because of Irvin's presence. Our contracts had not been affected by the sale, so we went about our business as if nothing had changed. At the outset of the 1980s Mattel fell on hard times and moved to sell off some of its assets to raise cash. In 1981, when they looked for buyers for the Ringling circus, the logical choices were Irvin and Kenneth. The Felds put up the bulk of the purchase price, borrowed the balance from Wells Fargo Bank, and closed the deal on March 17, 1982.

Before we came to America, I had met Kenneth when he accompanied his father on one of his trips to Germany. Irvin wanted to help his son learn the business by witnessing the negotiations surrounding Circus Williams. Kenneth and I started our friendship then, and it grew so over the years that today we call each other best friends.

I enjoyed a different relationship with Irvin. He treated me as if I were a member of his family. Before I came to America, I had hoped he would be that way. I would not have been able to function freely and do my best if I had been in a restrictive atmosphere, working under a tyrant. Whenever we were in Washington, D.C., or Florida, we visited Irvin at his homes, and whenever he showed up at the circus, we had dinner together. He never slipped in and out of town so that he would not have to bother with anyone. Irvin genuinely liked being around all of us.

We built a close, family-type relationship that grew stronger over the years, and Irvin became more like a father to me. Unlike Carola, who had sought my advice about almost everything and confided her personal business in me, Irvin had his son and other family members for that. He and I had a sincere relationship that went beyond business, and I always felt special and privileged when I was around him.

I was deeply moved by our friendship. Here I was, a German who had lived in Germany during World War II, with a Jewish man for my close friend and ally. One of the most stirring moments of my life occurred in 1984, when Irvin invited me to a Seder at his home. The Seder is a Jewish service held on the first and second nights of Passover. It is a solemn affair that includes a ceremonial dinner marked by special readings. Although I knew nothing of the customs surrounding this beautiful family holiday, Irvin welcomed me into his home to be a part of it.

Only someone who lived during the times in which I grew up and saw the terrible things I saw could fully appreciate how special I felt sitting at Irvin's table during that Seder. He accepted me as an individual and did not hold me responsible for acts committed by others. When, as a little child, I saw one of the Nazi concentration camps, I was too young to understand what was going on. I thought the people held there were being punished because they were criminals. I may not have understood what was being done to the Jewish people, but I knew what was happening to my country, and I did not like it. Even though during the war we were told that the Third Reich was the best thing that ever happened in our lives, I hated the Nazi regime. I still feel terrible about what happened to the Jewish people during the war, and I get upset about it all the time. I do not understand how the world let that happen.

Irvin and I sometimes talked about the Holocaust and

about our relationship, and I was always taken by his great insight and perception. He was not a hateful man, and he once told me that most of the people who worked very well and hard for him were Germans. Today many of my friends are Jewish. Sigrid and I have a network of doctor friends across the country, and they are all Jewish. I marvel at the way things turned out for me. If only it had been that way years before for all Germans and Jews.

We were playing in Charlotte, North Carolina, when Irvin and Kenny closed the deal that gave them back the Ringling circus. Irvin telephoned and asked me to meet him in Washington, D.C., so that I would be with him and Kenneth when they made the formal announcement. My family and I flew to the capital for the ceremony, and it was a great feeling to share that moment of triumph with the Felds. Afterward I spent some private time with them, and Irvin told me that he wanted to bring me into the company as a partner. He offered me the opportunity to buy a piece of the Ringling circus and everything else that was under the umbrella corporation of Irvin and Kenneth Feld Productions. He said I had earned it, and that he would be proud if I accepted.

I was dumbfounded, because Irvin and I had never discussed this, and I never expected it. But unlike in the past, when I turned down a piece of Circus Williams on the advice of Carola's friends, this time I made my own decision and accepted Irvin's offer. I was exceedingly proud when this happened because I knew how much Irvin loved his circus, and I was honored that he would share it with me.

This was another event in my life where people expected me to be overflowing with happiness, but I never get too excited about anything because I hate to be disappointed. I was always afraid to enjoy anything too soon because I thought it might be taken from me. I quietly accepted the partnership and remained under separate contract with the circus as an animal trainer and performer. It was never widely known that I was one of the owners of the circus. I think that made people feel a bit more comfortable around me and left me in a better position to work with them.

I was much more thankful to Kenny than I was to Irvin when I was made their partner, because I knew that if Kenny had not wanted this, it would not have happened. Even before Irvin sold the circus, Sigrid and I believed that Kenny was going to play an important role in the business and that if we were to secure our future with Ringling, it was important that Kenny like me and my family. When I accepted the partnership, I said to Kenny, "I thank you more than your father."

I understood Irvin's feelings when he bought back the circus, especially how he felt about working with his son. I had no compunctions about working with Kenneth. I had prepared for that day with the idea that because of either his father's retirement or his death Kenny would one day be running the company. After Irvin bought back the circus, I was never so stupid as to say to his son, "I don't have to listen to you because your father hired me." A lot of people made that mistake, but I did not. I gave Kenny the same kind of respect I gave his father.

Everything seemed to be on the right track under their joint leadership, and then, without warning, Irvin was cut down by an unexpected and fatal stroke. There was no long illness, no lengthy hospital stay, none of the things that would have prepared us for the worst. In the space of two days Irvin was taken from us. He died on September 6, 1984, and his death was an incredible shock for me.

I cared so much about Irvin, and he was taken from me as quickly and unexpectedly as Harry was. For the second time I felt as if I had lost a father. My stomach churned and I was depressed for some time afterward. As with Harry's death, I had much deeper feelings when Irvin left us than when my natural father died.

I was supposed to give a speech about Irvin at the circus following his death, but I could not speak. The words choked up in my throat and tears welled into my eyes when I tried to explain our loss. I am a tough man in many ways, but my emotions run deep. I felt like a boy again, hurt and alone.

It was extremely difficult on an emotional level for Kenny to come to terms with his father's death, but on a corporate level he had worked with Irvin long enough to be able to keep the business going without any long and unpleasant transition period. It might have been a delicate situation for Kenny to be my friend and also the man in charge of the company, but he never gave any signals that this made him uncomfortable. He was as good to me as Irvin had been, and equally caring. After his father's death, Kenny gave me his word that if anything ever happened to me, he would see to the well-being of my family. He told me, "Your kids are my kids." I knew he meant it, and that gave me peace of mind.

I also took consolation in Kenny's attitude toward the circus. I had as much freedom working with him as I had had with Irvin, and I knew there was nothing he would not do for me. In some respects Kenny was a different kind of man than his father. His attention was directed to the future and the stunning growth of the company, and he did not spend as much time with his employees as his father had. They could not show up at his office with their problems whenever they wanted, and he was a little more strict about the way they conducted themselves around him. His father was, well, more like a father to everyone. Kenny was more like the boss. He proved to be an astute, straightforward, no-nonsense businessman, and in the long run that was good for the circus.

Kenny and I always worked well together because I understood his approach to business. I was the same way when it came to the care of the animals and dealing with the people who worked for me. I made few concessions to my working men, because I knew how critical their jobs were to the safety and well-being of the animals. I bent no rules when it came to their care, and I only occasionally bent personal rules that applied to my workers. But like Irvin, I made time to listen to everyone and had a lot of empathy for their problems. Many times in my life I have helped people because I know what it is like to be in need or to feel you don't have a friend in the world.

I think the person on my staff for whom I have made the most concessions is Piccolo, the dwarf. Born Helmut Schlinker in Germany, he picked up the moniker Piccolo somewhere along life's way, and it stayed with him these many years. Piccolo started out in the circus business working for Adolf Althoff. I do not remember how he came to work with us, but he ended up at Circus Williams in 1964. When we went to Italy that year, I took Piccolo with me. For as long as I can remember, Piccolo has been an exceedingly tough guy who works hard and drinks hard. He also smokes too much. Because he does not spare any muscle, Piccolo became a valuable employee of Circus Williams and one of my assistants. The only problem I ever had with him was that he would disappear for days at a time, and no matter where I looked, I could not find him.

Piccolo has been very loyal to me, but sometimes the alcohol was stronger than I was, and a few times he was not around when I needed him. His disappearing act drove me mad, and I finally demanded to know where he was when he was missing from the circus. Piccolo confessed that he would retreat to a quiet bar, sit there drinking until he was out of money, and then come back to work. Regardless of how long he was gone, I always took him back. I could never be cruel to him. We had our ups and downs, but I always thought I was pretty fair to Piccolo, and he carried his load when he was around.

While we were still in Germany, Piccolo settled down a bit, and I did not have to go looking for him as often. He was stricken with wanderlust again after we came to America, and at one point he met a girl and went off with her for almost two years. I later learned that he had been in Venice, Florida, during that time. He turned up without her at the circus in the winter of 1988, and I took him back again. Who was I to argue with love?

I never had to worry about my children being around the circus while I was practicing and doing chores, because Piccolo looked after them. He made sure they did not have any accidents and kept them busy helping him. We did not have a baby-sitter, so Piccolo even stayed with our children in the evening if we had to go out without them.

Piccolo, who is now fifty-seven years old, can neither read nor write, but that never interfered with his ability to do any number of jobs, from polishing my shoes to caring for my equipment. In some ways he has been like a miniature butler, in others like my right arm. Doctors told him to stop smoking and drinking, and I tried to get him to do as he was told, but without success. Whenever I started lecturing him on the evils of booze and tobacco, he got on his scaled-down motorcycle and buzzed away, or simply walked out of earshot.

More than anyone in our business, Piccolo knows how often I change my mind. Everyone knows when Piccolo is upset with me over these changes by the way he acts. With great drama to illustrate his annoyance, he throws his cigarette to the ground, crushes it out passionately with his boot, flings his arms into the air, shakes his head sadly from side to side, and rants in German. I do not know if anyone else on my staff could get away with reacting like that when I tell them to do something, but Piccolo does.

Piccolo is an all-around man who fits in wherever he is needed. He works with the ponies, horses, and even the elephants. He has a lot of heart, and I respect that in a person. After so many years Piccolo is a part of my life, and I will keep him on at the circus until the end.

A few other workers have been with me for many years, and they are also part of our family. Pierre Kohnen, whom I call Peter, was born and raised in Luxembourg. He started at the bottom at Circus Williams some thirty years ago and worked his way up. Peter was first hired to work in the kitchen, but he showed an interest in the animals, which I understood and appreciated. He first learned to work with the horses, starting with the most basic things, then went on to work with the elephants and the tigers. By the time I retired as a performer, Peter was one of my top men. He left the circus business for a while, and he and his wife went back to Germany, where he worked in a zoo. I guess he missed our way of life, because he came back to Ringling, and I rehired him.

Alois Peier—Louis to everyone at the circus—is an Austrian who was the head usher at Circus Williams for many years. He started working with me in the 1950s when we were touring in Austria and has been with me ever since. He was an all-around man who had never worked with animals, but I believed he could be good with them. After we closed up in Germany and came to America, I put him in charge of caring for the elephants, and he proved to be very capable of handling himself and others around those behemoths.

Another person who worked with me for a while was Henry Schroer, the son of Carola's sister. When I was a young man, I spent time with his family in Germany and often ate at their home. Henry was not around so much in those early years because he attended a private school, and then trained to be an electrician. Years later he showed up at Circus Williams looking for work, and I made him my assistant when we toured Italy, and later in America. Eventually I allowed Henry to present a horse act, then a mixed act, but after a few years he returned to Germany to work at Circus Barum. A year later he came back to America and I rehired him. Henry never seemed to settle down in circus work. He always wanted to do something different, something better in some other place, so he left us again. With the exception of Louis, I think they all tried something different, but then came back to the circus.

I believe one reason I have remained so close over the years to this handful of men is because they are so hard-working and respectful. Those traits are at the top of my list of things I like most about people. Above all I hate ill-mannered people and people who do not take their work seriously. I have taught my children that only when they are sick, or have some other very good reason, should they miss work.

So many times I have seen performers carried out of a ring because they had an accident, or something serious supposedly happened to them. Everyone around the circus would be concerned and think the poor guy was dying because he could not move under his own steam, and two hours later he would be back on his feet again. I cannot see how in the hell anybody can do that. I would only let myself be carried out if I were a goner.

Throughout my career I hired working men who were willing to meet my standards of care and treatment of the animals. They were not allowed to interfere with their training; they were simply part of the team responsible for their care. It did not happen often, but if a worker tried to chastise an animal, I would tell him, "I am the trainer, and you are my helper. You do not take it upon yourself to deal with an animal the way a trainer does. When something is wrong, you tell me about it. You don't know when an animal should be scolded and when it should not. I don't ever want you to do anything to an animal that is not necessary." I despise men who go around acting like tough guys—if you kicked them in the butt, they would cry, but they act like big-shot tough guys with the animals. They push them, try to deny them food, and basically make their lives miserable. I would never tolerate that, and neither does my son.

I realize that I cannot step into other people's minds and bodies to get them to think and act the way I believe they should. No one should ever try to control other people. We can, however, learn from each other and try to surround ourselves with good people. I always tried to hire reliable, responsible workers who took pride in their jobs. Quite a number of young people left my employ over the years because they did not want to strive to meet my standards. I felt that I had a responsibility toward young people to teach them to be diligent and dependable. I told them that dreaming does not make dreams come true; hard work does. When you don't work, you cannot accomplish anything. Some of them learned and prospered from my example and philosophy of hard work and good conduct. Some did not.

I functioned this way not only in business but also in my private affairs. I always felt I had a responsibility to the people in my life. As a boy I often sent money to my mother to help her make ends meet. I even helped her after she remarried because her husband was an average man who was neither wealthy nor terribly ambitious. Money did not come easily to either of them, and it seemed as if my mother would have to work all her life just to make ends meet.

I did not have an opinion about my stepfather, Bernhard Poick, one way or the other, and I made no effort to like him, because I felt I did not have to. He was my mother's problem. I did, however, respect him because he was my mother's husband. Bernhard, an electrician, was a stoic, hardworking man who suited my mother very well. He was not worldly or impressive to look at, just average and tired, like so many other middle-aged people who had lived through the war. After he retired, my mother once again fell on hard times.

My mother always knew where to turn when she needed help. She wrote to me about her troubles, and I, feeling sorry for her, asked if she and her husband wanted to go on the road with Circus Williams. We needed an electrician, and I thought it would be a good experience for both of them because it would give them something to do and put extra money in their pockets. In 1966, two years before we came to America, I hired both of them. Bernhard became one of our electricians, and my mother was assigned small jobs, such as sewing.

I never argued with my stepfather or had any complaints about him, mainly because I paid little attention to him. He was not a troublemaker and did his work without any problems, and that satisfied me. I observed my mother, however, with a mixture of sadness and pity. I thought it was ironic that, after so many years and so much history between us, she had come back to live and work at Circus Williams. One might have thought that since I was by then an adult and she had so many years to think about the things that had happened between us, we would have grown closer. Regretfully that did not happen. She was as cold and indifferent as ever, and when I left for America, she shed no tears over my departure.

My sister did not seem to be distressed to see me go either. But what happened or did not happen between me and Rita I can blame on the war. I believe my sister knew that my mother was leaving me at Circus Williams when I was thirteen, but she could not help me—she had to worry about herself. Maybe that was the case later on, too, when we became adults, so our family never came together, never sat together at night and talked as other families did. I regret that, especially when I see how many families today, especially in the circus (including my own), sit together and share news about their lives and enjoy each other. It might have had something to do with our ethnic background. I believe other nationalities have stronger family ties than Germans, who are more independent.

My mother visited us several times in America, but she was always aloof. I thought she would exhibit some warmth when Mark was born, but she was as cold toward her grandson, even when he started growing up, as she had been toward me. She was not especially warm toward Tina either. I could only assume that she had been like that all of her life, or at least all of her married life. I was hurt that she treated her grandchildren so shabbily, but I finally realized that she was never going to change and I just accepted her the way she was.

We were living here quite a few years when my mother fell victim to Alzheimer's disease. Rita and my mother lived only a few blocks from each other in Düsseldorf, and so the responsibility for her immediate care fell on Rita's shoulders. But I regularly sent money because my mother needed specialized treatment in a nursing home. I was concerned about her and did not want her to suffer. Rita wrote to me periodically to tell me about her condition. I visited my mother in Germany during our winter break in 1986 and saw first-hand what a terrible toll the disease had taken on her. She did not recognize me at first, and when she did, she talked nonsense about her dress and things she thought she had done that day. She looked so pathetic as she spoke about riding her bike into town and shopping, and that was the image of my mother that I carried back to America with me.

On February 2, 1987, when our season was in full swing, Rita telephoned to tell me our mother had died. But I could not leave the circus to attend her funeral, so my sister made all the arrangements.

My emotions were in such turmoil when my mother died that I do not remember exactly how I felt. I certainly had some kind of attachment to her, even if I could not describe it. I had loved her when I was a child, and I remembered missing her terribly for the first few years after she left me at Circus Williams. When I tried to analyze my feelings about my mother's death, I experienced a peculiar kind of remorse, and I do not know which one of us I felt sorrier for, her or myself.

Although during her life I wished her the best, I do not believe I was very sad when she died. I did not cry. I remember thinking that death had been merciful because she was no longer suffering. I also recalled how broken up Sigrid had been when her father died in 1975 and, eleven years later, when she lost her mother. I wanted to feel that way about my parent, but I could not force those emotions.

My sense of responsibility kept me bound to Jeanette, even after she remarried. She left the Ringling circus in 1980 to open her own business, a restaurant in Venice, Florida, called the Continental Café. Her husband kept his job with the circus. She had been having some pretty serious personal problems, and all of a sudden they all caught up with her. She went home one night and became so hysterical that she scared her daughter, Caroline, half to death. Near midnight Caroline called my home and begged Sigrid, "Please, Auntie Sigrid, please help me! Mama is going to kill herself!" Sigrid heard uncontrolled screams in the background and tried to calm Caroline, in between telling me what was happening and rushing me and Tina out the door to the rescue.

It was a ten-minute drive from our home to Jeanette's, but I drove so fast that Tina and I arrived there in half the time. Sigrid stayed on the telephone with Caroline until she heard my voice in the background. Jeanette was in a terrible state. She was still screaming and ranting wildly. I shouted at her, even shook her by the arms in an effort to calm her, but she was out of control. I finally slapped her in the face to bring her out of it, and then she just cried and cried. I stayed with her until she was able to get a grip on herself and talk sense. When I went home, I left my cool, level-headed seventeen-year-old Tina behind to keep the situation under control.

Jeanette sold her restaurant in 1982 and went on to manage an animal-exchange business. She became self-reliant once she was able to sort out her life. When Jeanette's life stabilized, Carola finally had some peace of mind, and I had some peace.

Even though I was lax about writing letters after I left Germany, I tried to do as much as I could for Carola whenever she visited us—I even bought her a larger trailer so that she would be comfortable when she was in the United States for months at a time. In 1960, even though she had said she needed no one's help, I hired a driver named Peter Mandell for her. She was getting older and spending less time with us on the road, and her brothers and I were worried about her being alone. Peter was exceedingly loyal to Carola and stayed with her for twenty-seven years. Despite

UNTAMED

Peter's devotion I would have rather had Carola living in America, but no matter how I tried to talk her into staying with us, she refused. Carola always went back to Germany, and it was there that she died.

I always prayed that if Carola became fatally ill and was near death, I could be with her, or at least be able to go to her funeral. Death had played some wicked tricks on me. It did not hover around the people I loved and keep them ill for months or years before it snuffed out their lives. It sneaked up on them when they and I least expected it and stole them away. It had been that way with Harry and Irvin, and I feared it would be the same with Carola.

Death got a big surprise when it showed up for Carola. It had not counted on her iron will, or her deep affection for me. Carola knew my schedule better than I, and I believe she held on until the wintertime, when I would not be traveling with the circus and could be at her funeral. Carola left this world at the age of eighty-four on December 12, 1987. She died of natural causes, or, as they said at the time, old age.

Jeanette, who had been visiting her mother in Cologne at the time, telephoned at seven o'clock in the morning to give me the dreadful news. Carola's death was terrible for me. I had seen her only six months before when she was in the United States. She had told me then that traveling had become very hard for her and she believed that that was the last time she would come to America. It happened just as she had said.

Carola was a great woman. Growing up in troubled times made her tough, but she also had a good heart. She was not oppressive or selfish. She let me grow and gave me the opportunity to become all that I am today. I went to her funeral and did not try to hold back the tears when I stood at her graveside. While I was in Germany, I also visited my mother's grave. Standing in cemeteries, at two lonely gravesites, was a sad and difficult way for me to say good-bye to the two women who had done more than anyone else, good or bad, to shape my life. In my mind I tried to speak to Carola as I stood at her grave, but I was so stricken with grief that I could not organize my thoughts. When I went to my mother's grave, I remember looking at the headstone, then searching the sky, all the while wondering why our relationship had not been better and, once again, feeling very much alone.

So many times I miss having Carola to talk to, and it is too bad that she cannot see how far Sigrid, our children, and I have come after all these years. I used to tell her that if I had the opportunity, I would do this or that for her—the kinds of things sons tell their mothers—and she would say, "Don't worry about me. I want to be able to do everything for myself. Take the rest of your life and enjoy it and do your best."

More than the loss of Harry, Irvin, or my natural mother, Carola's death stunned me into the realization that nothing we want to say or do should be postponed. When Carola died, I felt like shouting, "Wait a minute. Don't go yet. It's too soon. I have to tell you something!" There was so much I wanted to say to her, so many things I should have told her when she was alive, but never did. I could not remember if I had thanked her—really thanked her—for rescuing me from a life of emptiness and despair. Had I told her that I would be eternally in her debt for the opportunity she gave me by allowing me to operate her circus? Had I thanked her for the food and clothes, the confidence and trust, she had given me? Had I ever told her how very much I loved her? I felt cheated because I had not been given the chance to have one last conversation with my stepmother.

UNTAMED

The day we buried Carola, I was with her brother, Adolf Althoff, whom I had not seen in many, many years. Adolf, and a few others, had done so much for me when I was a young man. I owed them a debt that could not be repaid with money. They had made certain that I was never hungry or alone and that I never felt like an outcast. The day of Carola's funeral I looked at Adolf's face, and he suddenly seemed very old. His hair was gray, his shoulders were not as squared as they had been when I first met him, and the years had etched tiny lines into his face. I realized how quickly time slips away, and I did not want to lose him without saying what was in my heart. I stood beside Adolf at the cemetery and allowed all these thoughts to wash over me. At first I felt shy about telling him what was in my heart, but as I looked at Carola's grave and realized how final death is, I resolved to speak with Adolf before the day was out. When we had a private moment after the funeral, I told Adolf just how I felt. I thanked him for being a friend and teacher and for taking me into his home as if I were a member of his family. He looked directly at me while I spoke, and I could see tears welling into his eyes. I thanked him for all the good he had done for me in my lifetime, and then I reached out, pulled him close to me, and hugged him for a long time. He was so touched by the things I said that he cried like a baby. He said no one had ever spoken to him as I had that day.

CHAPTER 13

I was never a stranger to unplanned events, even when I was a child. The war taught me to expect the unexpected and to count on nothing and no one. My exposure to death taught me that the world around us is very tenuous and can change from moment to moment without warning. As tough as my life has been at times, maybe it was a good way to grow up because it made me quick-witted, resourceful, and strong-willed—qualities that paid off in my work with the animals.

Most workers cannot comprehend the depth of the feelings my family and I have for the animals, or why I was so overly attentive and concerned about them. They understood that the animals needed us to give them food and water and clean their stables, but many did not understand that their dependency on me went far beyond filling their bellies and cleaning their stalls. I also had to protect them, because they cannot protect themselves. The elephants cannot tell a worker, "Hey, buddy, get me out of here. I'm in danger."

They needed me to allay their fears, warm their nights,

cool them when the sun was relentless, and get them past things they did not understand. I had to be on hand to let them know that they were not alone and that I would protect them. If they had been frightened by something, the animals would settle down as soon as they heard my voice and felt my touch, because they trusted that I would not let anything happen to them. As a father would sit beside his child's bed during a thunderstorm or after a nightmare, I stayed with them when they were ill or alarmed. In that respect there were many times when they came before my human family, because I knew that the children had Sigrid and each other, but without me the animals had no one to fill that protective, parental role.

I believe the animals relied on me the most when the weather was bad or extreme. One of the most critical factors governing the care and safety of wild animals is weather. They are, of course, subject to the same weather conditions as the rest of us, but they can do little to help themselves, especially if they are held in stalls and tents. They are troubled by extremes in temperature and become agitated when winds are howling around them or thunder and lightning are crashing and flashing outside.

In bad weather the people responsible for the animals must react quickly. Storms and animals are equally unpredictable, and there is no time to waste when they come together. I habitually moved the elephants and horses out of the tents before anyone else because they became especially nervous and agitated during storms. First I moved the elephants, because they are more dangerous than the horses in terms of the amount of harm they could do to the others. Everyone else would be rescued or secured after them.

While various animals react differently to particular weather conditions, a tornado is the worst of all storms because of its violent and destructive winds. We had a frightening experience with a tornado in Norman, Oklahoma, and it was one of those times where my wife and children had to fend for themselves. The animals were in tents for this particular stop on our tour, and there is only so much that can be done to secure a tent in very high winds. When the storm started coming up, I sent Sigrid, Tina, and Mark to the basement of the arena in which we had performed while I went to stay with the animals. The winds became so strong that street poles were picked up and carried through the air. I was so afraid that a caged tiger would be picked up and hurled through the air that I ran furiously from them to the elephants and back again. As the winds became more intense, I had to get Sigrid to help me because I needed someone I could trust to follow my instructions to the letter, and Mark and Tina were too young. My greatest concern was that the electric lights rigged to the tents might electrocute the animals if they blew down.

I told my wife to oversee the movement of the horses, and a couple of performers went along to help her. While they were taking the horses out of the tent, I ordered Sigrid to hold the light connection in her hands, and if she saw that the situation was worsening and the tent was in danger of blowing away, she was to disconnect the lights immediately so that the horses would not be electrocuted. I was worried that if the tent crashed down before we could move out all the horses, the live wires would fall onto them. If Sigrid broke the connection, the wires would be dead when they hurtled down to the ground, and neither she nor the animals would be hurt by them.

In the meantime I moved the elephants. When the elephants were nervous and knew they were going to be moved, they lifted their feet alternately as if to say, "Hurry! Hurry! Quick! Let's go! Help me!" We had a system whereby we could loosen the elephants' stays from both ends of the stable and get them out right away, and we always had security pliers on hand in the train, the tents, and our car so that we could cut the chains if need be to remove the animals more quickly.

We were able to safely move all the animals out of the tents and secure them inside the arena, and since none of the tents were blown away, Sigrid did not have to cut the lights. But it was a hair-raising experience. Once again I was certain that Someone was looking after me and everyone I love.

In 1989 we ran into every kind of weather, from tornadoes to blizzards. We had tents up, and it snowed so hard and so long in Hampton, Virginia, that I had to go up on the tents and brush the snow off throughout the day and night to keep the tents from collapsing. Inside, the elephants were scared to death every time I jumped up on their tent because they could not see what was making the noise above them. It was the same as when they were in a tunnel. The elephants almost broke their chains, and the horses got pretty nervous, too, and started jumping around, trying to run away. I had a couple of people working with me on the tent, and suddenly I turned around and everybody was gone. I was so preoccupied with what I was doing that I never even saw them leave. I did not shout for them because I knew they had been driven indoors by the cold and were out of earshot. I grumbled under my breath as my face was beaten by the freezing wind, and I beat my hands against my thighs to warm them. It was too cold for anyone to have to do that kind of work. I looked like an ice man, but I stayed and did what I had to do. No one can explain how scary and dangerous this kind of thing is. There was so much snow that we finally had to take the elephants and horses out of the tents and into the buildings, even though the show had been

UNTAMED

canceled because of the weather. No sooner did I evacuate the animals than the whole tent collapsed. It would have collapsed sooner if I had not removed the snow for a whole day and night. None of the performers helped me. There was no show because of the weather, so they were occupied with personal activities. It kept snowing, and everything looked beautiful, and I was a nervous wreck.

Weather can affect even the most basic of circus activities. Sometimes when we were in the midst of animal walks, the weather changed without warning, and we had lightning and thunder all around us. At times like that I cared only about getting the animals safely from the train to the buildings or tents, or vice versa. Early in my career, after a couple of run-ins with bad weather, I got into the habit of lowering the awning on my trailer at night and storing away whatever was portable, because I knew that if anything happened I would not have time to take care of my own property. Such precautions were designed to give me a clear head so that I could concentrate on the animals.

Heat is another villain that plays havoc with the circus. In the wild, animals seek relief from extreme heat by moving deeper into the forest, where thick ceilings shade the woodland floor, or by going to a stream or other body of water where they can bathe. Their source of relief when they are being moved on a train is also water, always water. In intense heat the train must be stopped several times during a trip so that we can water the animals. Heat is much more dangerous for the animals than cold. When it is cold, it is easy to close off tents and cages and put many bales of hay around the animals to keep them warm. We also place special heaters in their living quarters, which can be operated around the clock if necessary.

Snow and ice present the same dangers to animals that they do to humans. Ice really bothers the elephants, and I was always afraid that one of them would slip and break a foot. Fortunately that never happened, because elephants walk slowly when they have the feeling that they are not on solid, safe ground. They take such small, cautious steps on ice that they actually look comical, but there is nothing funny about moving them under such conditions. Ice is also dangerous for the horses, because it can lead to broken legs. We once arrived in Greensboro, North Carolina, and found the entire town under ice. I was concerned about walking the horses on that because after they have been on the train, they like to jump around when they get out into the open. They don't understand that they cannot safely play on ice. We were lucky that the town recognized our problems and provided us with a huge snow blower to clear the streets.

Bad weather presents a different set of dangers for the tigers. I was always scared to death about floods because the tigers' cages are low to the ground. Anytime it rained heavily at night, I took the tigers directly to the building where we would be working instead of leaving them inside a tent, which would have been dangerous. During the day people are around to protect them, but we cannot help them at night if we are asleep and there is a flash flood or super-heavy rains. In the stables there are two watchmen on duty around the clock wherever we are working, but I never counted on anyone but myself. I know the elephants and horses can survive flooding—I would simply cut them loose and they could fend for themselves—but tigers cannot. If there was a danger of flooding and I did not have a building to house the tigers, I would load them onto a truck and drive them to the highest spot in the area. I would take them to the highest spot in the world if it would keep them safe.

I tried to be prepared for any eventuality with the weather by listening to radio newscasts and special weather channels. I did not worry much if we headed into light thunder and rain because that kind of weather did not generally create serious problems. Thunder does not bother the tigers or elephants much, but it spooks the hell out of the horses. They jump around, and some of them get loose and run away, but that is not the worst thing that could happen.

We were always very lucky, because we were never hit with any real disasters. In 1989 we got especially lucky because in that year we missed what I think is the worst thing that could have happened to us. We performed in California only three weeks before a serious earthquake struck that state. The towns we appeared in were directly in the line of the quake. We traditionally played in Oakland and drove between that city and San Francisco every day to the place where our train was stationed. I cannot even imagine how the elephants would have reacted in an earthquake. Thank God I did not have to find out.

Weather is not the only thing that can play havoc with the animals. Commonplace things that do not bother most people can upset them greatly and create an opportunity for disaster. For example, the sounds of airplanes frighten them, and that makes walking them near airports dangerous. In Minneapolis/Saint Paul the building in which we worked and housed the animals is on one side of the airport, and the trainyard is on the other. We always had to walk them two or three miles around the entire airport, with one plane coming in or going out after the other. How much pressure can anyone take?

Planes especially bother the elephants because of their tendency to get spooked by sounds with which they cannot draw a visual connection. That, plus the strong vibrations that accompany the noise, frighten the living daylights out of them, making them dangerous. In Indianapolis we had to pass an aiport to get to and from the train, but the airport people were sympathetic to our problem and they changed the takeoff and landing schedule during our animal walk so that no planes went up over the elephants. Throughout my career I was able to avoid some dangerous situations only because someone was willing or able to make a change in our favor. But most people don't have an inkling of what it takes to move circus animals in and out of a town or around the country.

Animal walks could be dangerous even when we weren't worrying about planes and storms. We always had police protection, and that came in handy because whenever something happened, such as an animal getting spooked by a vehicle or people on the street, or I spotted a potential problem, such as a tunnel, I stopped the walk. If, for example, we were passing under a railroad bridge and a train was in sight, I would stop the walk until the train passed instead of taking the elephants under the overpass, where they would hear the noise but could not see where it was coming from. The police kept onlookers and traffic away from the animals while we waited for safe passage.

I conducted animal walks in every town I visited, both in America and in Europe, but I could never let my guard down simply because I had done something thousands of times. With all the children who often lined the streets to watch us, I did not want any accidents. Many mothers allowed their youngsters to stand right at the street corner or curb, and so many times I had to ask them to have their children stand back. It did not occur to them that if a horse got spooked, a child could be hurt, and if a child had been hurt by one of my animals, I would have felt terrible. Mark has been coming on animal walks with me since he was a little boy. When he was young, I would tell him that if something happened, he was to jump onto something safe right away and just stay there.

UNTAMED

With twenty elephants, I had to be prepared for any eventuality. It was never easy. When we came into a town like New York City, we had to unload the elephants in Queens, go through a tunnel, and walk into Manhattan. This was always incredibly nerve-racking because of the tremendous amount of traffic moving to and from Manhattan through Queens, the planes moving over the area to and from two major airports in Queens, and because the tunnel linking Queens to Manhattan is fairly long. Once we were through, I would think, "Oh, man, I've got to do this again when we leave." To make that walk safer, I would instruct everybody not to yell, speak loudly, or make any noise if possible.

Elephants run from noise, and they especially hate fireworks. When we went to Anaheim, California, our tents were close to Disneyland, where they display fireworks every night at 10:00 P.M. The worst thunder and lightning would not bother the elephants, and yet their reaction to the fireworks was nearly a stampede. Once, when we were playing in Los Angeles, where the sports arena and coliseum are opposite each other, nobody told us that they were going to have an opening-day football game on the day we arrived—complete with fireworks. It sounded like a war zone. I had to jump down and stand in front of the elephants to hold them back and keep them calm.

Because I made my work look easy, people outside the circus believed that nothing could happen to them if they got close to the animals. Not so. Some of my workers let down their guard a few times, and they paid a price. Accidents happened even when the animals were caged. The cage in which the tigers practiced and performed was deceiving because it looked stationary, but it was actually flexible hurricane fencing. If a person got too close to that cage while the tigers were running around the ring, and a tiger jumped against the cage, his claws could go right through the fencing and accidentally maul the person. They jump and have you! That happened to Piccolo, Henry, and a worker named Roger, but fortunately none of them was seriously hurt.

Animals created problems for each other as well as for humans. I had to keep the elephants out of the tigers' sight and their predatory thoughts when we practiced. Remember the story of my little elephant Prince, the tigers' favorite distraction. I could read their minds when they looked at Prince, and they were thinking, "One day I'll get that little elephant."

To prevent the tigers from watching the elephants during practice if they were housed in the same section of a building, I would pull the trailer portions of Ringling trucks between their cages and the elephants. It was the only way I could outsmart them. The tigers were in the ring to learn, not salivate over Prince or any of the others. I had to have their undivided attention when I was training them so that I would not become a blue-plate special when I was performing with them.

I lived with the potential for problems twenty-four hours a day, but it was the late-night knocks on the door that worried me most. It was one thing if a problem unfolded when I was up and around and could head it off or quickly solve it. It was another if something happened when I was in bed. Then I would feel guilty and blame myself because I was not there to help or prevent it. Sometimes I would wake up in the middle of the night thinking that I had heard a knock on the door, only to find that my mind had played a trick on me.

I worried about this so much because I knew that nobody would bother me at night unless something bad had happened. A late-night knock on the door always made me sick. It has not happened to me often—I've been lucky, but

UNTAMED

I was always under the pressure that it could happen. Even a telephone call from Peter, one of my trusted workers and friends, made me nervous. He had to preface any calls to me by saying, "Everything is fine, boss." For me the only good news is no news.

One late-night knock at our door brought word that a dear friend of mine, Mickey Antalek, had died. Mickey was a chimpanzee trainer who had worked for Ringling for many years. He was such a good man, so kind and helpful, always offering to do things for me because he knew how busy I was. The day he died, he had washed my trailer and taken it to be serviced and he was going to pick it up the next day. I reminded him that night before we went our separate ways. I went home, and an hour later Mickey was dead from a heart attack. He was one of my best friends, and I could not believe that I had been with him such a short time before and then he was gone. I was distraught over Mickey's death, and I never had time to come to terms with it because two days after we buried him, Irvin Feld died.

The only time I could ever relax was after the last show, when I would go back to my trailer, bus, or train car, and Sigrid would have delicious food waiting on the table for me, and I would sit down with a drink and watch *Johnny Carson* or *Nightline*. Sometimes I would start to watch a movie, but I would fall asleep before the end of it.

In so many ways animals are like children. They can easily become ill, and when that happens, they need constant, special attention. I always worried about the animals contracting diseases because they were given, out of necessity, so many different types of hay and water. Their housing also changed from place to place, and there was no way of telling what happened in a building before we got there. This can cause horses to develop extreme colic, which is characterized by abdominal pain.

All animals can develop colic. Although it is especially

common among horses, the incidence of colic among mine was very low—only about one case a year—and I attribute that to my feeding system. I fed the horses from the floor, instead of putting their feed and hay into buckets or troughs. When their food is placed in a container, horses just gulp it down and that can cause colic because they swallow a lot of air. But when it is placed on a floor that is dusted with some gravel or small stones, the horses are much more careful about what they eat, and consequently they eat more slowly.

To help keep our horses healthy, I made certain that they never stood in manure. That creates a lot of bacteria and endangers the animals. I have people constantly cleaning up after them.

A great deal of attention must be paid to what the animals are fed. I always personally checked on the hay because we used so much of it for the horses and elephants, and I wanted to make sure that they would not end up with stuff that was going to make them sick. As soon as we received a delivery of hay, I would grab a handful and smell it to see if it had a clean, fresh aroma. When new hay is harvested, it is too fresh for baling, but some people bale it anyway. This type of hay can sicken the horses. Sometimes bales of hay would be allowed to stand in the rain before being shipped to us, and the hay inside the bale would stay wet and become unhealthy.

I always put my hand inside the bales of hay to feel the temperature. Sometimes it would be cooking inside from the moisture contained in the new hay. That could not be fed to the animals, so I would have to open the bales to let the heat escape and the hay dry. I told my people over and over again never to put closed bales of hay on the train where I could not control the temperature or quality because I did not want the elephants or horses to get at it. I always kept old hay on the trains so that we could mix it with new hay to stabilize it, or use it instead of new hay if we got a bad batch.

Animals are not smart enough to know the difference between good and bad food. If something is bad, they will eat it anyway. Animals eat everything that is put in front of them when they are hungry and, like children, they tend to put harmful things into their mouths. Every three months my workers and I give the elephants pedicures, and for this job I wear gloves. Once, while I was preparing to work on one named Baby, I put my gloves on the floor beside me, and in an instant the elephant stole and ate one of them. None of the elephants had ever done that before. Fortunately the culprit did not become ill. Even though it is not designed for their consumption, elephants eat sawdust, if they find some on a floor, with the same gusto as they eat tender branches from trees. (They recognize the smell and taste of sawdust as being those of wood, which they like.) The sawdust might contain nails and other debris, but before you have a chance to get it out of their mouths, it is gone. The person who is in charge of those animals must know if their food is bad or good and what is on the floor that could be harmful to them.

Wherever we went, I was always concerned about what had been put on the floors before we got there, such as rat poison. Poisons are put out in every building, because they all have problems with mice, and many of them have rats, which carry diseases. Exterminators also use spray insecticides around arenas and coliseums. I inspected every building in which we performed before bringing in the animals, and I often asked the management to move certain things and take a broom and clean up others.

I made certain that any food fed to our animals was as clean as possible. We regularly received large shipments of bread for the elephants straight from local bakeries, and it would arrive still hot in the bags. The aroma would sometimes be too much for my workers to resist, and occasionally one or more of them would punch a hole in a bag of bread, grab a chunk and leave the rest. When I looked at a torn plastic bread bag and saw that the contents had been disturbed, I had no way of knowing if it had been done by a rodent or a man, so I would throw out the rest of the loaf. Before I retired as a performer, I put Mark in charge of the bread, carrots, and apples for the animals because he knew that everything had to be inspected to make sure rodents had not gotten into it.

Meat eaters, such as the tigers, get Nebraska-brand feed, which is a combination of nutritious foods. This is much better for them than meat, but since not everybody will eat this, those who refuse get meat. In 1990 our meat bill was two thousand dollars a week. I made sure that the meat was always fresh and that the tigers and other cats with whom I worked got fresh bones too.

Our animals' healthy diet was combined with good medical care. Richard I. Houck, or "Doc," as we call him, a veterinarian based in Wisconsin, has worked under contract with the Ringling circus for many years and is on call twenty-four hours a day. He is a dedicated doctor, the kind who will sleep in the stable with a sick animal.

We have had remarkably few health problems with our animals and very few deaths. The loss of an animal has never been easy for me. During my first couple of years with Circus Williams, I felt terrible whenever an animal died, and I would cry and be upset for days. Later I became a little harder and tougher because I realized that everyone must die sometime, but I still could never casually face the loss of an animal as others did. I felt that I had lost a friend and working partner who had done a good job and had never deliberately hurt me. The loss was not any less intense because it was an animal and not a person.

UNTAMED

I could never bear the thought of cremating or burying any of my five tigers who died, or my favorite leopard, Kenny. I did not believe that after all their years of friendship and service I should allow them to be consumed by fire or put into the ground to disappear. So I had a taxidermist preserve their skins, and they have places of honor in the living room of my home. No one is allowed to walk on them; we walk around them out of respect, because they are not trophies but dear old friends, and I am reminded of them every time I look at their skins.

All of those animals lived long lives, and only two of them died away from me. One of my tigers was sick and died at an animal clinic in Baltimore the first year I was in America. I brought him there for help, and eight days later he was dead. After that I promised myself that I would never put another one of my animals into a clinic or hospital unless I could be close at hand to supervise the treatment. I decided that sick animals would be treated on the road, where I could see what was being done for them and make certain that none of my animals went through unnecessary or prolonged suffering. Except for the one who had been sick, the other four tigers died of old age. The eldest was twenty-two years old.

Taking his place among the tigers in my home is Kenny, my leopard. Kenny was the first leopard I ever bought, and my mascot. He was also my favorite animal. Kenny was basically a gentle leopard and a nice guy. He was quite ill for some time, but I did not know it. That animal never missed a show, because he never showed any signs of pain or illness or even that he was upset and not feeling well. When he started showing signs of a problem, Dr. Houck treated him, and I took care of him. I became greatly alarmed when one day he began having nosebleeds. His nose would bleed on and off for days at a time, and then the bleeding would stop as suddenly as it had started. So many times I had to sit with him and apply pressure to his nose to stop the bleeding, and he allowed me to help him.

Perplexed and worried, Doc and I took Kenny to the veterinary hospital at the University of Illinois at Urbana, where it was discovered that he was suffering from a tumor that had filled his nasal cavity, destroyed the bones within his nose and above it, and taken the place of the missing bone, so there was no visible change in Kenny's appearance. Doctors said that the tumor had hemorrhaged on and off for months and that some of that blood escaped through his nose, hence the nosebleeds. With all the suffering this animal must have endured, he never whimpered, never tried to bite me, and never acted mean. You have to have tremendous respect for an animal like that.

The tumor was in the process of destroying the bone that separates the nasal area from the brain, so I agreed to let him have surgery. Because they anticipated that Kenny would lose a lot of blood during the operation, one of his fellow performers, a leopard named Snippy, was brought to the university as a blood donor, and Kenny received a transfusion before the surgery. Doctors removed the tumor during a tedious two-hour procedure. When the tumor's last attachment to the bony plate that separates the nose and the brain was severed, Kenny's heart abruptly stopped beating. The doctors knew that for his heart to stop beating so suddenly, there had to have been sudden damage to the brain, either from a hemorrhage or because the tumor had invaded the brain. He was given drugs to stimulate his heart, which got it beating again. A hemorrhage was found and then controlled, and while the surgery area was being closed, his heart stopped again. Kenny was given more heart-stimulating drugs and electric shock to get his heart beating, but after a while it stopped again. The doctors were able to bring him back one more time, but then his heart stopped forever.

UNTAMED

While Kenny was sick, I spent some private time with him each day. I knew the end was near when, the day before he died, I gave him water, then tried to help him to his feet but he could not stand. Surgery was his only chance. The doctors spent a full day preparing for his operation and a day in surgery trying to save his life. They did everything they could for Kenny, but he just could not hold on.

Doc later told me that because of the difficult nature of the procedure, the operating room had been filled with interested veterinarians, technicians, and students. They were really pulling for Kenny and fell into silence when he died. Many of them had tears in their eyes, and without exception they were overwhelmed with sadness. I know that Doc was feeling something extra for me, too, that day because he knew how much I loved that wonderful animal.

Veterinary medicine, like the medicine practiced on people, carries no guarantees. In the wild, if an animal becomes ill, it stands an excellent chance of being killed off right away by other animals. We tried to help ours live as long as possible, but I do not believe it is necessary to keep them suffering by prolonging the inevitable if they cannot be saved.

Several years after Kenny died, Blackie, a black leopard or panther, as they are familiarly known, became ill. Blackie had some unusual medical problems, and Doc pulled her out of scrapes with death twice, until she finally died of kidney failure. There was a tremendous amount of emotion involved with that cat. Even after she could no longer perform, I kept her at the circus out of friendship for about eight years. When she was near the end, Doc said we could do some things to keep her alive awhile longer, perhaps only days, but I could not see that. I said, "Come on, Doc, we let humans suffer. Why do we have to let an animal suffer? She's seventeen years old." Blackie had not eaten in ten days, could only drink water, and was nothing but skin and bones. We did not do anything to prolong her suffering, and she died peacefully in her cage.

I was very lucky because over the years, old age and not illness claimed the lives of most of the animals I lost. Part of my success in keeping them alive so long was that I was keenly aware of problems inimical to their species and tried to prevent them. Tigers, for example, are susceptible to liver problems. They are also prone to getting asthma; consequently I made sure their environment was virtually dust-free. Tigers with asthma could not be around all the dust that became airborne when the men cleaned up around them, so I had them placed elsewhere while their area was swept and washed. Some tigers were allergic to sawdust, so I insisted that it never be put in or near their cages.

My two asthmatic tigers were a mother and her son, and he had asthma worse than she did. Both received shots to control it. Sometimes a tiger's asthma gets out of control and he or she must be put to sleep. Unfortunately we had to do that with one of our tigers. We could not tell Mark, because he was just a little boy and would have been devastated if he found out the tiger had been killed, so we told him instead that the animal had been sent to a zoo.

I tried to keep my animals working as long as they were healthy and strong. Once they started getting old, I took them out of the acts so that they did not have to work hard, but some of them balked at losing their status as performers. This happened with a tiger named India, who was with me more than twenty years. From the first day of her retirement, India cried every time I passed her by and brought other tigers into the ring. I felt so bad for her that I let her come back into the act. That was a mistake.

India had always been the first tiger into the cage. The day I told my men to bring her back into the ring, they put her at the end, behind all the other tigers. Seeing that India was a little shaky when she walked into the ring, another tiger who had worked with her for years jumped down from his pedestal and bit India very hard on the neck. I separated them and saved her, but she suffered and almost died from that bite. When tigers become too old and weak, or too sick to defend themselves, the others go for them. That is their nature. No one can change that.

Although I always tried to treat all of my animals equally so that no one would become jealous or upset, I confess to having had favorites among each species. Bengal was my favorite tiger, Kenny and Blackie were special to me, and I have a soft spot in my heart for Congo, the African elephant, who has enough personality for a herd of her kind. I have a special relationship with Congo.

Elephants, especially African elephants, must feel that they have a personal relationship with their trainer, otherwise they can become belligerent, stubborn, and downright indifferent. Without a feeling of friendship it is virtually impossible to get an elephant to do what you want it to do. An elephant must be cajoled and carefully brought along so that it can be convinced to follow instructions.

African elephants differ from Indian elephants in several ways, most visibly in the size and shape of their ears. Africans have exceptionally large, broad ears, and Indians have shorter, smaller ones. Africans also have mighty appetites and are jealous of other elephants. Heaven help me if I gave something to one elephant and not to the Africans. I would hear complaint after complaint from them, and before long they would have the entire line of elephants talking at me and looking for whatever little goody I had slipped the first one.

In the order of elephants, when they were lined up in the stable, Prince always stood on the outside next to Congo, because he was so small. Congo always treated Prince as if she were his mother, but if I fed Prince and did not feed Congo at the same time, she would push Prince out of jealousy. She also had a bad habit of stealing his food. At one point I moved him farther away from her so that he would be able to eat in peace, but Congo developed some movements to get at Prince's food that would have impressed a contortionist.

When we fed the elephants, Mark and I started with Prince and Congo, then moved on down the line until everyone had his or her share. Since Prince often played with his food before he ate it, showering himself with the grain mixture and throwing his apples and carrots into the air, Congo knew she had plenty of time to carry out her plans. She would eat her food quickly, then, as soon as she thought we were out of sight, she would lie on her side facing Prince, stretch her body out as far as she could with one leg chained, then reach her head over to where Prince's food was, curl her trunk around it, and pull it all over in front of her. She would then nonchalantly stand up and eat his food, pretending that it was the original food we had given her. She thought she was sneaking his food away, but I was wise to her, so I would always make another pass at the end of the elephant line and give Prince some more food. Sometimes Congo even stole that.

Congo did not stand far from the horses, and whenever they got their sweet feed and she saw them eating, she would go right over and take the feed from them. The horses would get so upset that they would bite her, but that did not worry Congo. She would just shake her body, as if chasing flies, and keep trying to snatch all the horses' food.

Twenty years ago not many people knew how to handle African elephants. They had a bad reputation as being difficult to train, but I believe that it was the trainers who were difficult and did not have enough patience to put the necessary amount of time into teaching and practicing their African elephants. Africans are extremely smart and perform well if they are given a decent chance. Now we face another problem with African elephants. At the end of 1989 they went on the endangered-species list. Indian elephants are also becoming scarce. People everywhere must be concerned about this before these beautiful, wondrous creatures disappear from our planet forever.

Congo has been with me for most of my adult life. She has always been strong-willed and independent, and old age did not mellow those traits. I mellowed toward her by allowing her to be a bit flexible with some of my rules. On the elephant walks, for example, when they were taken out for exercise, Congo was permitted to walk at the end of the line so that she could take her time and nobody bothered her. She was told to catch up to the rest of the elephants only if she started wandering off to blaze her own trail. During the animal walks the horses walked directly behind Congo. Some other elephants would be scared to death of the horses, but not Congo. If the horses got too close to her, Congo would lift her foot and kick them right in the mouths.

Congo really is one in a million. She could have a tiger on her back and not show a bit of concern. She always walked around looking very secure in her actions, and she did scores of different things without anyone directing her. She worked totally on voice command. Animals like her took a lot of the worry out of training and performing and put a lot of joy into it.

CHAPTER

14

Danger comes in many forms, and around the circus it is sometimes masked by the excitement and pageantry or the hectic pace. It has at times come so close to audiences that my hair bristles at the thought, and yet those people were so enthralled by the show, they were totally unaware of the tense dramas unfolding behind the scenes. My friends and colleagues say that, like an animal, I sense impending danger.

I have a strange approach to it that, I suppose, boils down to a kind of veiled defiance. I never stupidly ignored danger, but there have been times, especially in bad weather, when I defied it by working around it. I never waltzed with danger—I respect it too much to toy with it. But I always met it head-on and quickly responded to dangerous situations with the attitude that I was a formidable adversary.

Because the circus is like a playground for danger, it is impossible to anticipate every situation. Human error often factored into the creation of these situations. There were times when the most honest mistake could bring us face-to-face with a crisis and even the potential for disaster. One night during the winter of 1988–89, we were playing in Hamilton, Ontario, Canada, and one of my workers, someone who had been with me a long time, forgot to check the chain lock on each of the tiger cages. All of a sudden four of the tigers who were not working that night got out. The tigers and elephants were located right behind the seating area.

The show was already in progress when this happened, and I was presenting the tiger act to a packed house. I had no idea what was going on, but suddenly I saw everybody around me running—all of my watchers took off, and other circus workers followed them. They all ran and did not tell me anything. At that time our show traveled with an enormous Indian elephant called King Tusk, but his familiar name was Tommy. Tommy was very unpredictable and dangerous, and it was to him that my mind raced. I thought to myself, "Tommy got somebody."

It was torture for me to be in the cage performing and not know what was going on. I was concerned that something terrible had happened. It would have been dangerous to take my attention off the tigers who were inside the cage with me, so I kept my cool and moved the tigers through their paces so that the audience would not become alarmed. As soon as the act was over, I hurried to see what was wrong.

I found out that Sigrid had been in an office in the arena and heard the elephants screaming. They never do that unless something is wrong, so she sent somebody out to check it, and he never came back. Sigrid went to look into it herself and saw the tigers standing out in the open. They were confused and frightened, so they just stayed there sizing up the situation. An elephant named Sabu was standing nearby so frozen with fear that he looked as if he were paralyzed. An hour later he was still standing like that. Sigrid sent a message to my watchers that the tigers were loose, and they had gone to get them. That left me without any watchers around the cage in which I was performing, but it had to be done. If the tigers had run between the elephants, we would have had lots of problems, because the elephants would have panicked. Luckily my men got them back into their cages without further incident. The same thing happened in New York City and New Haven, Connecticut, but by then I knew that if I saw people running, the tigers were out.

A dangerous situation like that can be indirectly related to the weather. When it was cold, we had to put hay in the bottoms of the tigers' cages for insulation. To do this we had to open the cage doors. If a worker was distracted for even a second, a tiger could get out.

The elephants and tigers were usually kept near each other so that I could get to both groups quickly. While playing in Oakland one season I went into the arena to work with the elephants, and one of my workers suddenly appeared saying, "Quick, quick, boss, two tigers are out." I ran back and got one into his cage very quickly, but the other one jumped right on top of the horses and jumped from one horse to the next. The tiger was not hurt, and after the third horse he was pooped. I jumped on him, threw him down, and scolded him like mad. That was dangerous because I had to be between the horses, who were already upset about a tiger leaping onto their backs. I put a canvas over the tiger, then my men brought a cage, and we got him back inside of it. Every horse was terribly hurt, with skin hanging off and big claw marks everywhere. It took months and months to nurse them back to health, but we saved them all and they worked with me again.

One day, after an animal walk to the Boston Garden, Mark, who was still a youngster, was pestering me to take him home. At that time, we had forty cages between the leopards and tigers, and I had to clean out every one of them. I had worked all morning and was tired and hungry, but I could not go home until all the cages were clean. I had three or four leopard cages left to finish, but Mark was impatient and followed me all over the place, pleading with me to go home and arguing that someone else could finish the cages. I said, "No, Mark, I must stay here and do this myself," and no sooner had the words left my mouth than a leopard was out of the cage. He took advantage of my divided attention and moved like greased lightning.

A leopard is not like a tiger, who stays on the ground and takes a few minutes to get his bearings. In a few leaps a leopard is gone. The moment I saw the leopard dart out of the cage, I was on him and grabbed him by the tail. I scolded him and put him back into his cage, then turned to Mark, who was standing there wide-eyed, and said, "Tell me who in this building would be able to catch a leopard. Do you see what could have happened if we both went home?" Mark had learned a lesson that would serve him well in the future if he chose to work with such dangerous animals, and I learned one that I used as soon as Mark was old enough to drive: I bought both him and Tina their own cars so that they would not have to wait for me at the end of the day. I had to make sure that everything was okay before I could go home.

I have always said that animals do not make mistakes, people do, and almost all of the injuries I have sustained over the years have been directly or indirectly caused by human error. For many years I checked all my own props for my acts. When he became old enough, Mark took over that responsibility, and during a show, after the tiger cage was raised, he went inside to set up everything for me. Even though I trusted him, once I got into the cage, I quickly looked everything over to see that it was okay and then I

UNTAMED

opened up the cage to let the tigers or other cats in. If something is wrong with a prop, it is not up to the animals to know that. When Kenny bit me during the filming of the American Express commercial, it really was not his fault. The film crew did not understand that he could not be rehearsed and kept waiting like a human being. I have received a few bumps and bites and been knocked down by a couple of elephants, but I have survived everything and handled almost every kind of emergency with animals.

I did not, however, handle births. The veterinarian had the job of bringing the babies into the world. Only once did a tiger take me by surprise. She was pregnant, but I could not tell, since she did not look pregnant and she worked during the whole time. Then one day she had two cubs. When the tigers had cubs, we tried to get the mothers to take care of them, but most of the time tigers reject their cubs. We let them stay with their mothers for a couple of hours, but if we saw that they were stepping on them and not caring for them, we had to take them out, otherwise they would have died soon after birth.

To avoid emergencies with the elephants, I took extra precautions whenever I thought it was necessary, and I never felt that any safeguards were a waste of time. One of our African elephants, thirteen-year-old Daisy, had long pointed tusks, and since she had become pretty frisky around my working men over the years, I cut and filed the points of her tusks in 1987 to make her slightly less dangerous. The next day she hit a groom and knocked him to the ground. I ran between them to save the groom, and as he rolled out of harm's way, she hit me straight on with her tusks and I was thrown backward onto the concrete floor. Luckily, I was wearing a fleece-lined jacket, or I would have been seriously hurt. Even luckier for me and the groom was that her tusks had been trimmed. Afterward I was sore, and the groom gave her a wide berth. I thanked God for letting us escape serious injury.

When we were in Chicago in 1989, I had more evidence of God's care. The temperatures were in the twenties every day, and I was worried that it would be that cold when it came time to bring the animals to the trains. When I utter my silent worries, they are like prayers. The day we left, the temperature was in the forties. I was truly grateful.

I had this feeling of protection all the time, not just when I was working, and my life was spared more than once. I had an especially close call when the circus train on which my family and I were living at the time was stationed in Washington, D.C., where we were performing. After a morning rehearsal, I went back to the train, put a deck chair outside our train car and rested in the sun. I had rolled onto my stomach and was sleeping when suddenly I awoke and sprang to my feet. As I leaped from the chair, the front tires of a large sewer truck, which had come to empty the train's sewer car, crushed it. I was shocked, but unharmed. The truck's operator had been driving forward but looking backward at a hose used to empty the sewer car, and he never saw me or my chair. I do not know why I awoke when I did or what made me jump up so fast. I only know that if I had not, I would have been killed. I have had a number of accidents that should have left me dead, and my friends were always surprised that I walked away from them.

I am grateful today that I have been fortunate enough to work with many different species of animals, and always successfully, unlike most trainers, who work with only one species. At Circus Williams I worked with horses, elephants, big cats, and a tremendous assortment of animals for the menagerie, including camels, llamas, and zebras. Llamas and camels required special care. Their bodies could be brushed, but only their feet and legs could be washed. Llamas originally come from high, cold regions, and we found it difficult to move them around in extreme heat. Many times during the summer when it was very hot, we never let them walk. We put them in the show bus with Tina's dogs and let them go back and forth that way.

I seldom had to organize special exercise sessions for these animals because the circus moved every second or third day and the animals got plenty of exercise walking to and from the trains. When we were touring, I rarely even found the time to practice with the animals before a show because of all my other responsibilities. Many animal trainers practice in the morning so that the performance will go smoothly in the afternoon or evening. Once I started creating many new acts, I did not have time to practice all the animals. I only had time in the morning to train the new or young animals. That is one of the reasons why my animals had to be so well trained, and why I had to concentrate so intensely during the show so that I would not mess up and cause the act to fall apart.

In America I also found that my mornings allowed only training time, and sometimes even that had to be worked into other parts of the day if we had a 10:30 A.M. show for schoolchildren. There is only a little bit of time between shows to work with the animals. Some people have the misconception that animal trainers go off to some mysterious place where they hole up with the animals and do not return to civilization until they are perfectly trained. That is not the case. I always had to find time to train them between shows, traveling, animal walks, and the myriad of other things the animals and I had to do. By 1990 I was working with twenty-one elephants, thirty-five horses, twenty-two tigers, four zebras, four ponies, three camels, three extra horses, and a couple of llamas.

Animals are not objects that can be put someplace and allowed to do nothing but stand there. After I got them and cared for them, they became part of my family—they became part of every one of us, Mark, Tina, and Sigrid. Whenever one of Tina's dogs became ill, we would all be concerned, and Tina would cry with worry. Our little elephant, Prince, was sick for the last two weeks of our 1989 engagement in Chicago. We were quite concerned and sad, and I did not sleep well until I knew that he was in good shape again. These animals are so close to my heart that I worry about them just as I would worry about a person. Each animal was as important in my life as a dog is to a person who has only that pet.

My philosophy of animal training, as I have said, was that above all else I had to respect each individual animal and each animal had to respect me. I believe that when respect drops out of the picture, or if it was never there to begin with, that is where cruelty steps in. In my lifetime I was never cruel to any animal, and I would be the unhappiest man alive if I had to work with anyone who was. I wish that kind of person would go through life without any luck. My luck comes from my animals and what I do with them, which makes me very happy. I can go to sleep at night very easily knowing that I have done right by my animals. My whole family is like that.

People have watched in awe as I worked with tigers and leopards, horses and elephants, and they wanted to believe that I have some strange power over them. What I had was the pure and unconditional kind of respect that I have been talking about. I never tried to destroy an animal's personality or break its spirit. I did not want a tiger to sit on a pedestal, hunched over, with its tail not moving, and be scared to death whenever I showed up. When I went into their quarters in the morning, the animals were happy to see me. I had to be firm and give them the right commands if I wanted to get the right response during training or a performance, but I wanted everybody to retain his and her personality.

This does not only apply to wild animals. It is the same with dog training. A person cannot work well with a dog who is scared to death and always crawling along the ground on her belly or walking with her tail between her legs. People want to see happy, lively dogs. They may not always do the right thing during a performance, but at least they are happy and they show it. The tigers would literally jump up and move around in their cages when they heard my voice in a room. They would push against the sides of their cages as I approached, waiting for an acknowledgment from me. When I first acquired them, all the tigers would want to do is play, and that is all I could let them do. I put each new animal in a large arena cage and let him run loose for a while so that I could see what kind of a creature he was and get an idea of his capabilities. As the animals got older, they had to understand that they could not play all the time, and that was when proper training and the right signs and commands became important. While they were being trained, I never beat them or punished them. What would that accomplish? My tools were touch and voice, and they are now my son's tools also.

Some people become upset when they see a trainer working with an elephant hook. A hook is basically used to give the animal direction, not to hurt it. When you see elephants fighting with each other, and how much power they have and the tremendous strength behind their thousands of pounds, you realize that it is impossible to hurt an elephant with a hook. They are so much more powerful than us. In the forty-three years that I have been in this business, I have never been able to figure out why elephants respect and obey us. Mind you, not all elephants are like this. There are animals who can never be trained and who will never respect a person. This kind of animal usually has an exceptionally strong mind and a mean personality. Captivity does not make them this way. Like people, animals have individual personalities, and some of them are mean.

I will not tolerate the use of drugs in animals or people. If I found out that someone on my staff was using illicit drugs, he was fired immediately. There was absolutely no chance that he would be kept on. I never gave drugs to my animals, and the most I ever took was a painkiller when my teeth were knocked out. My entire mouth was repaired by a dentist named Richard Hammett, who is also a dear friend, and I never even took a shot. People can, for the most part, control what goes into their bodies, but animals cannot stop a person from giving them drugs, and that constitutes cruelty.

There are people who believe that animal cruelty is part of the circus way of life. This is not true. I have never seen it where I worked in Europe or America. Of course I cannot speak for others, but I do not believe you can get any animal to do what you want if it is mistreated.

An animal-rights newspaper once wrote that when we load the elephants onto the trains, we repeatedly hit them. If we beat the elephants, how long would they continue going onto the train? We do the complete opposite. We move them onto the train with the same commands that are used during their walks. Mark carries two large bags of carrots with him so that when everybody is aboard, they are rewarded for another good loading.

In each of the Ringling troupes we have about 120 performers, between the ages of nineteen and twenty-five, and all are animal lovers. I cannot believe that any one of them would remain silent if he or she saw someone abuse an animal. Everybody is always around to see what we are doing. We have an open policy and open practices. You must do the right things under those conditions because everyone can see how the animals are handled. We are not working with people from old circus families, who will keep quiet about circus business, good or bad. We hire from the general population. Anyone can be a groom, a clown, a showgirl. We have all kinds of people walking around, and everyone can see what the others are doing. I have fired people because I did not like the way they treated the animals. Mistakes can happen. Grooms are bitten and kicked all the time, and sometimes animals and workers get hurt accidentally. Our rule for our workers is well known: Be careful. We do not want anyone to get hurt, but if you do, you do not punish the animals.

Animals know when they do something wrong, and they understand the difference between happy talk and when they are being scolded. One day a big African elephant with tusks pushed Piccolo to the ground. Piccolo never hurt anybody—he is much too small and much too concerned about the animals—but this elephant got ornery and lashed out at Piccolo for no particular reason. I was concerned, not only because I wanted to protect Piccolo but also because the elephant had to know that he had done something wrong so that he would not do it again. Mark and I stood at his left and right and yelled at him. You cannot soothe an animal when it does something bad, and say, "Ooooh, don't do this anymore, elephant." You must correct him and let him know that his conduct was improper. As with children, the tone of the voice is important. An elephant might remember being scolded for doing something wrong for as long as a year. Then it becomes history, and he might do the same thing again. For that reason Piccolo was not allowed near that elephant anymore. Scolding does not work with every elephant. I once had an elephant who pushed so many people, I was afraid he was going to kill somebody, so I gave him away.

Elephants are wonderful creatures to work with, but they are dangerous. I emphasize that because many people perceive them as being gentle giants. I always had to remind people that elephants are wild animals. Even my workers needed this reminder. I was always yelling at them to pay attention to how they approached the elephants, because I was the one who ended up hurt every time I had to save one of them.

My extreme concern about working around the elephants comes from my personal experiences. As much as I enjoyed working with them, there were times when the elephants gave me a big headache, literally. Although I have had a number of brushes with the elephants, one of the strangest and most harrowing experiences I had with any one of them occurred with our King Tusk (Tommy).

Tommy, an Indian elephant, is nine feet six inches tall. His tusks are eighteen inches in diameter at the base and six feet long, making him one of the largest male elephants in the world. At the age of forty-four, he is very powerful and weighs thirteen thousand pounds. At good times Tommy is quite gentle, and at bad times he is not so gentle. Kenny Feld bought Tommy in America and hired the trainer who had worked with him for twenty years.

One season we took Tommy and his trainer on the road with us. The trainer had already been with us for a year and a half, and although he and I had had a number of arguments, he worked well with Tommy. We never argued over the elephant, only personal matters. He had a drinking problem, which caused family problems, and I always told him that he was his own worst enemy. When he was drunk, he would become angry and terrible to deal with. He would

UNTAMED

talk badly about me to people at the circus and say that I was trying to get his elephant away from him. If I had wanted Tommy, I could have had him from the first day he joined Ringling, but I never wanted him. I had enough to do with the other elephants, and enough problems. I just wanted this trainer to stay sober and do his job correctly. But it did not work out, and in the middle of the season, on a Saturday with three shows, he disappeared. He performed Tommy at the first show and then did his vanishing act.

I had never been close with Tommy, and I did not know the commands this other trainer had used with him. The man had been so disagreeable that I never tried to learn what he did with the elephant so that if something went wrong I could step in. This was my fault, and also Kenny Feld's, because from the beginning he should have told the other trainer, "I want you and also Gunther to perform King Tusk so that if something happens, he knows what you are doing." We both made the mistake, and it never happened again, but we learned the hard way. After this experience I made certain that I knew the commands of every other trainer who was involved with the show.

When his trainer disappeared, Tommy immediately became my responsibility, and I had to go out and perform with him. I used my commands, and he responded well enough to do the night show on Saturday and two shows on Sunday. I then spent some time practicing with Tommy to teach him my commands and improve our performances, and I presented him in the show perfectly for months, until he went into musth. In that phase the levels of testosterone in male elephants rise extremely high, and their attitudes change. They become terribly aggressive, cranky, brooding, and unpredictable. They hallucinate and swing their trunks wildly at imagined objects and refuse to eat. During such periods, which occur several times a year in some elephants and once a year in others, they do not give a hoot about anything and will challenge anybody.

I had been giving Tommy quite a bit of exercise, which the other trainer had not done. I took him out every day and walked him around, and after a while the elephant really looked good and was in good shape. On September 8, 1988, a few months after taking over Tommy's act, we were working in Kansas City, and I organized a morning practice for some new horses so that they would get exercise. The time I spent with the horses cut into the time I would have spent walking Tommy, and I felt guilty. If I had left him on his chain and just went ahead and did the two shows that were scheduled for that day, perhaps nothing would have happened. But I looked at him and said, "Come on, Tommy, we'll go out a little bit, too." Normally there would have been nothing wrong with this, but Tommy was in musth, and I made a mistake by taking him out in that condition. Then I did two other things wrong. I stepped the wrong way and made the wrong movements while telling Tommy to move on, and I had people around him with whom he was unfamiliar. I moved too far in front of the elephant, and in an instant he jerked his powerful head, hit me with his tusks, and sent me sailing into the air. People who witnessed this said I flew backward about eighteen feet.

I slammed against the concrete, hitting my back, head, and shoulders and jamming my elbows and arms. I was unconscious for a few seconds because my head was badly hurt. When I came to, I remembered a dream I had had a few nights before. Normally when an elephant pushes somebody to the ground, he immediately goes right in behind him for the kill. In the dream the exact same events had occurred between me and Tommy, but he did not charge me after I was on the ground. I asked him in the dream, "Why don't you kill me?" and Tommy replied telepathically, "Because I don't want to." It seemed ridiculous at the time, so I told no one about the dream, not even Sigrid. Now I was on the ground where Tommy had put me in real life, and I had to see if he was going to follow through with the attack. I could barely move, but I managed to lift my head a few inches so that I could look for Tommy. My vision cleared enough for me to see his ponderous frame, and Tommy had not moved at all. He was still in the same place he had been when he hit me. I knew he was not going to kill me, and I tried to get up, but collapsed.

My workers crowded around me, and although they did not want me to move, I made them help me to my feet. I felt awful, but I had to let Tommy know that I was still in charge. I shouted at him, then took him back to the stables and yelled at him at the top of my lungs. My workers summoned Sigrid from the train, and when I finished scolding Tommy, she took me to the hospital. My hip, back, and elbows were bruised, and my head was split open and I was dizzy. A doctor wanted to admit me to the hospital, but I refused. I let him treat me with stitches and bandages, and then Sigrid helped me out to the parking lot. My knees gave way before we got to the car, and she had to help me to my feet and into the car. She was worried about me and wanted me to rest, but I insisted that she take me back to the circus and Tommy.

Tommy had to see me. He had to be shown that he had not destroyed me and that I was still the boss. I made my way over to him and stared him square in the eyes. I was badly hurt and could hardly move my head, but I looked long and hard at his face, then left the stable.

Elephants are like tanks with no drivers. How do you stop them? There is nothing in the world that can stop elephants when they want to do something. I simply had to trust them that they would not kill me, and they had to trust that I would be humane and attentive to their needs.

I did so much to get close to Tommy, but it never

worked out. He never did anything again to hurt me, but we never developed a close relationship. He shut me out, and sometimes he was so distant and still that it was eerie. Tommy was the only animal I ever worked with who gave me a bad feeling right from the beginning of our relationship. He always made me uneasy, but I never let him know it. I was in charge and tried to treat him with as much respect and warmth as I treated the other elephants. Adding to the weird feeling I had about the incident with Tommy was that it had happened close to my birthday. It seems that things always happened to me around my birthday (and Sigrid's, which is September 8), and I still have to be extra careful during that time of the year.

Tommy gave other people who worked with him the willies too. He always had to be handled with greater care than any of the other elephants because sometimes he seemed like a time bomb. I believed that if I was ever going to be killed by an animal, it would be by Tommy. I worked with him until the end of the season and then never did anything with him again. I told Kenny Feld that I did not want to handle Tommy anymore, so he moved him to the Blue Show. To this day Tommy is a member of the Ringling circus. He receives the same care as the rest of our elephants, but unlike them, Tommy does not perform. He is displayed only in the opening and finale.

I believe that when Tommy hit me, he was actually challenging my authority. Elephants have a great sense of their individual capabilities, and I am certain that Tommy knows he is "King Tusk." He was showing me that he could take me out any time the circumstances permitted. Tommy and I had a showdown, and it ended in a draw only because he wanted it that way.

From my other elephants I have felt love and affection. Assan, Nellie, Congo, Tetchie, and Prince are still very attached to me. Assan nuzzles up to me as if hugging me. If I am nearby and Assan is loose, nobody can hold her. She comes straight to me and stays with me. She rubs her head against my shoulder as if to say, "I love you, I love you." I let her do that for a while, and I pet her and talk nicely to her, but then I have to say, "That is enough," because if I do not, I will lose control over her. I had to know where to draw the line because these are dangerous animals, regardless of any emotions they show.

Some animals, including elephants, never want to grow up. They always want to act like children. Mary is close to forty years old, yet she always acts like a little baby. She likes to roll around and put her head on the ground. Assan and Mary love the water. They roll in it and spray it over their heads more than any of the other elephants. They can only be allowed to do that for short periods of time because elephants have to be washed carefully to ensure that they are thoroughly cleaned, and it is tough to do that when they are doing whatever they want. Elephants can get out of line very quickly. You must let them play for only a few minutes, or they start acting silly and the next thing you know they are fighting.

Trainers can never let a big group of elephants out on their own in a fenced-in area because of their inclination to fight. I occasionally let them graze on grassy areas so that they could change their diet, but I could only let them do that for ten minutes at a time, because after that they started messing up the grass and pushing each other. As long as they are hungry, they concentrate on eating and not on each other, but once the hunger is gone, they start playing.

Elephants, like people, have their own little quirks and idiosyncrasies. I discovered this one day when I was sitting in the elephant tent and got hit on the head very hard. I looked around to see what hit me and found a stone near my foot. I picked it up and threw it away in the direction of an elephant named Sabu. The stone rolled near his foot, Sabu picked it up with his trunk, and threw it back at me. I was surprised because I never expected him to do that. A few seconds later he threw another stone at me, which hit me in the mouth and split my lip. I had to move because as long as I sat there, he threw stones at me. He now plays catch with the workers during the day, with everything from stones to apples. During the summer Mark collects tender branches from trees for the elephants to munch on. When the branches are fairly large, the workers have to run away from the elephants because they throw the branches around.

One of Congo's few quirks is that she always liked to lag behind, even when she was young. She has never liked walking single-file with the other elephants. She simply does not want to be bothered. Over the years, during animal walks and exercise sessions, I would have to shout at her every once in a while to bring up the rear and hold the group together.

Suzie, a fifty-six-year-old elephant, is known as a chronic complainer. She becomes especially vocal—making noises and trumpeting—whenever she is told to do things. Cheetah is the same way. Cheetah and another elephant named May are very fat, and all their extra weight can make walking tiresome for everyone. In 1989 we bought a big trailer so that when the train is far from the arena, May and Cheetah can be driven instead of walked.

Elephants can suffer from allergies, too. I established a policy many years ago whereby every winter we oil the elephants' skin. Their skin can dry out, and unlike elephants in the wild, who can rub against trees to remove dry skin, our elephants must rely on us for relief. Oiling keeps their skin supple. We oil their bodies once a year, but once a week we use it around their eyes. Elephants' eyes water heavily—it is their way of cleaning them—but that can dry out the skin around them. Oiling helps prevent that. We also put it around their toenails to keep that skin soft. We have one elephant named Rhanie who is allergic to oil. The first time we used it on her, her eyes and feet swelled and became itchy, so she never got the treatment again.

Although elephants thoroughly enjoy baths and would love to be washed every day, I never bathed them unless the weather was warm. Elephants are highly susceptible to arthritis, and they shiver and freeze easily and take a long time to warm up. If I felt the slightest chill in the air, the elephants had to wait for their baths.

I have been with some of these elephants for forty years. Tetchie joined Circus Williams in 1948, and we have been together since then. Nellie showed up in 1951. Congo arrived in 1956. I got all of them when they were babies, so young and small, and have watched them grow to be so much bigger, taller, and more powerful. We are all growing old together. It is rare for someone to buy an adult elephant, unless one knows the background and who the trainer was and what he did. (That is one way to avoid the kinds of problems I had with Tommy.) I always thought it was better to work with an animal who was brand-new so that I could start a relationship with someone who was never hurt by a human and had no bad memories of people.

Elephants seem to remember everything. I believe if I taught an elephant a trick and then did not do it for twenty years, after rehearsing it two times the elephant would remember exactly what to do and would do it. I did not see Tommy for a full year, and when I went to the winter quarters to see him and I talked to him, he recognized me right away. He shifted in his place and moved his ears as he had done in the past anytime I spoke to him. I was no more comfortable around him during that visit than I had been when I performed with him.

Working with the elephants is extremely pleasurable,

and I had a lot of fun teaching them to do everything from standing on their heads to break dancing. People love elephants, but if something happens suddenly—a train goes by; a truck backfires; a bat, pigeon, or mouse gets in their tent—they can either explode or continue to be gentle and do nothing. If something goes wrong in their minds, even if they have worked with you for twenty years, elephants can hurt or kill you. They can be like the neighbor you have known for forty years who was always a nice guy until one day something goes wrong and he kills somebody and no one can believe it. This happens to animals too. It has nothing to do with them being in captivity. It just happens. Anyone who works with animals—including the seemingly domesticated horses—can be killed at any time.

I find horses very spooky. Most of them do not develop close emotional ties with people and are dangerous because they kick and bite. I have worked with horses since I was a little boy, but I have always preferred working with animals with whom I could have a closer relationship. With the horses you just practice, then send them away.

I did not dislike training horses, especially when everything worked out well, but it took a lot of practice and a lot of attention. They are smart, but require a great deal of repetition before they learn an act or trick. I presented horses until the day I stopped performing, and I was always proud of the work I did with them.

I used only stallions, who are very territorial, so there was a lot of fighting among them. I was always concerned that somebody would get hurt, and I had a number of accidents with them myself. I have been kicked, stepped on, thrown over the chain to which they are tied in the stable, and thrown off their backs. I have been kicked right in the face and in the elbow. Kicked. I was always kicked. Horses are forever kicking. Once I was kicked in the teeth and my lip was split open so badly across the bottom that a specialist had to rebuild my mouth from the inside out. I have been through everything with the horses. I was lucky not to break any bones in those accidents, but the injuries I did receive hurt very much.

Only two of the teeth in the front of my mouth, top and bottom rows, are my own. The rest have been replaced several times. One incident that cost me my teeth occurred when I was loading the horses onto a train. Whenever the horses are loaded or unloaded, they must be brought close together, and that is a dangerous thing to do with stallions, because it gives them the opportunity to fight. On this particular occasion there was a lot of sporadic fighting among them. Anytime the horses fought, I had to run over and separate them, and later on, when he was old enough, my son did the same thing. When horses are locked in combat and hanging close together, the odds on us getting hurt are high because we have to get in close to loosen their leads and separate them. That is what I was doing this day when the horses started kicking, and one of them kicked me right in the face.

I was stunned at first, then the pain hit me. There is really no way to describe the pain associated with being kicked in the face by a horse. It is incredible. My face and shirt were covered with blood, but before I took care of myself, I separated those horses.

This happened not once but a total of three times in Germany and America. Whenever the horses fought, I could not tell someone else to endanger himself by separating them because I had been hurt before and wanted to protect myself from further injury. I intervened myself, and was hurt time and again. I could never allow myself to become afraid of being injured, because getting hurt could not be separated from the rest of my work. If I had dwelled on past injuries, how would I have been able to step into a cage filled with leopards?

One of the great things about my business is that I could change the types of animals with whom I worked and go on to develop new and different relationships. I worked with lions in Germany and America, but I found that they are like bears, and that kind of relationship is not for me. I was never a lion man. Lions can be either very nice or very mean, and because they are also more family-oriented than other cats, they are harder to train. Tigers and leopards live independently, so it is easier to build individual relationships with them.

Everybody called me a lion tamer after I did some work with lions in America, but I never was. I created an unprecedented act in which I rode two horses with two lions sitting in front of me on the mounts. I presented that act for two years. I next tried to create a new mixed act with horses and lions, but it did not work out. The lions never really offered the kind of friendship I look for with animals, so I did not create any other acts with them.

I felt that of all the leopards with whom I worked, Kenny and Blackie really loved me. They were very affectionate toward me, which confused anyone who knew just how vicious leopards can be. Whenever I got close to Kenny, he would rub his head against my face. Blackie did the same thing, but she always had to be watched because she liked to bite my fingers and slap at my hands.

Though I did not always feel loved by all of the animals, I never felt hated by any animal. I did not integrate exceptionally mean animals into my acts, and I would not keep a disagreeable animal long enough to let him hate me. We received one leopard who was already pretty big, and he was so mean we could not even take him out of the cage. I immediately sent him back to the supplier. I never wanted to have to hurt animals to get their respect, and I did not want uncooperative, unlikable animals around.

I believe Kenny enjoyed lying on my shoulders. Performers at other circuses had placed leopards on their shoulders, but they never took them outside the cage before an audience. I used to drape Kenny over my shoulders, then walk out of the cage and around the floor with him. That made that part of my leopard act different from what other people had done.

Kenny was not docile. He was a single-minded individual with a strong personality. I often worked with him in promotional spots and commercials for the circus, and he never wanted to do what I told him to do. Above all else he hated to sit very long in one place. I constantly had to remind myself that he was a leopard with all the will and determination of the species, and when we were in front of cameras, I had to find the right moment to get him to do the correct thing so that we could get it on film.

I broke up the leopard act after six years at the request of Kenny Feld. He knew how much time I was spending with those animals and how taxing it was for me. They certainly had become the focal point of my work. It took a tremendous amount of patience to handle them, and if I were asked to do it again, it might not be a question of having enough patience. Now that I know what it is like to train these animals, I think I would be too afraid of being hurt to work with them.

Each leopard had to wear two lead chains during training. They were the only animals I had to train with chains (except for tigers who were trained to jump on elephants' and horses' backs); otherwise they would have jumped out of the cage and attacked people. None of my tigers or lions ever wore collars when they were trained or performed. The leopards never liked wearing collars, and every day that I had that act, I had to bring twenty leopards into the cage, put collars and leashes on each of them (a nerve-racking thing to have to do before a practice), then take them off when practice was finished. The leopards moved so fast that before I would have a chance to move my hand, I would see a flash of claws and teeth. They tried to maul me every time I put the collars on or took them off.

When I first began working with the leopards, before I had a relationship with any of them, they constantly threatened to attack me. Once they were trained to come into the cage alone and jump up onto their pedestals and sit there and I knew they were not going to try to attack me anymore, they did not need the chains. But for the first couple of months it was terribly difficult work, and chains were a necessity. The chains were always put directly onto the leopards so that I could grab the links if one of the animals took off or got into a fight. I never chained a leopard to a prop, because I did not want to take a chance that he would jump down and accidentally hang himself. The chains were removed for performing, and that meant that the cage in which the leopards worked had to be completely closed off so that they would not jump out through the top and get into an audience.

I had only one accident while working in the cage with the leopards, and that happened when I tried to protect Henry Schroer, who was acting as my assistant, and a leopard jumped on me. I was not badly hurt, just scratched up a bit. My hands and arms are covered with traces of scars from incidents like that.

The leopards presented a number of problems for my working men and train crew because they were so fast that the men could not always get out of their way before they struck. Our train master has a big scar on his left side from a swipe by a leopard. Leopards slip their paws through the bars of the cages, and then they swipe at you so fast that you can barely see their paws move. Blackie was the worst one for this. When loading the leopards onto trains, we had to cover their cages and make sure that their long tails were protected so that they did not get cut or torn. Upon arriving at our destination, the leopards went to the arenas in cages, along with the tigers and bears. Sometimes the cages were included in the parade of the animals, but most of the time they were transported separately.

Because we could not even pass close to their cages without being hit by them, I sometimes became so upset that I would open the cage of whoever had tried to claw me or someone else, slap my hand on the cage floor, and shout, "Okay, come on! Let's go! I'm inside now!" And the leopard would do nothing. I do not think they ever believed I would open the door and go into the cage, so they were stunned when I did it. But as soon as I closed the cage, the offender would swipe at me again.

They also tried to hit us while we were giving them food and water. We had little room to pass between the cages, and everyone was always jumpy during feeding time and whenever they worked around them. The leopards had to make only the slightest movement to get someone to practically jump out of his or her skin. Once, in Portland, while one of my men was giving water to the leopards, I sneaked up and grabbed him from behind as a joke. The guy let the water can fall and screamed, "They got me, they got me, they got me," and ran out. That is how spooked everyone was working around those leopards.

At the height of the act we had thirty leopards—more than twenty spotted ones, three black ones, two mountain lions, and all their little babies. When the mothers did not take care of the babies, Sigrid did. Life around the circus was much easier for everyone after we got rid of the leopards. They were beautiful and made a fantastic act, and two of my best friends came out of that group, but I do not believe I would accept that challenge again.

When I broke up the act, I kept Kenny and Blackie, gave the mountain lions to a private family in Oregon, and Ringling sold the rest of the leopards to a large South American circus. Henry was hired by the owner of that circus to take care of them, but that did not work out. Once I was not around to protect and work with him, Henry was not safe enough or sure enough around the leopards to perform with them. Those leopards ended up in a South American zoo.

The tigers offered quite a different experience. Like leopards, tigers do not naturally live in groups, so it is tough to bring them together as a group every day for practice and performance. They do not always have a good time when they are together. I had to make sure that I did everything correctly every day so they did not get hurt or fight. After two tigers fight, the relationship between them is never the same. One will always be scared, and the other will attack him or her again at any time.

Although my tigers seldom fought, when they did, I always jumped in to separate them so that they would know that I was doing my best to protect them. Sometimes they were hurt, and sometimes I got hurt. If a tiger was unhappy with me or blamed me for something, he showed his displeasure by being nasty, or "talking back" when told to do something, or refusing to work. I would have to reassure him with treats and touches, backed up by firmness so that he would know that I was still in charge.

People have asked me which is more ferocious, a lion or a tiger. I believe the lion is a big showman and has a way of blustering to frighten people. The lion has a bigger mouth than a tiger, and opens it wide for shock value when he is really upset. Blustering aside, however, I would not want to have a fight with a big lion or a tiger. I do not know who is more powerful, stronger, and faster, and I would not want to find out in a hand-to-claw confrontation.

I did not get all of my tigers when they were cubs. Cubs are easier to train and to build deep affectionate relationships with. I got some tigers who were two years old and had never been handled by a person. They took a little longer to train, and I never had extremely close relationships with them, but we respected each other, even though they did not particularly care to be touched.

When he closed his act, Charley Baumann gave me two Siberian tigers. They are bigger and slightly tougher to train than Bengal tigers. They have much longer backs, which make it difficult for them to sit up, so they need more time in training in learn even simple tricks. I trained both of them, but I never touched them. Some Bengal tigers like to be touched, but Siberians absolutely hate it and will not tolerate touching under any circumstances. I trained them only with rewards of meat and hand signals, never by touch. Sometimes, just to make the effort, I would walk past the Siberians and touch them lightly on their backs, and right away they would be on their feet, very upset. Tigers are like house cats—some become affectionate toward people, and some do not like to be touched.

I had no compunctions about coming up from behind and pushing some tigers to give them direction or get them to move off their rumps. Giving them a nudge on the butt is part of their early training and a way of teaching them to get down from the props a little faster. It must be done from behind, since tigers will not tolerate pushing from the front and will assert themselves by using their claws.

A trainer can only physically push tigers as long as they allow it, and that is usually only while they are young and small. They are like little kids—you push them in the right direction until they will no longer tolerate it. When the tigers became much bigger, I never went behind them, because I knew they were powerful enough to hurt me, and I respected their status as adults who did not want to be pushed into anything. I then substituted other training techniques for pushing movements. For example, to get an adult tiger to move faster from his pedestal, I would throw a piece of meat to the ground so that the tiger would quickly jump down to get it.

While I was training tigers and leopards, Sigrid was raising them. She took care of quite a few cubs, which involved a lot of work. Like human babies, cubs must be fed several times during the night; someone must clean their bottoms when they move their bowels until they are big enough to do it for themselves; and they must have the proper mix of milk, as well as the right vaccinations. It is better for the cubs when their mothers raise them, but often the mothers push them aside. When that happens, the best thing to ensure a cub's health is for the veterinarian to get a bit of the mother's blood and put it under the cub's skin to help build up its immune system. When cubs do not get milk from their mothers, their immune systems do not work correctly, and often the little cats die. The mother's milk contains antibodies which are necessary to provide a cub with immunity to bacteria. Her blood contains the same antibodies. We lost some cubs when they were small, but the longer we worked with tigers, the more we learned from the doctors about how to take care of them and nurture them.

Raising those little guys was always touchy, and a lot of time and love went into their care. Then Sigrid would have to give them up, and it was like sending a child to school for the first time. We raised the cubs on the road and kept an eye on them around the clock. They were never left alone, because they required constant attention. When we were working, we had to take them from the train to the dressing room, and from the dressing room back to the train. Sigrid went so far as to put a television set in our dressing room so that when we were not there, the cubs would have "company." We always had cartons filled with little leopards and tigers.

Sigrid cleaned a lot of manure in her life, but she never complained. When you raise cubs, they quickly become part of the family. And as with children, you have to know when to let them go because they must learn to be individuals and grow strong enough to survive in a group. Sigrid kept the little cubs clean, prepared all their food, and made certain that they always had fresh boxes. I did whatever I could for them during the day, and I set aside time to play with them and just be near them so that they would get to know me. When they were sick, Sigrid, or I, or both of us sat with them through the night, just as we did when our own children were ill. We held and caressed them reassuringly, kept them warm, and made certain that they were seen by a veterinarian if we could not help them.

When the adult cats were sick, I offered them the same reassurance I had given them when they were babies. Many, many nights, I stayed in the stable with sick tigers or leopards, I gave them water, encouraged them to eat by hand feeding them, and stayed while the doctor examined them. They knew I was there, and they looked to me for this kind of support. I would not leave their sides for a minute when any of the tigers or leopards were sick.

It was also incumbent upon me to make sure that their cages and bodies were clean. When we washed the tigers' cages, we also washed the occupants, and that was a sight to see. Some tigers loved water and lay in their cages relaxing while it washed over them. Some were scared to death of it, and as soon as the hoses were turned on, they were on their feet trying to get away from the water. They scrunched up their faces and closed their eyes like house cats in a bathtub, nervously waiting for the bath to be over.

I found that the best animals were the easiest to work with. There was always a tiger like that. The tiger who went on the elephant's or horse's back in the mixed act had to be a favorite because he had to wear a collar and leash while he was being trained to jump onto the elephant or horse. A favorite would allow me to touch him while putting the leash on and taking it off, but there was still a danger of being bitten. Whenever I performed big cats outside a cage, such as in the mixed acts, I did everything myself instead of working other performers or assistants into the acts, because I was worried about them being bitten or clawed.

Each tiger must be treated individually, because everyone is different. Some tigers are more likely to go for people than others. When I worked with new tigers, I would be consistent with each, and while working with them their distinct personalities emerged. One tiger will learn something fast. Another will take a couple of months, or maybe even a year or two, to learn only to sit up. You may use the same amount of time and the same style with each, yet abilities and the speed with which they learn differs from animal to animal. Sometimes I would become irritated because they did not learn at the same speed, but I knew I had to have patience. There was no way to estimate how long it would take to train each tiger.

One tiger, named Madras, has lousy balance. Because of that I never took the time to teach him to sit up. He is not one of the nicest-looking tigers I ever had, but I kept him in the act for many years because his character is so pleasant. I never wanted any animal to be kept in a cage if it was not going to have a chance to perform. Nobody was ever locked up and forgotten about. If I decided not to keep an animal, I found a place for it in a zoo or with private owners.

I always taught each tiger several different tricks so that they could stand in for each other when necessary, and also keep busy. Every trick was easy for them, but they did not necessarily want to do every trick, so I always had to find the right one for the right animal. In my farewell tour, during 1989–90, I had two tigers who could hold a fire stick. It was not easy to teach, because some tigers were afraid of fire, and I had to find out which tigers were not. Then the work began. Teaching a tiger to hold a fire stick or baton requires special techniques. First of all, to get them to hold the baton, I could not open their mouths as I would a dog's to take something out of it. By repeatedly placing sticks in their mouths I taught the tigers to take the sticks and hold them indefinitely. When I rewarded them with a piece of meat and said, "Good," they knew they could let the sticks fall. After a while a tiger knows what is going on and performs his tricks without rewards or prodding. That makes it look easy to the audiences.

People seldom had any conception of how long it took to train the animals before they could be presented in a show. One of the mixed acts I created for Circus Williams took two years to perfect. It took that long because I only had time to practice two or three days a week. It is tough to train animals when you have so little time and want to do so many difficult things. The years went by as if they were days, and suddenly there was this wonderful act with horses, elephants, and tigers.

The mixed act with the leopards and mountain lions was difficult to create. Every leopard required an exceptional amount of training time to get it to sit on a prop, listen to my voice, pay attention to my words, and follow commands. Do this twenty-two times a day with each leopard and it eats up a lot of time. If we were going to spend that much time together and not be the worse for it, my animals and I had to have good relationships. I had so many accidents in the tiger and leopard cages that I cannot count them, but they occurred when I broke up fights, not because the animals attacked me. It is the same as with humans. Many times you go between two people to stop a fight and you are the one who gets hurt. Does it take courage to separate fighting animals? Absolutely not. It requires years of experience and time spent building relationships with them. When I moved in on fighting animals, I was separating my old friends, not my old enemies. That made a big difference, but it was still perilous.

An animal trainer must always expect the unexpected. Nobody knows when the serious or fatal accident will occur. But it is easy to believe your life is in danger when you see two five-hundred-pound tigers fighting. The sweat beads up on your face in seconds, and you must react instantly. There is no time to think about the danger that, in a situation like that, increases with every breath. I have been in many situations that could have led to accidents, but quick reactions saved me and the animals who were involved. From one minute to the next you never know what is going to happen when you are dealing with wild animals.

One of the secrets to reducing the risk in my work was finding the right animals for each act. Many elephants, for example, run from horses. I had to find horses and elephants for my mixed act who were not afraid of each other. Unlike the tigers, many of whom fear fire, the leopards were not afraid of anything. It never bothered leopards to jump through hoops of fire. When I was looking for animals, I turned to several different sources, including animal suppliers. Zoos are very particular about giving animals away, but they were not afraid to entrust them to my care. A zoo once gave me five free tigers, two of whom worked with me until I stopped performing. When I was rounding up animals for the leopard act, five leopards were given to me free by a zoo. Kenny was the best leopard of all, and I paid nothing for him.

Audiences cannot appreciate the variety of training methods employed to create each act. Working with so many types of animals from such a wide variety of places showed me that all animals really are smart; they only have to be taught differently. Camels, for example, are much smarter than horses, and much easier to work with. They kick and bite as horses do, but they respond faster to commands and tricks. I worked with my share of camels over the years and enjoyed them enormously because funny situations were always unfolding around them.

Camels jump around like crazy, with all four legs flying in the air, and this makes them look comical. The grooms were always afraid they would be kicked while working around them. Camels are slow to get started, so someone must go behind them and push them by the butt. The moment they are touched, they start jumping, and heaven help anyone in their way. But they also act funny when they are free to play, always giving us something to laugh about during camel practice. They run around and flail their legs and sometimes do splits and slide down to the ground. They also spit, bite, and kick, and they can be mean too. They can take a man's finger off in one bite. But in the end they are likable animals.

Llamas share some bad habits with camels, one of which is spitting. They spit so much that it is hard to get near them. Believe me, it is not nice to be spit on by a llama. The saliva smells terrible, and there is so much of it every time they spit that it gets all over you. I always tried to be nice to them and feed them special treats like carrots and apples or whatever they wanted to eat. I would give them the food, then try to get close to them and make friends . . . but for what? All of a sudden they would tilt their heads back and spit at me. They deliberately aim at your face, and before you have a chance to duck, you are hit. Whenever they did this to me, I would get so upset that I would jump around as if I were walking on hot coals. It made no sense to punish them, though, so I did nothing and hoped they would not do it again. But they always did.

Zebras are also difficult animals to work with because they act so wild. This also makes them dangerous. Whenever we ordered zebras, they would arrive in a box directly from Africa and they would be completely out of control. Zebras' hooves grow unevenly and must be cut and shaped. It is extremely dangerous to lift their feet to work on them because of the possibility of being kicked. Someone was always hurt while working on them.

The only protection zebras have is their ability to bite and kick. They kick with the same concentrated power as giraffes and can kill a person with just one blow. They also kick very precisely. I could hold a stick behind a zebra, and it would kick the stick and make it fly twenty feet into the air. They spook quickly, even faster than horses, and consequently must be handled with terrific care. Yet I was able to create an act in which I put harnesses on zebras, rode them, and got them to perform as well as horses. I was proud of them.

The only animal I have found to be completely untrainable for performance is an average house cat. These small cats take advantage of their owners' love and, for the most part, do as they please. They are totally independent and take over their environment from day one. Every animal can be trained to do some tricks, but house cats are limited by their personalities. As big and powerful as they are, buffaloes can be trained to do tricks over and over again. Pigs, cows, and yaks—all can be trained. It is just a matter of how much repetition each animal needs to learn something. In Germany we always had buffaloes in the show. When you get them young and raise them yourself, buffaloes can be trained without a problem. If you get them a little bit older, there may be problems, especially if they are mean. In Germany I created mixed acts with buffaloes, camels, and yaks.

One of my biggest undertakings, literally and figuratively, was the care and training of Dickie, the giraffe. Circus Williams had owned one in Germany, but he had been part of the menagerie and never performed in the show, mainly because I was too busy to train him. I was certain that giraffes could be taught to perform, and in my quest to create unusual acts for Ringling every season, I set out to acquire one. That is how Dickie came into my life.

Dickie was born in the Busch Gardens wild animal park in Florida, and the circus bought him when he was only three weeks old. The Ringling Brothers and Barnum & Bailey circuses had exhibited giraffes long before I came to America. A giraffe was part of Barnum & Bailey's 1895 show, and for three years, beginning in 1893, the Ringling Brothers Circus had one named Mamie. More were added to both operations, and after they merged in 1919, their new show included four of the spindly creatures. In 1938 a giraffe named Edith (also called Soudana) became the last such animal to perform in the United States, but they were displayed in menageries until 1964. I thought it was time to bring a giraffe into the spotlight again.

Because Dickie was so young when he joined our family, the responsibility of caring for yet another baby animal fell on Sigrid's shoulders. She bottle-fed Dickie four to five times a day and helped keep him clean. My job was to build a relationship with him, and that was not easy because giraffes are not very family-oriented. It took a long time for me to form an emotional bond with Dickie. I knew of only one way to build that relationship, and that was by spending every available minute with him and, once he was weaned off the bottle, doing everything for him myself. This turned into a project as time-consuming as it was with the leopards, but I was not about to give up.

Dickie needed special treatment. Giraffes had traditionally been worked on mud out of concern for their fragile legs, but because we were primarily working inside modern arenas, I had to work with him on concrete floors over which we had lain rubber mats. I had to be extra careful that the giraffe never stepped off the rubber, because with one slip he could have broken the middle bone in his legs, and that would have been disastrous. This was especially stressful during his early training, when all he wanted to do was play and jump around.

In the past, performances by giraffes had generally been limited to being paraded around the rings during big production numbers. I had no intention of walking Dickie around the circus at the end of a halter when I was doing such a variety of things with other animals. I wanted him to be featured in a special way, so I created an act in which he worked with elephants. A giraffe had never before been teamed with pachyderms. He also joined in several production numbers, including one in which Mark rode on his back.

Training Dickie was not like training tigers. At times he seemed so distant and caught up in his own little world that I could not make any mental connection with him. That was frustrating, especially since I was spending so much time with him, day and night. After months of work I still did not see any significant progress. I would go home at night totally disheartened and wondering if Dickie would ever respond to my training or show any signs that he was developing a warm relationship with me.

After several months of bottle-feeding, I changed Dickie's diet to hay, sweet feed, corn, oats, molasses, and treats of raw vegetables. I personally brought him all of his food and water and stayed with him while he ate. I would not even allow my working men to exercise him. I made the time to do all these things myself in order to show him how much I cared, and because I was always worried that something would happen to him. I even groomed him myself. Had I been two feet taller, it would not have made that task any easier. Giraffes are so tall that a person must stand on a ladder to groom them, and this is what I did to brush Dickie's neck and body and damp-sponge his coat. Ladder climbing around a giraffe can be pretty spine-tingling because they like to kick at anything that disturbs or annoys them and, when happy, they jump around like children. Like a zebra, a giraffe's only protection is its legs. They are very agile and can kick to the front, back, and sideways. They miss nothing. A giraffe can kill a lion, its only natural enemy, with one kick.

We took Dickie on the road with us as we had all of our other babies, and he thrived under my care. He had his own customized semitrailer, which I drove from town to town. By the time he was two years old, Dickie was eating some fifty pounds of hay each day—about one-third to one-half of what the average elephant eats. He was healthy and growing steadily toward his adult height and weight of eighteen to twenty feet and 3,500 pounds. He was a combination reticulated and Masai giraffe, with dark chestnut-brown markings and narrow white lines on a rich, dark background. Dickie was a beautiful animal, and I grew to love him. After months of working with him, I believe he came to love me too.

I trained our giraffe as I had the other animals, primarily with voice commands. Once Dickie began responding to my voice, I introduced him to whistle commands, which turned out to be fun for both of us. Giraffes are mute, so the only way Dickie could communicate with me was by knocking his feet against the wood that surrounded his pen. Dickie was enthusiastic when he used his special form of sign language, and he always made me laugh. We practiced for quite some time before Dickie was ready to be incorporated into the show. Finally, when he was two and a half years old, I introduced him to our audiences, and he was an immediate sensation. Dickie became the first giraffe to perform in the Ringling Brothers and Barnum & Bailey Circus in more than forty years.

Dickie had to have unique living and traveling quarters because of his height. We bought a truck—an eighteen-wheeler with air-conditioning, and heating—to transport him to wherever we were performing. I regularly had to go inside the truck to feed him and spend time with him, which was risky because of the potential for being kicked. Dickie never did kick me, but he sure came close a couple of times.

I performed with Dickie for two very stressful years. Fans loved him, and he certainly added a unique touch to the show, but he required much more attention than I could continue to give him. I felt guilty that I was spending so much time with a single animal—time that had to be taken away from everybody else. I did not want the other animals and acts to suffer, and I knew that my responsibilities with Dickie were not going to lessen with time, so I decided to give him up and close that act.

UNTAMED

That was one of the most difficult decisions I ever made, but I believed it was for the greater good. I had not stopped performing with the other animals nor had I given up my other responsibilities while working with Dickie, and it sometimes seemed as if I were going nonstop, twenty-four hours a day. I was under constant tension. The slightest, most innocent-looking things had the potential for disaster, and I lived with that stress every day. Something as simple as changing a costume could mean big headaches for me.

I had problems with the animals every time we changed the colors of the circus. Different-colored plumes confuse them, and they react accordingly. Every second year, when I changed the color of my costume for the new season, I had to introduce it to the animals carefully. Wearing the costume, I would slowly walk between their cages or around the elephants and horses, while talking as I went, to let them know it was me.

Even with the precautions I took, I had several problems because of costume changes. During one visit to Chicago, I was wearing a white costume with gold trim, which included a short bolero vest. I usually wore tights and that type of vest when I performed with the tigers. Tina was concerned about me because the arena was so cold, and she suggested that I wear a closed jacket. Each of my costumes had a full-length matching jacket, so I changed from the vest to a jacket in the same color with identical trim. When the tigers came into the cage, they acted as if an enemy was in their midst. They moved to their positions on the props very cautiously, with backs dropped and heads craned slightly forward to scrutinize me. They were extremely suspicious, and even after I started giving them orders they looked at me carefully and strangely. Every tiger, without exception, acted in this peculiar fashion when they saw me dressed in something other than the abbreviated costume to which they were accustomed. For the second show I switched back to the vest and told Tina, "Better that I should die of pneumonia than die in an accident with the tigers."

During a visit to Seattle, Washington, I had an accident that indirectly created a much more serious problem involving a costume. I had been helping my men to move props inside the building where we would perform. In my rush to get the job done I jumped down from one of the props and twisted my ankle. It was quite painful, and my foot swelled to twice its size, but I still had to go on that night. The problem was that I could not wear the boots that were part of my regular costume. The only alternative I had was to wear a tuxedo so that I could wear a small shoe. This was an almost fatal mistake.

I am certain the tigers had seen me in a tuxedo many times, but I had never worn one inside their cage. When the time came to present their act, the tigers were sent into the cage, then I joined them. The moment I stepped inside, they became highly agitated. They were so alarmed that I quickly removed my jacket while talking to them very loudly so that they would recognize me. It was a really dangerous situation, and initially my voice did nothing to calm them. The tigers were becoming more and more tense, so I ripped off my tie, and practically tore the buttons from my shirt to get it off as quickly as I could. I stood in the center of the ring, bare to the waist and completely surrounded by tigers, talking a blue streak to convince them that I was Gunther. They finally settled down enough for me to present the act, but it was one of the most disturbing experiences I ever had with them.

It was times like that, when I stayed inside the cage instead of moving to safer ground, that made people believe I had no nerves. My reactions in those situations were so spontaneous and smooth that people often thought I was

UNTAMED

scoffing at the danger or that I did not even realize how great it was. I realized it, but I could never have thought about it at the time those situations were unfolding. What people did not know is that if I had left the cage under those circumstances, I would never have been able to perform with those tigers again because I would have surrendered control.

Animals need consistency, and that is why changing things abruptly can create havoc. Colors seem to excite animals, and when colors and styles are suddenly changed, and the animals have not been given time to adjust, they become exceedingly uneasy. Their brains do not work in such a way that they can say, "Wait a minute. The color is different, but this is the same man who has worked with me for so long." Something blacks out in their minds, and they lose their composure. This happened to me once when I changed the colors of the elephants' blankets and the tigers who were supposed to jump on their backs attacked the blankets.

Once something is in an animal's mind, it is difficult to change it. I have also seen this with elephants. Before I could safely change something in the elephants' acts, I had to introduce it to them gradually. The changes that upset them most involved my costumes. And yet, when I practiced with them, I was out of costume. I always wore blue jeans and casual long-sleeved shirts rolled up to the elbow for training and rehearsals. The animals know the difference between practice and performance. They are accustomed to seeing me in jeans and a shirt for practice, and so they accept that under those circumstances. During performance they are accustomed to another set of clothes, and that is all they will allow. I also had to be careful when making the transition from winter break, when we only practiced for weeks at a time, back to performing, because by then the animals expected to see me in blue jeans and long sleeves all the time.

Even changing the colors of the plumes on the horses presented a problem. Out of twenty-four horses, at least six acted up when the colors were changed. I had horses who had to have their eyes covered when we changed colors at the beginning of a season so that they would not go haywire.

With all of these variables at work, getting physically and emotionally close to wild animals and keeping myself and them alive at the same time was quite a challenge. On a daily basis, external factors affect the way animals interact with human beings. People have seen me hug and pet wild animals, but they have also seen me keep them at bay. I never let the tigers choose the times when they would get physically close to me. I chose the times, so that I could be in control. When they wanted to show me something, or to touch me affectionately, the first thing that came in my direction was a paw with claws. The body is always far away, but the dangerous claws are always close. It is a cruel quirk of nature that even when the tigers wanted to touch me to show me that they loved me, they could not do so without inadvertently hurting me. I used to hug them, but it was always a brief exchange, and not without danger.

I trained tigers to sit up, roll over individually and as a group, play leapfrog, walk in a regimental line, leap through fire hoops, hold fire sticks, and even walk forward and backward on their hind legs. Teaching a tiger to walk backward was a difficult trick because I had to find one who could do it without tripping on his tail. I taught them to work smoothly and precisely with elephants and horses even though their natures told them that they should be eating them. Twenty percent of all baby elephants in the jungle are killed by tigers, and yet I had them working side by side. All of those accomplishments were to the credit of the animals who achieved them.

Every one of my animals knew his or her name and responded instantly to it. If Congo or Sabu, the elephants, were misbehaving, I could shout their names from where I was standing in the stables or the arena and they would hear me and stop in their tracks. All of my cats knew their names, too, and they reacted when I called to them. Yet as well as my tigers knew me, I had to be careful not to make any rapid movements with my hands when I was near them, because such actions alarmed them, and they would bite.

The only place I ever dared to hit the tigers was on the head with a stick, and that was restricted to when they fought or gave me a dangerously bad time during practice. A person might see me hit a tiger on the head and call that abuse. It was not. I had to make certain choices when working with them. One of them was that it was better to whack a tiger on the noggin with a stick to let him know that he was being bad than to have two or more tigers in a full-blown battle that could endanger their lives and mine. Most people did not realize that when tigers were fighting, the stick I used to separate them was in effect merely an extension of my own arm.

During our 1989 winter break a horse who had been with me for about twelve years started acting up. He had gotten something in his foot, so I rested him for a few weeks, and when he was healthy, I wanted him to do a bit of work to get him back into the act, but he refused. He had become lazy and did not want to do anything. How does a person get a horse to do something it does not want to do? If you hit a horse with a whip, it kicks right away. When a horse is angry, it tries to hurt people, step on them, and kick them. I told this troublesome horse, "Look, if you want us to keep you, and you want to stay here and make a living with us, you have to do something." Then I got three grooms to bring him into the ring and walk him around to get him moving. Some people might have called that abuse, but it was not. That horse, Favory, is still working at Ringling.

It was always my habit to visit the animals after the last show to make sure they were fed, their cages were clean, and everyone was secure for the night. During those visits I rewarded animals who had done an especially good job and reprimanded those who had not. I did this every single night that we performed, and many nights when we did not. The animals expected to see me after a show. One night I was exceptionally tired, so I decided to skip my regular visit. Before I left the arena, the animals made such a fuss that I had to go back to see them. The tigers made noises and were restless in their cages, the elephants trumpeted—everyone was so upset that I had to stay longer than usual just to get them to settle down.

It took two years to train the leopards; three years to train the mixed act with three tigers, two horses, and an African elephant; and another couple of years to train the teeterboard act, in which an elephant hit a teeterboard on which I was standing, sending me backward into the air and somersaulting onto the back of another elephant. Whenever tigers were retired or died, I had to replace them with new tigers. When I brought the new tigers into the cage with the others, there was always the possibility that fights would break out. I have scars up to my elbows from breaking up such fights, but I am alive to tell about all this.

I never fed the tigers until after the last show. There were people who said this was cruel and that I kept them hungry to have control over them. Untrue. Tigers are like people. After a big meal they become sleepy and want to doze. I could not work with a bunch of drowsy, sluggish tigers, and people did not pay to see them lounge around in the cage. My tigers always ate well after our work was finished.

Although I am against giving drugs to animals, I accept that under certain conditions, such as when a veterinarian takes blood for tests, an animal must be given tranquilizers. A tiger needs a tranquilizer when an ingrown nail is removed. I always spotted a tiger with an ingrown nail right away because I would see him licking his foot. When Doc was not around, I removed the nail myself, using a pliers and cutter. We had a small cage into which we put the tiger for this procedure. I then put a longe around its foot, pulled the foot out of the cage, and cut the nail. But I never did that by myself. I needed Mark and a couple of people to hold the tiger and keep him from moving in the cage so that nothing would happen to me.

The strange thing about wild animals is that they are as delicate as they are ferocious and powerful. I could never wear cologne, aftershave, or even scented deodorant when working with any of the animals. Perfume-type odors annoy some of them and adversely affect others. Tigers, for example, are allergic to heavy scents and tobacco smoke, and smoke can be harmful to asthmatic tigers. I had twenty grooms, animal handlers, and assistant trainers at Ringling, and no one was allowed to smoke near the tigers. I actually preferred that they not smoke in the stables at all. We all made sacrifices.

With my feelings for the animals and the circus, people were confounded by my decision to retire as a performer. It would have been extremely difficult if I were one of those who retires and never again does anything related to his work. But I did not completely remove myself from my work. I simply stopped performing and training so many animal acts. I am still involved with the Ringling circus as one of its owners, and my son and daughter still perform and work for the circus. I spend time looking in on the animals and meeting up with the circus on the road, because Mark works with the horses and elephants now, and I want to see what he is doing and how the animals respond to him.

When I stopped performing with them, the tigers were put into temporary retirement at our Venice winter quarters, but I did not sever my ties with them. They had to be exercised regularly and given the same type of care they had received while performing, and those jobs fell to me. I also have in mind that if the day comes when Mark decides that he wants to work with tigers, I will take them out of retirement and teach him to present them.

I have continued to train some animals, but now I have the flexibility to practice in the morning and have the rest of the day to myself. It is not the same as having to do so many jobs, including performances, that you are on the go from early morning until late at night. I have a bit more time to enjoy things that I never experienced before, such as ball games.

I made the decision to retire in 1988 while touring in California. I was having dinner with my wife, Kenny Feld, and his wife, Bonnie, when Sigrid said, "You have two years left on your contract. Do you really want to renew it? You could stop tomorrow if you wanted." I said, "Let me do these last two years, and then I will stop performing." Kenny decided to give me a farewell tour and build the entire show around me.

As I toured through the last two years of my contract on my way to my last performance in Pittsburgh, on November 18, 1990, I felt that each town was the last town. The audiences were wonderful, and so sincere. I was simultaneously looking forward to a time when I could have a little change in my life, after forty-three years of performing, and regretting that the end was so near. Audiences would scream and cheer and give me standing ovations, and I could not keep the tears from my eyes. But I knew the time had come to step aside.

I did not want to be forced to step down for any reason—accident, illness, old age. I tried always to be on top of everything, and I knew that I could perform for another two years, and another two, but we have to realize that at some point, all things must come to an end. I did not want audiences to come back to see me in five years and compare me to the way I was in 1988 or 1990 and be dissatisfied.

At first I found it very strange to not have to be in a predetermined place every day of my life, with every minute of my time spoken for. It has been a short time since I stopped performing, so this is new to me, and apart from writing this book, I am still toying with things I want to do. I would like to do something special for Sigrid. She might want to spend time at our home, since we have never really been there long enough to enjoy it. She might want to take a somewhat belated honeymoon. It has been years since I went to a movie, and even though I never felt that I missed anything, I am glad to have enough time to sit through a film if I want. But I think that once we have rested and indulged ourselves with some treats, I will be back on the road with the circus for at least a couple of months to see how things are going for Mark. I want to be there to give him all the help I can until I see that he can do everything alone, and then I will take my first vacation.

I have not dreamed of where that might be, but after so many years of traveling with my own coach, there are many parts of America that I would like to visit. I want to see a bit more of this country outside the parameters of the circus. So many times we stopped overnight in places, and I thought, "This is so beautiful that I would like to come back here someday." Places such as California and Arizona. I believe I will go back to some of the towns I never had a chance to enjoy.

I also always dreamed of performing in a cowboy movie. In addition to being able to ride, I can shoot and even act. This is something that has been on my mind since I was a young man in Europe, and I certainly would enjoy working on a movie set again.

I have no regrets about not performing anymore, because I got so much out of it over the years. There was always enough enjoyment to keep me at it, through good times and bad. Long ago I reached the point where I could not remember how many times my teeth had been knocked out or how many stitches I had received, but I never stopped to wonder why I stayed with it. I accepted everything that happened to me as part of my life and my job. I was hurt, things were painful, and maybe I was upset that an animal would hurt me, but after three days the pain would be gone and everything was over. It is only the first three days that are tough.

I often think back about the early years, when it all began, and about my mother. She saw me perform at Circus Williams and also in America. I am certain that she was proud of what I did. I think she even told me so once. I never spoke with her of my childhood.

I was lucky while I was growing up to have several mother figures who took care of me. Carola's sister Jeanette Schroer (Carola had five sisters and two brothers), Henry's mother, was great to me, and so were Carola, and Maria Althoff. One Mother's Day I sent four cablegrams to Germany to the four "mothers" I had in my life, including Elfriede Gebel, and signed each one, "Your son Gunther." The wire man said, "You know, young man, I've seen kids with many fathers, but I never saw a kid with so many mothers." I always tried to remember, at least one day a year, what they had done for me.

Many happy things stand out in my mind when people ask about my past, but unless my memory is prodded, I do not easily recall events. When a life has been filled with as much activity as mine, it is easy to forget the good things and the bad. I was a kid from a little town between nowhere and nothing, where I never had anything to do, and suddenly here I was with Circus Williams handling animals. That was a happy time for me—a time when people made me part of their family affairs and took me into their homes and let me sit at their tables and eat every day. Nobody ever gave me the feeling when they saw me that they were thinking, "Oh, God, this guy has shown up again."

I was always welcome, and for me this was one of the greatest feelings I could have. I was a favorite with Franz and Adolf Althoff, even if I was not popular with their children. They always chose me to do special things, then they would say to their children, "Look at how Gunther works." I believe many feelings were hurt because people trusted me a little more than they trusted their own children. I felt very self-conscious about this.

Carola gave me so much opportunity and trusted me to do everything right. Nobody I worked for in Germany was rich enough to say, "Okay, do whatever you want to do." That only happened after I joined the Ringling circus. But I knew what I was doing in the early years and did not squander circus money. I think back on that and I am proud to have known that kind of trust. Today the only people from the old clan still living are Adolf and his wife, Maria. Maria was so kind and generous that we would say, "You already have your golden chair in heaven because you are so good to us." I have seen very little of them, but now that I am no longer performing, I hope to visit Germany to see them.

I am grateful that we were persuaded to pack up Circus Williams lock, stock, and barrel and come to America, especially when we had such security and success in Germany. We knew of circus people who had left Germany and went to work in Greece or Turkey and failed miserably. They lost everything. That could have happened to us.

I am very proud that I am an American. The only thing that bothers me is that I do not speak English well. However, I will not go back to school because I believe that what I have learned through my experiences is enough to get me through to the end of my life. My son chides me about my German accent and the funny way I pronounce some English words, and I laugh at myself over my language problems. There are even times when I cannot speak any language very well. I have so many bumps in my lips from scars that sometimes, especially when it is cold, I can hardly speak at all. I am proud that my children and wife read, write, and speak English fluently, and although I do not like to fumble with English-language newspapers, I make a point of watching television news programs to keep informed.

My children appreciate living in America, but they cannot draw the contrasts that I can between this country and old Germany. They never saw the war or what happened after it, so they never knew how hard it was during those years and what a difference it is living in America. Tina spent some time in Germany, but Mark never did. He was born in a different era, and I can only tell him about the past. It is so hard for him to believe it, so hard to understand what it was like to be young and struggling to stay alive. My children can only read about the years in which I grew up, see it in the movies, and try to understand what a different life they have and how lucky they are.

I have shared my experiences with my children so that they will understand why I am who I am. I have told them, "Whenever you feel overpowered by me, and you want to do something different, the door is always open for you to leave, and I will always be happy if you come back to be here with me."

One of the things for which I am most thankful is the good health we all enjoy. The circus carried high insurance on me, which required that I have a physical every year. I was always in great shape. Sometimes I grin when I think that after the life I have led, the only health problem I have is high blood pressure, which I control with medication. I used to think that only fat or lazy people developed high blood pressure. I was never overweight in my life. I eat anything I want and only what I believe is good, and I gain no weight. I eat fast food when I'm on the run, and such goodies as ice cream, German salami, and smoked pork chops. I think I always stayed so fit because I was active and performed and practiced so much. Maybe after being out of the spotlight for a couple of years my profile will change.

Sigrid changed my life. She is enormously kind and always there when I need her. She never missed anything special in our lives. Sigrid was able to concentrate more on being a wife and mother because, unlike Jeanette, who was heavily involved with all aspects of Circus Williams when we were married, Sigrid was there just for me. She only started working when we joined the Ringling circus, and even then she was still there for me, but she had to do more work. It is a wonder that Sigrid never developed high blood pressure.

We tried to work out her schedule so that she would

be able to do less as our family grew and have more time for us. It was very stressful for her to take care of me, Mark, and Tina; perform; do housework and cooking; and still look good. And she always looked good!

From the first day we met, Sigrid knew that good looks are important to me and that it means something to me to have a beautiful woman in my life. If I couldn't be the best-looking man, at least I wanted to have a good-looking wife. Sigrid was always that. She never goes anywhere unless she is perfectly turned out. One of my fetishes is that I like her to wear high heels all the time, even in the house. People say, "Let her relax when she's home," but I like to see the way a woman's legs look when she is wearing high heels, so why should I not be able to enjoy my wife's? Sigrid dresses in high fashions, changes for dinner every evening, and always wears high heels. It is tough for her sometimes, walking around in those shoes for so many hours, but she does it for me. She buys any clothes she wants, and if I don't like something, she doesn't wear it again. She would never argue and say, "But I like it." She makes these concessions for me. I have not made many concessions for her.

I am not a foolish man, but I have always been a sucker for beautiful women and beautiful cars. I have always pampered myself with cars and inevitably complain when I sell them. I would spend so much money on a car, then sell it after only a couple of thousand miles, and even if it looked good, I never got enough money back. Every time I lost money on a car, I would tell myself, "This is the last time." I did that with my Corvettes. I bought five Corvettes at different times in my life, and after I sold each of them, I said, "That is the last one. It will never happen again." Then I bought another one. In twenty years I have owned five Corvettes and a couple of Cadillacs. But that is the only luxury I treated myself to in all of my forty-three years of

UNTAMED

work. Nobody suffered when I bought a new car—not me or my family—so it was not such a bad vice.

Cars, motorcycles, and animals are the only things I have ever shopped for. When I have to buy something else, I get my whole family involved because I do not know how to shop. I have never bought presents for anyone in my family, not even Christmas presents. Tina buys presents for me to give to Sigrid and Mark, and Mark or Sigrid buys things for me to give Tina. I never felt that they were upset by this, and Sigrid never complained. She would always say, "Don't worry. You do other things that are good for us." I never stopped in a shop even to buy flowers for my wife. I didn't have the time. Tina always did it for me, and I must admit that sometimes I felt strange about that. But I am not a romantic person. I am the most unromantic person alive. I think I have always been too realistic to indulge in romance.

I never even allowed myself time to be sentimental about things. My sister sent me letters that I had written to my mother in my early years, and pictures. Jeanette put photos from Circus Williams in an album for me. If they had not done this, I wouldn't have any of those things.

When I look at those pictures, they bring back a myriad of feelings, but no regrets. I would do everything over again if I had to because I have had a good life. I always tried to do the best things for my family. We were together as much as possible. I don't know if my children were always happy with that arrangement, but at least I knew we were together, and I could see what was happening with them. I believe a family affair, where everybody is concerned for one another, is very important.

I have been so firm with my children because I was concerned about losing one of them if I was not around to protect them. I worried about them taking what I perceived to be high-risk actions, such as unnecessary trips. We spent our lives in places that were unfamiliar to us, and that made me fear for their safety. When you live and work in one place, you know the location of traffic lights, railroad tracks, and things like that. But we were always in different places, and I was uneasy for them.

I was also pretty tough on Tina when she started dating because I did not want to lose her to someone unworthy. I tried to protect her, and maybe that was wrong. A boy is much easier to raise than a girl because he is expected to be able to handle himself. But fathers are always afraid that they are going to lose their daughters to someone who will end up divorcing them.

We moved around constantly, and I tried to hold on to everybody as long as possible until they found the partner who was right for them. I told them, "When you are really in love and you have somebody you want to marry, then that new family will come first. Until then this family must come first." Tina found love at the circus, and on February 8, 1990, she married Edward Del Moral, an acrobat who works for Ringling Brothers. Mark is still single.

Sigrid has been the greatest wife, compassionate and able to survive so many hard things without any anger. I'm sure she felt it, but she never let me see it. I believe the woman holds the marriage together, and Sigrid sure was the glue in our home. I have always been very controlled around the animals, but not so controlled around my own family. This was because I was under such constant pressure and had to have complete control for my work. When I got home, I sometimes became explosive, like a valve being released on a pressure cooker. I believe they understood this, since they have been extremely forgiving toward me.

I left my animals in good hands. Mark knows how to teach the horses and elephants, and I believe he could even train the tigers if he wanted. When the tigers were young, he was inside the cage with them many times.

I did not prepare Mark for the day when I would leave the circus and he would become the featured animal trainer. He prepared himself the same way I did at Circus Williams. He was around for every practice and every performance, and he learned to do every job. He is only twenty years old and needs time to develop his own identity and image now that I am no longer performing. We must also give him new acts so that audiences won't compare him with me. All of these things will come to him with time and experience.

Mark knows what to expect from circus life. Above all, he understands that there is no such thing as a typical day. Every day starts out the same, but each one unfolds and ends differently. And that is part of the allure of our business. Not every day is one that merits remembering. There were days when things were falling on my feet and on my head, when I hurt myself, and seemed not to be able to do a thing right, but I never had a day that was so bad that I said to myself, "If I have another day like this, I'm going to quit." I hope it is no different for Mark.

The older an animal trainer gets, the better he is able to gauge and manage the risks in his life. I said earlier that there is no such thing as a good young animal trainer because the fine-tuned judgment a man needs to survive as a trainer only comes after years of experience. That special type of judgment helped me many times, and at least once, recently in fact, it saved my life.

In January 1990, while I was making my farewell appearance in Savannah, Georgia, a tiger named Flappes became the first of my cats to attack me deliberately. This was my closest brush with death, even though it left me without a scratch. Flappes is a scrapper—he has been since he was a little bit of a cub. I got him when he was six months old, and as soon as I started training him with the other tigers, he started fighting. I expected to have trouble with him someday. After you work with animals for a long time, you can judge changes in their personalities, and I noticed that as Flappes grew older, he became more hostile toward his fellow tigers.

After six years Flappes was instigating so many fights that I trained another tiger to take his place, and I had already put him into the act, but I had not yet taken Flappes out. We were performing an afternoon show when Flappes attacked a tiger named Syrus. I jumped between them to break it up, as I had done in other tiger fights, but instead of backing off, Flappes immediately turned on me. He snarled and threatened, and I tried to hold him back with verbal commands and my stick. Mark, who was working as one of my watchers outside the cage, thought that Flappes was going to leap on me, so he quickly got a fire extinguisher and sprayed it in the tiger's face to make him snap out of it. Flappes was not afraid of anything, and he ignored the spray in his face. I thought for sure that I was a goner, but I knew I could not show any fear. My men opened the door that leads into the cage so that I could back Flappes out, but he held his ground and flailed at me with his paws. He moved to attack me while the other sixteen tigers in the cage were held onto their props by commands from my watchers.

Although their props are very heavy and almost impossible to lift single-handedly, I somehow found the strength to pick up a prop with one hand and send it crashing to the ground between me and Flappes before he could carry out his attack. This startled him, and I was then able to get him to leave the cage. If ever I have been granted a miracle, it was coming out of that fracas alive, and the Lord received thanks from me that day.

I had put off taking Flappes out of the show until then. Usually when tigers fought, I took them out of the act for a while so that they could cool off, then I brought them back. With only ten months left for me to perform I decided not to tempt fate, so I took Flappes out of the act permanently and asked Doc to find him a good home. After this incident Flappes acted friendly toward me and tried to get me to talk to him and touch him, but I knew I could not take any chances with him. If he turned on me once, he could turn on me again. Until then I never had the feeling that anyone wanted to attack me. If I was going to continue working comfortably with the tigers, Flappes had to be sent packing. That kind of judgment does not come by osmosis, but from experience, something the young lack. I believe Mark learned a great deal from watching me that day.

This judgment affects every aspect of training, including knowing which animals to buy—being the proverbial good judge of horse flesh—and recognizing when your animals are sick. Once, in my early days as a trainer, I bought four tigers from a supplier in Switzerland. I trained them as part of an eight-tiger act, and suddenly they became ill and three of them died. They had such severe cases of worms that the worms were in their stomachs and intestines and also affected their brains. They had been sold to me this way, and I did not recognize that they were ill because I was so inexperienced.

I would not be afraid for Mark to work with the tigers, but I know how much pressure he would be under for the rest of his working life. He would have to be the same person every day. You cannot be moody, you cannot do your work well one day and badly the next. When an accident happens, you cannot be afraid to do the next show, which may be only two hours later. If Mark decided to accept the challenge of the tigers, I would have a serious talk with him that I would begin by explaining that he would have a much easier situation if he worked only with horses and elephants. Afterward the choice would be his.

I don't know if Mark will become famous. I do know that he is very happy now, but how far he goes in this business is his own decision. Everything in life has two sides. Whenever you do more and become better at your work, everyone expects you to do even more and become even better. Eventually Mark will have to make a decision about how far he wants to go and the extent of the commitment he is willing to make to circus life. He is much too young to make that decision now.

I was thirty years old when fame knocked upon my door. I came to America when I was thirty-four, and I soon found myself trying to do more and more all the time. In this work, once you are in, you cannot get out, so each person must find his own level of commitment. That will happen with Mark. I am not worried about Tina. She is a fine young woman, and I am certain that she will remain with the circus, if not as a performer, then in a position behind the scenes or in the business end of the operation. With her ability to adapt, she will be at home in any career situation she chooses.

I made my own commitment to circus life and my work as an animal trainer. It is difficult to speak of that commitment and all that it has meant to me without occasionally sounding arrogant or vain or even boastful. But, as I said before, I am really a very simple man, with simple tastes, who actually is embarrassed by the outward symbols of success. I feel for people because I understand what it is like to be hungry, cold, alone, and struggling to get ahead.

I would be foolish to deny my good fortune and my accomplishments for the sake of being humble or modest. I am proud of my life and respectful enough of my fans to want to talk about it openly.

UNTAMED

This year, 1990, was very eventful for me, and another turning point. It was highlighted by many firsts and lasts. I was a spectator in a circus audience for the first time since I started working for a circus. I attended the opening night of Ringling's Blue Show at Madison Square Garden in March because it featured some of my lifelong friends, the Togni family. Ringling had approached them about coming to America to work, and they were as reticent about it as I had been when asked to leave Germany with Circus Williams. But I assured them that this really is the land of opportunity and the place where they should sink their stakes, so they picked up their circus, just as we had done twenty-three years before, and came to America to join the Ringling operation. I have known that family for thirty-five years. I watched their children grow up and perform in the circus. I was proud to be in the audience for their first American performance.

I gave my last performance several months later in Pittsburgh. I had not been looking forward to that last town, and certainly not to the last show. I had such butterflies in my stomach that I felt like a child starting out all over again in my German circus. I hoped that it would be over quickly, and that would be the end. The audience could easily have been the best I had ever had, but I said that about every town I performed in during my farewell tour. I had a terrible lump in my throat when I performed my animals that night, and a strange sensation in my chest. I think it was the tremendous sadness I was feeling. I did not allow it to affect my work, and I did not want to go into the tigers' cage that way, so when I presented that act, I looked at them and said, "Come on, guys. This is the last time we're gonna do this. Be great!" They were.

One of the things I would like to do now that I have stopped performing is compete in the Olympics as a Dressage (High School) rider. I believe I could win America a gold medal in that event. I have been called one of the greatest Dressage riders in the world, and I would feel mighty good about putting my abilities to work in competition on behalf of my country.

I want to give something back to America and to the people who came to see me perform for so many years. I have been told that I have given much to the world of animal training. I do not know if I actually caused training styles to change, but I have advised and helped other trainers when they asked for my assistance. I never tried to interfere in their work, but I wanted them to know that I cared about what they were doing and that whenever they needed me, I would be there for them.

Although in the course of my career I have received extravagant praise, I believe I am simply a man blessed with a special gift that I have been able to share with some of God's most beautiful creatures.

INDEX